Panthers over Korea

George Schnitzer

PublishAmerica
Baltimore

First printing

ISBN: 1-4241-7942-4

PUBLISHED BY PUBLISHAMERICA, LLLP

www.publishamerica.com

Baltimore

Printed in the United States of America

Dedicated to the memory of my roommates who paid the full price

Richard (Dick) C. Clinite
Laurence (Larry) L. Quiel

Acknowledgments

After 50 years of an exciting life in the computer business I retired to take on new challenges. I became interested in recalling what went on during those many years ago, beginning with my naval career through training and flying combat missions over North Korea. It got a needed kick start in 1997 when the air intelligence officer of the squadron's second deployment, Robert Lee, started the successful search for the former officers of VF-153. This began my e-mail correspondence with many who were still alive. The squadron commander, Jerry E. Miller now a retired Vice Admiral, during several lunches encourage me to write what this "forgotten war" was like from the cockpit of a Grumman F9F jet fighter/bomber. This seemed to be an impossible task, but my interest was awaken to his challenged, and I started digging. At the same time, I also start as a behind-the-scenes volunteer at the National Air and Space Museum in Washington DC. This opened other avenues where I had access to more information written about the conflict. This also let me connect up with the goldmine of information on the individual official action reports written by the carriers and air groups. These came from the archives at the Navy Historical Center in an electronic format.

Using my pilot log book, personal notes, letters, and photographs, plus my roommates' writings and their photographs I started my manuscript. I augmented these with a few official Navy photographs taken aboard the carriers, USS *Antietam* and USS *Princeton*. I began the construction of the frame work of this book. Former squadron mates H W (Bill) Jones, George M. Benas, and the late Charlie J. Clarkson were generous with their own information on their flights under very difficult conditions. Admiral Miller was helpful in many ways to move the project along.

I am deeply indebted to the help I received from Marion Ashley in making my ramblings into readable text. She forced me into writing clearer text with as little jargon as possible. To assist the reader, the appendixes and glossary will be useful to understand many of the technical words for non flyers that I used through out the text.

I would like to extend my special thanks for those friends and relatives who read this book in the draft form and gave me important critically suggestions to clarify events.

—George C. Schnitzer
Manassas, Virgina

Table of Contents

Introduction

It was a dark, cold morning before dawn as I walked carefully to my jet fighter/bomber aft of the deck edge elevator of the USS *Antietam*. It was difficult to see objects and without the help of the plane captain with his red flash light I might have walked right by my aircraft. Climbing in he helped me to get comfortable in the cockpit. Strapping my parachute was a struggle, as was hooking up the shoulder straps and seatbelts. I wiggled to insure everything was tight. All strapped in the next job was plugging in my radio cord, "G"-suit tube, oxygen tube, and finally pulling on the hard helmet. Pulling my oxygen mask over my face I checked the oxygen blinker by breathing normally. The next important job is to do my cockpit check. Touching each of my switches to assure they were properly set I looked up to see a thin sliver of light appeared in the eastern sky as the task force was moving with the wind so as to gain sea room for the upcoming launch. Tightening my chin strap, the sounds of the flight deck became a rumble. The sound of the air boss's voice, however, suddenly boomed across the flight deck. "Start the jets." Almost simultaneously the carrier started to heel over starting into a 180 degree turn. This was the start of another mission, and the tingle of apprehension flowed strongly through my body. The starter jeep wheeled close to my airplane aft of the wing and the electrical line was plugged in. When the cockpit lights glowed red I pressed the starter switch. The tachometer moved quickly from zero, and at 9% I pushed the throttle outboard hitting the micro switches that fire the two igniters as the fuel lines opened. There was a rumbling sensation as the tail pipe temperature-gauge needle climbed quickly and stopped at normal. A good light off! Signaling to the jeep driver with a thumbs-up he disconnected and was quickly gone. Now the apprehension in the ready room and during the cockpit check gave way to, "I'm all business." I was alert, well trained, and ready to move out to do my job. The light of dawn was a little stronger, and I could see the rockets mounted under the wings ready for delivery in a short time. How did I get to this professional state?

My first flight was in a World War I "Jenny" when I was four years old. My uncle Charlie was the pilot, and I sat on my father's lap. I have no remembrance of this, but it must have made a big impression because I caught the flying bug. I built model aircraft powered by rubber bands and thrilled to the successes and failures on these creations. Oh, to be in the cockpit of these machines became my dream. How I filled that dream to become a Navy flyer is where this book starts. It covers seven years of my life that were exciting, terrifying, and challenging. I met many fellow pilots in my journey though these years and laughed, drank, and told wonderful stories about our flights. Some of the stories were really good without stretching the truth!

The down side of combat deaths left deep emotional scars within me that never will go away. The loss of roommates was especially difficult to handle. The reader will learn of the boredom that can come from flying "safe" flights boring holes in the sky and the terrifying, heart-stopping events of missions when I came under heavy enemy anti-aircraft fire. Included are many pictures from my personal collection and from others as well to highlight the action. Naval air operation aboard a World War II carrier during the Korean War goes on out of slight for most citizens. The action is difficult, dangerous, and physically exhausting for pilots as well as the crew. Now start the reading and follow me into a new world. Thank you for your willingness to dive into a life that only a few will ever follow.

Chapter 1
Getting Started—Pre-flight

On August 13, 1946 the United State Congress approved the Hale Plan, also known as the "Flying Midshipman" or "Aviation Midshipman Program." It was part of a program designed by Captain James L. Holloway Jr. when he was Chief of Naval Personnel. At the time of this action, I was blissfully unaware of the impact it would have on my life. In the fall of 1946 I learned about this program as I started my senior year at Rogers High School in Newport, Rhode Island. I applied to the Navy in January of 1947 when I learned enough about the program to be very interested. Soon after my application I made sure I would fulfill all the educational requirements. This specific Navy program was for six years. The first two years were to be spent at a college of my choice as a seaman recruit, then two years of active duty as a midshipman, first as a flight midshipman in training and after graduation the remaining time in a fleet squadron. The last two years of the program I would either be a full-time naval officer or a civilian active in a Naval Reserve Squadron attending college for my last two years. The Navy, in return for my service, paid all expenses for my education, plus $50.00 a month for living expenses the first two years. Not much money, but being careful I could make it. It was my ticket to a college education, and I sure wanted to complete the entire educational experience. To receive four years of college and become a naval aviator were the two major goals I had set for myself, and I was determined I was going to reach them. The only thing I didn't plan on was a war. At the end of May 1947, I received my acceptance into the Navy program, and on June 8, 1947 Brown University accepted me as a freshman.

I soon found out that Brown was a tough academic school, and it was all study with very little outside activity. Majoring in mathematics I found I had to study at least six hours almost every day. I made good grades by the end of my freshman year and worked during the summer to add to my savings for the coming year. During the beginning of my fourth semester a fellow student asked me to go out with him on a blind date. I met a very delightful young lady and was very taken with her. I thought I had an unusual last name, but Beverly Greensides had even a more unusual one. We enjoyed each other's company but realized that I was going away at the end of the semester, so we kept in as light as possible. At our good bye date, she agreed to write, and we sadly parted in June of 1949. I would not see her again until March almost two years later. So at the completion of my second year of college I left Brown after receiving my Navy orders to Pensacola, Florida, to start my aviation career.

On the morning of July 12, 1949 I picked up my small bag, and after all the goodbyes had been said I walked out of the house where I grew up. With a sad look back I walked the three blocks to the bus stop at the One-Mile corner. At twenty years old, my life was about to dramatically change forever. I rode the bus to the Providence, Rhode Island, railroad station to catch the train to New York City. From NY via a slow, two-day ride in a Pullman car I arrived at a small town in northern Alabama for the final train ride to Pensacola, Florida. It was very early in the morning with over and an hour to wait, so I walked over to a small café for some breakfast. My first surprise was the mound of white stuff that showed up on my plate. I found out that it was grits. There would be many more surprises in store for me. It was later in the morning of July 15, 1949 that I found myself on a bus to the naval base. At 11:00 I reported to the officer of the day at the Pre-Flight School at the Naval Air Station (NAS) Pensacola to start my training and a new life.

"Apprehensive" was a mild word for my feeling as I settled into a strange new world. I had never been very far from home before. The first two weeks at "Main Side," as it was called then, were filled with the processes all too familiar to anyone who entered the military service. You were given a number and everything else needed for your future. I was assigned to pre-flight class 16-49 along with 38 others. One of the first persons I met when I arrived at the Pensacola cadet barracks was Laurence (Larry) L. Quiel. It turned out that Larry and I roomed together as we moved from one airfield to another, completing each stage in the flying syllabus and gaining flying experience. We continued together further even after graduation to the same fleet squadron

Once processed into the Navy I started my two weeks of pre-flight indoctrination. Anyone who has been to the Gulf Coast in the summer knows it is hot and humid. We marched to all our activities no matter what the weather was like. The frequent afternoon rain showers just added to the humidity. Being from New England I was not used to this kind of weather, and I suffered from the heat and especially the humidity. Just to add to my misery, our class lived in a non air-conditioned WW II-built barracks, so sleeping was not pleasant. At least the classrooms were air conditioned.

It wasn't all work and no play, however. One of the funnier things that happened was when we marched down to the dock area to try our hand at navigating a small flat-bottomed landing craft. I never knew what the enlisted man that showed us how to operate the craft must have thought about these cadets.

I could tell that I should stick to learning to fly. That damn boat did not go where I tried to make it go. I once hit the dock hard, generating jeers from the others in the class. Some of them were good seaman, but I sure wasn't. The physical training (PT) classes, held in one of the old seaplane hangers located on the bay, were the toughest. It was during these first two weeks that we were measured on our physical fitness. Part of this fitness testing was the infamous "step test," and it was the "terrible two steps." I thought that I was in good shape from carrying heavy cans of ice cream and trays of glasses during my after-school and summer job at the Newport Creamery, but it was one of the toughest tests I had ever taken. I was determined to make it no matter what they threw at me.

We were quickly introduced to the military side of life by the Marine officer and his three drill sergeants who ran the barracks. We slept four to a room and lived a Spartan life. Each week one of us was designated as room captain. It was the room captain's job to make sure everything was shipshape. Our day started with the sound of reveille over the loudspeaker system. We jumped out of the bunk, and then stripped the bedspread and sheets from the mattress. These were folded carefully in a perfect square. The mattress was folded over on its self. Once done, we stood at attention for the inspection party. We had five minutes for all of this to take place. The inspection party consisted of the Marine officer in charge and a Marine drill sergeant. If they found anything that was not perfect, the room captain was given one or more demerits. Each demerit given was to be marched off on Saturday instead of relaxing. One hour per demerit under the supervision of the drill sergeant was the penalty. One of the interesting things I learned was that toothpaste and brush was just as good for cleaning the faucets as for cleaning my teeth. My toothbrush served double duty. I had spotless faucets as well as teeth.

I managed to survive the stress and pain of this military discipline and physical introduction, and after these two weeks of indoctrination were over our class started the 16 weeks of pre-flight school training. I was commissioned a Midshipman at the beginning of pre-flight on July 28, 1949, and I received the princely sum of $75.00 per month. It didn't go very far because I had to pay for my laundry and other minor items. There were four midshipmen in the class, four commissioned officers, and 31 Naval Aviation Cadets. It would be a mentally and physically grueling period for all of us. Classes started at eight o'clock and were held on the subjects of meteorology, aerial navigation over water, Morse code, Navy Regulations, Essentials of Naval Service, and Theory of Flight.

The classes in navigation were based upon WW II fleet operational searches. We used the plotting board to set up our track and then learned how to adjust our heading to compensate for the winds aloft at our assigned altitude. It was fun, and I usually aced the test because of my math education. These problems were fine for a slow moving search pattern, but would be completely outdated in two years. I later discovered that the F6F "Hellcat" made by Grumman I flew in advance training had this same plotting board at the bottom of the instrument panel that could be slid out for use. I never used it. The advent of the jet aircraft and its impact on aerial navigation did not seem to influence the course contents. We learned how to judge the wind velocity by looking at the wave motion and height. Having lived by the sea, I was personally aware of the effect of the wind and the resultant wave motion. Meteorology was another subject that had interested me from an early stage. We received a good grounding in all types of weather and how to understand the various wind conditions within the frontal systems. This was a good course, and I gained important knowledge that stayed with me throughout my flying career and beyond. Again, the class contents did not take into consideration the weather effects at higher altitudes where I later flew in a jet aircraft. The flying world was changing, but the response by the training command at this time ignored these changes completely.

The classes in the subjects of Navy Regulations and Essentials of Naval Service were interesting, but often taught in such a dry way that the real challenge was to stay awake. I did not understand why these classes were taught after lunch. That is the worst time of day because lunch relaxed the body, and it was tough staying awake. I think I learned how to nap with my eyes open. The examinations in these two courses, typically forty true or false questions, were too easy. I don't think anyone failed them. The course on Theory of Flight was easy because of my gasoline-powered-model-airplane hobby as a teenager. I again aced these classes as well.

We were frequently shown movies with Hollywood actors doing the narrative. The only problem with them was the aircraft used. The movies were produced for WW II training in either the Naval Aircraft Factory N3N biplane, the "Yellow Peril," or the Boeing-Stearman N2N "Kaydet." During WW II the North American SNJ was used as an advance trainer, but we were going to learn to fly it in primary training. I would not have the opportunity to hear the wires "sing" in the slipstream flying the older biplane. They were fun to watch, however, and there were still some basic lessons to learn from them. With the exception of Morse code, which I just managed to get by, I finished Pre-Flight with great grades.

Afternoons were spent either in military formation marching in the hot afternoon sun guided by our Marine drill sergeants or PT in all its forms. The best PT activity for me was the three weeks of swimming. We were pushed hard to build up our endurance to be able to pass the swimming tests. The first test was to swim a mile with just a bathing suit; the second test was to swim the mile clothed with shirt and pants. We were assigned a number, and as we swam around the perimeter of the pool we gave our number to the officer in charge. I came out of the pool each time looking like a prune. The latter test had a painful side effect on me. The movement of the khaki shirt over my nipples as I swam rubbed them raw. I sure wished I had worn a tee-shirt. Both of these long-distance swim tests were plain exhausting. The last test was to be able to swim the length of the pool under water. This one was just difficult. I had done a fair amount of underwater swimming since childhood either in the ocean or the lake so I completed it on my first try.

Near the end of the three weeks I got my first taste of real water survival with training on how to land in a parachute in the water. Being thin, I had no problem with the technique. As explained by the instructor the technique was simple and straightforward. The execution was not so simple. The first step in preparing for a water landing was to maneuver the parachute around so as to be facing in the direction the wind was taking the chute. Then we were to put our thumbs under the leg straps and slide our butt as far back on the seat strap as possible. That was so the leg straps could be loosened enough to unbuckle

15

them. Next thing to do was to unbuckle the chest strap keeping your arms crossed. When you were descending and getting close to the water you tried to judge your height above the water. Just before hitting the water, you uncrossed your arms and slid out of the chute. Sounds easy, but it was tricky. Judging how far above the water was not easy even over a swimming pool. If you didn't do it right you ended up getting caught in the harness or the shroud lines of the chute. If there was little or no wind over the water, the chute could collapse on top of you. In a bathing suit it was not too difficult. What I didn't know was I might have to use the parachute after having the aircraft hit by enemy gunfire and then landing in ice cold water. The thoughts of combat were far from my mind as I prepared myself for this training. The bigger classmates got some taste of water as they tried to get out of the parachute harness after dropping into the water from ten feet.

The last activity was really fun but a difficult one using the "Dilbert Dunker" trainer. This trainer was a mockup of the North American SNJ primary-training aircraft cockpit mounted on an incline ramp. The trainer was designed to roll down the rails, hit the water, and turn upside down under water. The student had on a dummy parachute, as well as being strapped into a regular shoulder harness and lap belt. When all was ready, the machine was released, quickly slid down the ramp hitting the water, and flipping upside down. The student found himself in the water upside down five feet under the surface. This simulated a ditching into the ocean and having the aircraft turn over on its back.

The task was to release the seat belt and shoulder harness, push out of the cockpit with the parachute on, diving deeper, and then to the side to clear the cockpit of the trainer. It was one wild ride. Down I plunged into the pool. The water sprayed, and I was upside down in five feet of water. I had grabbed a big lung full of air and was able to follow the instructions. Even so, it was scary to be in such a condition. I popped to the surface with the two life guards and climbed out feeling great! This trainer impressed me what could happen if I had to ditch the aircraft into the water and it flipped over.

During one of those hot August day the cadet mess hall served cold tuna fish salad for lunch. It looked too full of mayonnaise for my taste, so I bypassed it and piled other things on my tray. I lucked out in one way, but not in another. The students who ate the tuna fish got very sick, and then what a mess. Those few of us who didn't eat the tuna fish salad and get sick were the bucket brigade cleaning up after everyone else. The barracks smelled for days, or maybe I finally just got used to the stink.

A few days later a notice was posted on the barracks bulletin board that announced the formation of a Pre-flight Drill team. I had been part of the Junior

ROTC in high school and performed in a small drill team, so I thought this would be a good way to get out of late-afternoon battalion sports. I was slight and tall and usually got roughed up by the bigger cadets playing either football or basketball. The ones who didn't sign up razed those of us who did sign up. However, the worm turned on them when the event schedule was posted. The drill team made up of 60 students and one student leader were going to perform at half time at a series of college football games. During pre-flight, all cadets were restricted to the base. The only alcoholic beverage that could be drunk was a weak beer at the cadet club. For members of the drill team, it was freedom! The members of the team got out of class at 3:30 on Friday afternoon, rushed back to the barracks for our uniforms and gear, to be bussed to the Naval Auxiliary Air Station (NAAS) Saufley Field on the outskirts of Pensacola.

Once at Saufley we boarded a four-engine Navy DC-4 to fly to an airfield that was the closest to the game site. Often after the game we were free to go our way. Our only requirement was to be back to the airfield to board the airplane for the return trip. We traveled to New Orleans, Louisiana; Austin, Texas; Columbus, Ohio; Pittsburgh, Pennsylvania; and Washington DC, to mention a few places.

The one performance that stuck with me was the performance at a Washington Redskin's professional football game in the old Griffin Stadium. The transportation aircraft landed at the Naval Air Station Anacostia, and we were bunked in one of the barracks that night. Even though there was no liberty on this trip, it sure was a welcome relief from the rigors of the academic training. The flying back and forth in the R5D (DC-4), however, was no picnic. It was noisy, uncomfortable, and slow. We ate box lunches and slept wherever and on whatever we could find. It had bucket seats along the sides that were almost impossible to sit or sleep in. Of course, no matter the difficulties, we certainly lorded it over the non-members when we returned with our tall tales of wild college parties. Ha! After all, we were in training to be naval aviators with a reputation to uphold.

Just before graduation, I learned that I had been "volunteered" to attend a dance to be held at the officer's club. It seems that the Navy and a girls' finishing school in Mobile had an agreement to have two dances to be held each year. The spring dance was held at the girls' school, the fall dance was held at the Pensacola Officers Club. It was a lot of fun because most of us hadn't had a date in months. The girls were all dressed up in long white dresses, and we were all in our best starched whites.

The dance was heavily chaperoned, but that sure didn't stop a bunch of eager youngsters. There were many moments when a pair could slip out the door into the garden. I was not sure which side was the instigator, but those girls were really boy crazy! Of course we were perfect gentlemen! Unfortunately for me nothing came from this contact with a lovely southern beauty because I was too broke to be able to do any traveling. My monthly pay of $75.00 did not go very far after I paid my laundry bill and other expenses. I also had to wait until I finished Pre-Flight because we could not leave the base.

The sixteen weeks passed quickly, and as the weather cooled our excitement increased. Before we could graduate, however, we had to go through the PT examination once again. We were surprised at how easy it was. Those weeks of workout and marching had turned these flabby civilians into a bunch of hard-bodied cadets in far better condition than when we arrived. That wonderful day came on November 19, 1949 when we received our Pre-flight diplomas. I was on my way to learn to fly!

At graduation I learned how to keep a straight face under a very funny condition. A Marine officer was designated to call out each graduate's name over the loudspeaker. The graduate was to march up in front of the admiral, salute with his right hand, accept the diploma with the left hand, and shake the admiral's hand with the right and marched back to his place in the formation. Before the ceremony the Marine officer searched me out because he wanted to make sure he would pronounce my name correctly. He said it a few times and everything seemed okay. At graduation, when it was time for my name to be called, he called out, "Midshipman Shitzer," instead of "Midshipman Schnitzer." I wanted that piece of paper no matter what, so I just marched up and accepted my diploma.

After the event was over, he found me in the barracks and apologized for such an error. I smiled and told him that wasn't the first time my name was mispronounced. I had my diploma and was off to the actual flight training. I couldn't have been happier.

Chapter 2
Primary and Basic Flight Training

After Pre-flight graduation, Larry Quiel and I, along with the others members of the class received our transfer orders to NAAS Whiting Field. Whiting was located near Milton, Florida, where I was to begin my actual flight training. Primary training consisted of the first two stages in a long list of stages that made up the primary and basic flight-training syllabus. They were simply known as the "A" and "B" stage. The first stage, "A," was to learn to fly the North American SNJ well enough to solo on either flight A19 or A20. After settling in the cadet barracks at Whiting, I attended ground school full time for the first two weeks to learn all about the aircraft I would be flying. The engineering course covered all of the operation of the engine systems, fuel, oil, electrical, and the hydraulic system. I was taught the use of the variable-pitch propeller and how it was managed along with the engine power controls. Other courses covered air safety, flight patterns around the airfield I would use, and the layout of the Whiting Field flying area. Whiting Field was close to the Elgin Air Force Base, which was to the east, and we were forbidden to cross over into this area. There was much to learn about the SNJ and many a night I spent studying the material I was given. How to put all these pieces together was going to be a challenge. NAAS Whiting Field was far enough away from Pensacola to discourage me from going into town and spending what little money I had. I also needed to save some money for the trip back to New England for Christmas leave. I stuck with the simpler life of study, ground school, and most of all, learning everything about the SNJ and how to fly this airplane.

I was assigned a flight instructor with the last name of Parr. He was a short, red-haired lieutenant with an easygoing manner. I was happy that I had been assigned to him, because other students complained about their flight instructors shouting and cursing at them. He was knowledgeable and very good at explaining what was to take place on each of the scheduled dual flights. As it was, he would turn up again in my future flying education while in the Pensacola area. We also continued ground school on a half-day basis to study more navigational training along with the study of the night sky. We were exposed to and learned to use the sextant. The aerial navigation training was basic stuff; unfortunately the new electronic technology and the introduction of jet aircraft would make much of it moot for those of us who would go into carrier aviation. I hardly could wait for my first flight. The tension and excitement was thick enough in the student's ready room to cut it with a knife. The immediate problem was the weather. There was too much rain and low clouds for a number of days. Finally the weather improved enough for student flying, and I was assigned an aircraft. I checked out the parachute from the parachute loft and fitted the shoulder straps over my skinny body and snapped the chest buckle so it wouldn't fall off. I had been taught the proper way to carry the chute and helmet while walking out to the flight line. The chute was carried on the right hip, not bumping on your butt. The worst thing was to have the ripcord accidentally getting pulled and the chute fall to the ground. I waited nervously at the schedule desk for my flight instructor to show up. He walked up to me with a smile and a pat on the back. We walked out of the hanger and towards the ramp area where our plane was parked. Fortunately they were parked in the numerical order of their side number. I was not sure I walked out or floated out as if in a dream.

Unlike a Piper Cub that I flew in as a passenger in college, the SNJ was a high-powered airplane to learn to fly. During World War II, this aircraft was used as advance training. It had enough big airplane characteristics to make it a really big challenge. There were still many lessons to learn, however, before I climbed into the cockpit for the first time. The first major lesson was how to pre-flight this airplane. Lt. Parr talked to me about the pre-flight of an aircraft as we walked out to the flight line from the hanger.

Waiting while other students taxied their aircraft out to the runway Lt. Parr discussed safety procedures and the dangers walking around the nose of the plane. We parked our parachutes on the wing so we could inspect the plane easily. He led me around the airplane we were to fly on my first flight.

He showed me what to look for by pointing out the possible areas on the underside that could get damaged by flying rocks or other pieces of metal kicked up by the propeller blast. Together we examined the tires to make sure there were no cuts or worn spots that could cause a tire to blow out and end up in a ground loop or a nose over. I carefully checked the engine section for leaks of oil or hydraulic fluid. Probably the most important was to check the fuel levels in the two wing tanks. It was a simple check, but there was no question about why to do it. Unscrewing the cap and sticking my finger in proved the tanks were full. All set. Then I was ready to climb in to the cockpit. Boy was I nervous, but excited. The first time I primed the engine and upon a "thumbs up" from the ground crew I hit the starter switch. The propeller spun, and with a roar the engine caught, and I was fired up. Even though this was a trainer, that 600-hp engine was really something. Now I had to remember all the positions of the needles on the engine instruments. After the engine had warmed up the instructor told me to check the magnetos. The line crew gave me another "thumbs up" that the area was clear behind me, and I smashed down on the brakes and pushed the throttle forward until I reached the required 30 inches of manifold pressure. I moved the switch from first one magneto to the other. No drop off, so they were both working, and I went back to "both." It was a cool day, but I was sweating! It seemed that everything was in order, and I was ready to taxi the aircraft. I mashed the brakes down and gave the hand signal to the ground crew to remove the chocks. With the chocked removed one of the flight line crew moved out forward and to the left of the aircraft and checked the taxiway for other aircraft. All clear. With my heart rate really up there, I slowly added power and began to move the aircraft forward. With my tail clear of the other near by planes, he gave me the hand signal to unlock the tail wheel and then to hit my left brake to turn the aircraft to head down the taxiway.

Out in the taxi way he signal me I was clear to go by pointing down the taxiway. I was on my way for my first flight. Now my next big event in this unfolding challenge was to taxi the airplane. The SNJ was a little tricky to move safely when taxiing to and from the runway. My first experience in the SNJ was in a ground trainer. It was an old SNJ non-flyable aircraft that was had fitted with an extra wheel under the engine, so if the student hit both brakes at the same time it wouldn't nose over all the way and damage the propeller or engine. Trying to taxi this trainer quickly showed me the difficulties that were to be overcome to move this airplane around on the ground. For one thing, the pilot had to make a series of "S" turns while taxiing because it was not possible to see straight ahead over the nose of the aircraft. It took most of us some time to master the use of each of the main wheel toe brakes on top of the rudder pedals, engine throttle, and rudder in the right combination so the airplane could be taxied safely down the taxi way to the runway for take-off. No one wanted to chew the tail off of the plane ahead. The take-off was started from the intersection of the runways which was at the mid-point of the length. That meant the feet did two jobs, activating the brakes with the toes as well as moving the rudder pedal with the entire foot. It reminded me of trying to rub your stomach and pat the top of your head at the same time. The same thing was necessary after landing and taxiing back to the parking slot or in pilot's lingo, "in the chocks" after landing. There wasn't any part of the learning process that came naturally. I learned to drive a car in a few lessons from my father. But with this aircraft, it all had to be learned and repeated over and over until it became a part of my vocabulary. Slowly the technique became easier as I gained experience, and it wasn't long before I could move the aircraft with positive control.

One interesting feature about the SNJ was the hydraulic system that was used to raise and lower the landing gear as well as the wing flaps. The fluid pressure was only available when a lever on the left side of the cockpit was activated. This lever had the fancy name of "power push." After pushing this lever down I could raise or lower the landing gear and also to lower the wing flaps for landing. After learning all the things I had to do to be ready for takeoff, I still had to use the check-off list that was on a card in a holder on the instrument panel. Knowledge was important, but your memory could play tricks with you under pressure so this was the insurance factor not to do stupid things. The worst cases were to land with your wheels up or try to takeoff with the propeller in high pitch. Mistakes like these could be costly to yourself, the aircraft, and other personnel. The development of good discipline in the cockpit was essential for a long life.

Unlike taxiing, takeoffs were a lot easier. The three runways at Whiting field were 6,000 feet long. The runway in use was posted on the side of the control tower in big block numbers. I taxied to the mid-point because the upwind half were used for takeoffs. The downwind end was used for landings. When I was ready and the runway was free of traffic, I rolled out to line up on the center line straight down the runway. Locking the tail wheel was just about the last thing to do before adding full power for the takeoff. Landing, however, was especially difficult for the new student. This tricky characterization of the SNJ was created by its short wheelbase of 8.5 feet.

That short wheelbase meant the student pilot had to be very careful during the landing touchdown and in the landing roll out because it was easy to "ground loop" this airplane. A "ground loop" occurred when the plane was allowed to make an uncontrolled fast turn on the runway or leaving the runway for the taxiway. This could cause the plane to tip over on one wheel and drag a wing tip on the ground. It was especially true in learning how to land in a crosswind. Later on my instructor and I went out to an outlying field to practice crosswind landings. He was very good at it, but it took me a couple of flights to begin to master the technique, though by now I was gaining experience and did well. When it starts getting fun, then you feel it in your bones. Gads, what a great feeling! A number of these ground loops occurred with other students, but I mastered the landing technique and managed to get through this stage without coming close. One good thing about learning to fly was my pay increased by 50% now that I was in flying status. That meant I was making the princely sum of $112.50 a month.

I started my actual flight training on the first day of December. In the earlier part of this primary "A" stage I did not have very much confidence in my ability but had no problems. Although some of the flights were a little rocky I was given no incomplete so I didn't have to repeat any of the flights. Just trying to stay up with the airplane was a job. I was still reacting, not being proactive.

Unfortunately, I had flown only seven flights in the first two weeks when it was interrupted by Christmas leave. The training command shut down completely, and we all received two-weeks leave. I traveled with a group of cadets packed into one cadet's car headed to New England to spend time with my family in Newport, Rhode Island. Every member of the class but one returned after the Christmas and New Year holidays, and we resumed flying. (He washed out for either poor flying ability, or he didn't want to fly.)

Back from leave, I had two warm-up flights, which were repeats of my A6th and A7th flights. During January I progressed slowly because of poor flying weather caused by low clouds, fog and rain. Often the foggy weather did not clear until late morning and the morning group did not get to fly. I had a check ride on my A10 and repeated this with my instructor almost a week later. January was a slow month for all because of this poor flying weather. I only managed to fly nine times during the entire month. After another week of poor flying weather in early February, the weather improved and I was flying almost every day. Near the middle of February I was often flying two flights a day.

I moved slowly at first through the schedule, but things picked up. Finally had my check ride with another instructor on February 17 and got a "thumbs up." I flew with another instructor on the morning of the 18th and I was now confident that all would go well for the final step. I began to really feel that I was flying the airplane, not just going along for the ride. On that afternoon I flew to an outlying field, and my instructor had me practice touch-and-go landing as well as full-stop landings in anticipation of my solo flight. Then on this one landing in particular, he said that I should taxi over to the side of the field because he had to go to the bathroom. As he climbed out he came forward from the rear cockpit and said to me that while he was there for me to take it around. So on the afternoon of February 18, 1950 I flew my first solo flight. What a thrill to taxi out from the side of the field and turn into the wind. After checking for other landing planes I was ready to go. All was clear and with full power I rolled down the field and took off on my first solo flight. My heart was pounding and my mouth was dry but there was now no turning back. I was going to get my wings one day.

Larry Quiel did the traditional honor of cutting my black necktie four inches from the top. To this day I can still see that flight in a picture I have in my mind's eye. I was on my way!

The next stage, "B," was to practice more landings and takeoffs, light acrobatics and emergency engine failure procedure drills with the instructor on board. On my own I repeated the acrobatics to sharpen and smooth out my flying skills. During this stage I flew one flight with the instructor, then two flights on my own to practice what he had taught me. On solo and instruction flights I flew to a large grass field and entered the landing pattern with other student-flown aircraft. On each approach I practiced the entire process from flying downwind at 1,000 feet with wheels and flaps down, completing the check off list and then being ready to start my descending left hand turn as I flew abeam of the spot I was to land. This would be a little earlier if there was a breeze blowing. At the 90-degree point in the turn I shot for an air speed of 65 knots and 500 feet altitude. A steady turn was ideal so as to arrive at the final approach without overshooting or undershooting the assumed runway. With a short straight away, I started slowing my descent, reducing the throttle, and flaring out just above the ground in a three-point attitude. The SNJ settled nicely on to the field just above stall air speed. Once on the ground, after a short roll, I advanced the throttle smoothly and the airplane quickly became airborne again. Sounds simple to talk about a good landing, but it took me many practice touch-and-go landings to become good at making smooth landings.

During the later part of this stage, I was introduced to crosswind landings. With a crosswind blowing 30 to 45 degrees from the landing runway heading, the approach and landing became much more complicated. The approach pattern had to be changed depending upon the wind direction. A wind from the left meant that the turn from the downwind leg was steeper because the aircraft was being blown to the right. As the plane reached the last 30 degrees of the turn it was very easy to overshoot, and often a steeper turn was needed to compensate. On final approach the heading was maintained by dropping the left wing slightly and applying top or right rudder to slip the aircraft just enough to maintain a constant heading. A wind from the right had another pattern to fly with the reverse action of the controls. Just before landing, the aircraft was leveled out just as the touchdown was made. The rudder and wheel brakes were used as needed to maintain a straight heading down the runway. To learn to make good crosswind landings, practice was once again all-important. Flying had become the most important part of my world. There wasn't anything else I wanted to do.

The acrobatics were really fun, and flying through loops, barrel rolls, split "S" and wing over was terrific. Before each maneuver, it was necessary to make a clearing turn to ensure that there was no other aircraft in my immediate area. Once done, the acrobatic maneuver was started. Learning to fly in any attitude, upside down, right side up, tight turns was challenging and demanding. The SNJ was a good acrobatic airplane and handled well in all attitudes. To perform a loop after the clearing turn, I let the nose drop into a shallow dive to build up the airspeed. With the proper airspeed I started the loop by the pulling up smoothly but rapidly with about four "Gs" tugging on my body. While going straight up the airspeed continued to drop as I rolled the airplane over on its back. It felt terrific! At the top of the loop, the sound of the slipstream almost disappeared and there was a sense of weightlessness. The nose of the aircraft dropped through the horizon and the airspeed began to build. Easing off the throttle on the way down, the sound changed and as the airspeed increased I began pulling "Gs" until I reached level flight. This stage was where I also learned to do stalls, spins, and most of all, clean recoveries. It was important to recognize all the signs of an approaching stall. A stall is not so bad at high altitude, but could be deadly at low altitude. Once the stall was mastered, then it was on to the spin. The SNJ was spun to the right because a spin to the left was tighter and more dangerous due to the torque from the engine. The aircraft wings were rigged to offset this, and so the student pilot did not do left-handed spins. It was great fun to enter a spin on a compass heading or lined up on a farm road and to stop the spin after exactly two turns ending up back on the same heading. I felt at home in any attitude, upside down, steep turns, it didn't make any difference.

The aircraft emergency drills were of two types and the instructor could call for one at any time. A high altitude emergency was to teach the fledgling pilot how to plan for a forced landing as well as to have time to make possible corrections to the engine controls to restart the engine or improve engine performance. The SNJ carburetor was subject to icing that could cause engine failure or reduced performance. With altitude it might be possible to find a clear field and to be able to make a safe wheels and flaps down landing. If it was to be a ditching into the water, then it was how to plan for a wheel up and flaps down landing. The low altitude emergency was to teach the student how to line up for a forced landing with little time or altitude. I was finally coming into my own, and I went through these 17 flights without difficulties with great grades from my instructor. With the improved weather conditions I was able to fly almost every day. I completed the "B" stage on March 7, 1950. In three months I had accumulated 13.8 hours of solo flight time and over 55 hours in the air.

After completing these two primary stages at NAAS Whiting, I moved on to NAAS Corry Field for the next three stages, "C," "D," and "E." These basic training stages consisted of more acrobatics, introduction to instrument flying, and introduction to night flying. Prior to the actual instrument flying in the airplane, additional hours had to be logged in the Link Trainer, the instrument trainer or simulator. This "sweat box" or "panic box," as the cadets often called them, was used to practice instrument procedures, pattern, and low-frequency-radio-range instrument-approach flights. There wasn't one time when I finally climbed out of this machine at the end of the class period without being soaked with sweat. Instrument procedures were demanding and it took a lot of effort to handle the simulator. I marveled at how easily the instructors "flew" this monster. During this same time I also completed the "C" stage, acrobatics without any repeats. In addition to refining the acrobatics taught in "B" stage, I learned how to recognize high speed-stalls and to perform the violent acrobatic maneuver, the snap roll. This was, however, not one of my favorites! By, April 18, 1950, I now had accumulated a total of 79.6 hours in the SNJ with 29.5 hours as first or solo pilot. It was everything that I could have imagined. There wasn't anything I would rather do than fly. I knew I had found my calling.

The next two basic stages were "D" and "E." The "D" stage was basic instrument training, and during this stage the student sat in the back seat of the SNJ. The aircraft was fitted with a cloth hood that could be pulled over the pilot's head on guide wires attached to the inside of the canopy. This was done so it would not be possible to see the horizon. It consisted of 16 flights in the back seat and four regular solo flights to keep up my flying proficiency. I enjoyed the challenge of flying with instruments, "on the gauges." Mastering the technique and flying smoothly would stay with me for the future. The training in the simulator had been a big help in getting the procedures down pat, but there was no comparison between the simulator and the actual airplane. The sound, sights, and smells were all missing in the simulator. Flying on instruments required knowledge, smooth aircraft handling, and staying ahead of the aircraft at all times. At the same time this stage was going on, the night flying stage "E" was conducted. This stage consisted of two flights with an instructor who flew in the back seat and two solo flights. Night flying was a real eye opener to me about the complexities of night visualization and the need to keep a good instrument scan going while being aware of the sky around you. All the flying up to this point was done in the sunshine, which helped keep me warm. That was not so at night. Without the sun, flying around at 5,000 feet with the canopy open it was cold even in the Pensacola summer. I found that I enjoyed the challenge of instrument flying and four years later I would teach this type of flying. I continued to do well and aced my check rides in all three stages. My last check ride was on May 19th and I was ready to move on to the next stage at the next air base. After completing these three basic stages at

NAAS Corry Field my flight hours continued to build. I had over 38 solo fight hours and 119.1 total hours in the air.

Larry and I were transferred again in locked step to NAAS Saufley Field on May 20, 1950. Saufley was home for two exciting flying stages for the budding pilot. The first stage was the formation stage "F" and the even more exciting stage was the gunnery training stage, "G." These stages created the sense of being part of a group. Formation flying was exciting for me, but some of the students had difficulty with these flights. The formation stage was designed to teach us how to join and leave a formation, plus practicing the free-cruise technique. Free cruising allowed the aircraft to slide back and forth behind the plane ahead as the flight leader made turns. It allowed the pilot to reduce the use of the engine throttle movement, yet maintain airspeed and position in the formation. The normal flight consisted of six students and an instructor. While at Saufley there was an accident in which two students' aircraft collided during a join up. One student was able to bailout from his crippled airplane and landed safely by parachute. The other student did not leave his crippled airplane and was killed when it crashed. It brought into sharp focus to all the students that this type of flying could be very dangerous. One misjudgment could be your last. I made sure that I kept my eyes and ears busy at all times during these flights. Even at the airspeed I was flying, 130 knots, a mistake can be very dangerous. To add to the excitement, several times the formation flight I was flying with had to race back to the airfield to beat an approaching thunderstorm. In the summer along the Gulf Coast these storms were short lived, but contained some strong winds and heavy rain. There was no place for a student pilot to be flying. We were certainly not the best flight of students in formation training, but there were no close calls. By the 12th I had finished ten formation flights mostly with an instructor in the back seat. On the 14th to change the pace, I flew my first cross-country flight to the Naval Air Station outside of New Orleans and returned. It was all dead-reckoning navigation, but it was easy as it was along the coast. The following day was a more difficult cross-country to Selma, Alabama. This one required more awareness to the landmarks to find the town and return. I finished all the formation flights on June 26th.

To fly in formation was great, but the gunnery flights, the "G" stage, was the big adrenal flying experience up to now for me. For gunnery training the SNJ was armed with one 30-caliber machine gun firing through the propeller on the right side in the cowling above the engine. I had to learn the two firing tactical approaches using the technique called deflection shooting. The first approach was called the flat-side approach, which was done by making a shallow dive on the cloth sleeve towed by another SNJ and firing when within range. The other was the high-side gunnery run, which was a steeper dive on the cloth sleeve. The flat-side run was made with an approach dive angle of about thirty-degrees from above the sleeve. The high side run was at a sixty-degree dive angle. This was to teach the ability to hit an airplane from the side using deflection shooting.

Deflection gunnery required that the target was led by enough mils using the gun sight so as to have the bullets arrive at the same time and place as the target did in the air space. It brought home very quickly that I needed to keep the plane in perfect trim by keeping the ball in the turn and bank instrument in the center. That was so the bullets went where I wanted them to go and not wide of the mark. It may look like you are aiming correctly, but if the airplane was out of trim, or "yawing," you simply missed. The maneuver started at a higher altitude above the sleeve. The flight was in a slightly strung-out formation, and when it came my turn, I passed the lead to the next pilot and then a moment later dropped the wing and nose over at the same time. As the aircraft started gaining air speed and losing altitude in the dive while turning, I rolled the plane the opposite way to start the final approach for firing. A continuing turn was made to bring the plane's nose slightly ahead of the sleeve and then correct for what was needed to keep it in that position. When the plane reached within 1,200 feet from the sleeve, I fired a short burst from the single machine gun. Before getting too close, about 500 feet, I made a breakaway by leveling the wings and started a pull up. Adding throttle, I climbed back for altitude on the opposite side, located the flight, and crossed over to join up in the last position of the formation. As each pilot did this, you moved up in the formation until it was your turn again to dive down for another firing run.

The flight instructor flew in the rear seat of the tow plane that dragged the sleeve so he could grade the students on each pass. I flew the tow plane three times during this stage. The sleeve was stored in a container under the wing, and when it was to be released, the SNJ was pulled up in almost a stall altitude. Once the air speed was reduced the release handle was pulled and the sleeve deployed at this low speed. After deployment the pilot dropped the nose to pick up normal air speed. This airspeed was maintained with the engine at a normal setting. The student flew the plane on a specific altitude and compass heading out into the Gulf of Mexico.

Halfway through the flight, the course was reversed and the firing continued until we reached the end of the gunnery area. All but one of the students in the firing flight departed for the airfield. One student was designated to fly formation on the sleeve as it was towed back to warn other aircraft of the presence of the sleeve. When the tow plane approached the airfield it received the control tower clearance to fly alongside the runway and drop the towline and sleeve. Once a clean drop of the sleeve was made the tow plane and escort entered the landing pattern and both made a normal landing in turn. Tow flights did not relieve the tension because I wanted to make perfect landings to impress the instructor. I was after every high mark I could get, plus sharpening my skills.

After returning to the airfield, landing and parking the aircraft, all members of the flight gathered around the sleeve when it was brought into the hanger and laid on the hanger deck (floor). We eagerly checked for our color to show up around the holes in the sleeve. Each member in the flight had his bullets dipped in different colored paint. The student who drew plain always lucked out because often the color didn't come off when the bullet went through the sleeve. Some exciting discussions took place when the color was doubtful. We all wanted to do the best we could because we were a competitive bunch. All together I flew nineteen gunnery flights. I was well aware that these few flights were only the tip of air-to-air gunnery knowledge. What would it be like when I was faced with someone firing at me while I was firing at an enemy aircraft? That sent a shiver down my back bone. At this time of the year, weather in the Pensacola area was great for flying and we went through the course in a short time. We finished up on July 21, 1950. I now had 179.6 hours in the SNJ including 88.6 hours solo time. It was during this time at NAAS Saufley Field that the Korean War started on June 25, 1950. Everyone had the same feeling that we would end up there if the war lasted any length of time if you selected single-engine advanced training. Now our training had more than the goal of getting our wings. We were learning the basics of combat flying and air-to-air gunnery. We were only about seven months from completing our flight training. Little did I know what would be in store for me in about one year's time!

The last stage in basic flight training, carrier qualification or "CQ" took place from NAAS Corry Field with Field Carrier Landing Practice (FCLP) done at a small auxiliary airfield, NAF Spencer. These training flights were to prepare the student pilot for the final step in basic training: to land the SNJ six times on an aircraft carrier steaming in the Gulf of Mexico off the coast of Pensacola. These FCLP flights were designed to teach us the technique of flying around the carrier, making the 180 degree turning approach, landing aboard, being arrested, and then making a deck run for takeoff. A flight of six students flew out to this small airfield in formation and practiced this type of flying under the watchful eye of a Landing Signal Officer (LSO) instructor until we were proficient in all aspects. This type of flying really honed my flying skills to another higher, sharper level. I flew at 125 feet above the ground on the downwind leg, making a 180 degree shallow descending left hand turn to approach the outline of a flight deck area marked on the runway. Flying a few knots above stall speed and about 20 feet above the ground I watched for the LSO out of the left side of the windscreen as I approached the runway. The LSO using his paddles guided us through the approach. When the aircraft reached the final straightaway, the LSO gave the signal for a "cut" or reduce the throttle to the idle position. At the same time the throttle was pulled back, the nose of the aircraft was lowered slightly to start the descent and then back pressure to make a smooth three-point landing. Once on the ground, the throttle was pushed to full power, and the SNJ took off. A slight clearing turn to the right was made to keep your prop-wash from affecting the aircraft approaching behind you. Each pass was graded by the LSO and after the flight our approaches were analyzed at a debriefing.

On one of these flights I had just taken off after a landing and was climbing up to get ready to make my turn to the downwind leg when all of a sudden a large bird appeared dead ahead. Even with fast reaction, I could not take any evasive action and hit the bird with the right side of the engine. The bird was torn to pieces by the propeller but enough got through to knock off the radio mast. The right side of the windscreen was also smeared with blood and some of the bloody bird feathers landed in the cockpit. On my next pass I made a full stop landing and taxied to the center of the field and parked the airplane. Because my radio mast had been knocked off, my radio was not working; I could not notify the LSO why I elected to stay on the ground. When all the other students had finished and left for the base he drove over in the jeep to find out why I stopped my touch-and-go landings. When I pointed out to him what had happened, he was amazed that I had hit one of these birds. Seems that they are around all the time, but no one had ever hit one. It was just my luck to be the exception. Because I did not have a radio, I flew formation with him back to NAAS Corry Field. Besides fixing the plane with a new radio mast and antenna, the maintenance crew also had to steam clean the airplane because some parts of the bird had been cooked on to the engine. My flight suit went into the washing machine. It turned out that it was spotted with blood as well. It wasn't one of my better days.

On another August day I headed out to NAF Spencer for another round of FCLP landings. I flew what ever airplane I was assigned, but it was the first time to fly his particular SNJ. There was nothing unusual about it to alert me what was about to happen. I entered the landing pattern on the downwind leg with gear and flaps down. I started my turn and slowed the aircraft down as I complete half the approach. The approach was going well, and I arrived at the runway on speed and altitude. The LSO held his paddles in the "Roger" position and then signal a "cut." I pulled back on the throttle and started to lower the nose when all of a sudden the right wing dropped, and I hit on the right main landing gear. I hit with a real jolt. I was able to get the plane under control and instead of adding power I elected to stay on the ground. I taxied over to the shack in the center of the runways and shut the engine down. I was really shook up. I also was mad because I would probably face an accident board.

After the flight had completed their landing and left to fly back to Corry Field, the LSO came over to inquire what had happened. I couldn't explain to him or myself what had happened. I left the plane at the field and flew back in the rear seat feeling really upset with myself. The next day I was scheduled for an accident board meeting at the Operation Building. I sat in the outer office dreading what was going to happen to me. It seemed like a long time, but it was only about 10 minutes when the LSO came out of the inner office. I figure it was time for me to meet my fate. He smiled at me and said, get your flight gear on, you are going to keep flying. From the depth of despair I was soaring again. He had explained to the members of the board that he believed that the aircraft should be checked because it stalled when it shouldn't have. I was flying an excellent pass. There was minimal damage to the right wing tip without a problem with the right landing gear. I wasn't written up, which I expected. My record was still clean. I floated out of the Operation Building and dashed to the barracks to change clothes. I was back into the game.

It spite of this bird strike and my hard landing, I made 76 FCLP approaches and landings on the runway outlined like a carrier deck at NAF Spencer Field.

In a nine short days, our flight as well as others was ready for the big day. The carrier used for basic qualification was the USS *Wright* (CVL-49), a small escort-type carrier whose flight deck was 75 feet wide and the landing area about 300 feet long. The SNJ had a wingspan of forty-two feet, so that did not leave much room for landing. The major goal was to land the aircraft in the middle of the deck on the white line and have the tail hook grab the number-two or -three arresting wire. That may sound like an over-simplification, but there was one small difference between the FCLP flights and landing aboard the carrier. The carrier was moving. Instead of starting the final turn abeam of the end of the runway, the turn was started abeam of the island structure of the carrier. During the turn, the carrier moved forward so that the airplane reached the stern with about 20 to 30 feet of straightaway. If the straightaway was too long, the nose of the aircraft would block the pilot from seeing the LSO. Losing sight of the LSO caused an automatic wave off. The exact spot to start the turn varied depending upon the wind speed over the water and the speed of the ship. A low wind in the morning had a different start point than a stronger wind in the afternoon. This was just one more variable to add to the approach and landing equation.

The approach and landing were similar to what I had done on the field except that I flew at a slightly higher altitude over the water to compensate for the height of the flight deck above the waterline. After the "cut" and the landing, the tail hook snagged an arresting wire, and the wire stopped the aircraft with a rapid de-acceleration, slamming me against my shoulder harness. Once the aircraft came to a complete stop, the taut arresting wire pulled the aircraft backwards a few feet so that a member of the arresting crew could stow my aircraft's tail hook that was free of the arresting wire. If the aircraft was still okay I gave thumbs-up to the flight deck plane director. He then give me the signal to go to full power, release the brakes, and make a deck run to takeoff. At this point my right wing was only about 12 feet from the ship's island. As soon as I was airborne and clear of the flight deck, the standard clearing turn to the right was made. Although the technique was the same, landing on a ship was a brand new experience for any student pilot. From my very first landing, this was high adventure for me. On my last landing I left the aircraft with the engine running after the wheel chocks were in place for the next student. I would make many more in the future, but that first landing stayed with me forever as one of my all time highs. I knew I had what it takes to join the ranks of those select pilots who could do this on a daily basis. I loved the adrenal rush that came with the entire process. It was the challenge, not the danger that propelled me forward.

On the afternoon of August 10, 1950 I completed the six qualifying landings in the SNJ-5 on the carrier without a wave off or coming close to the barrier. I had finished my basic flight training in high spirits. There is no way I can convey the level of excitement, awe, and personal satisfaction that surrounded these six landings. For me it was something that had grown inside me ever since I first became aware that people could fly. I had built model airplanes out of paper and balsa wood before I was ten years old. By the age of twelve, when Pearl Harbor was attacked and WW II began for the U.S., I was into flying in a big way. I made solid-wood scale models for the military to be used for aircraft recognition at Munford Junior High School. My older brother and I shared a bedroom, and we had it strung with wires that supported our ever-increasing collection of model aircraft built by us. At night before going to sleep I used a flash light to spot individual airplanes. I soaked up everything I could get my hands on to read and dream about flying.

Now, suddenly I realized as I sat on the railing of the bow of the ship, below the flight deck, as the carrier steamed into port that I was going to reach my goal. Gads, I was one happy guy. Larry and I had made it this far, and we were now graduates of basic flight training. I had accumulated 192.8 hours in the SNJ of which 101.4 hours were solo time. At the end of basic training, the student pilot could elect to go to single engine carrier advance training or opt for multi-engine training. We both had chosen the single-engine route. The challenge and excitement of carrier aviation was already in our blood. For Larry, it was a family affair. He had an older brother who was already flying with Air Group 19 from a carrier off Korea.

Chapter 3
Advance Flight Training

In the middle of August 1950 right after our successful completion of basic training, Larry and I received our transfer orders to report to NAAS Cabaniss Field just out side of Corpus Christi, Texas, for advance training. When we arrived, Larry was assigned to the Advance Training Unit (ATU), flying the Grumman F8F, "Bearcat," and I was assigned to the training unit flying the Grumman F6F "Hellcat." There were two other training units at this airfield. One trained in the Chance Vought F4U "Corsair" and the other in the Douglas AD "Sky Raider." I was assigned to a group of students to make up three sections of two planes each.

After spending almost two weeks of intense ground school learning all about the aircraft I was scheduled to fly, boy, was I was ready for the actual flying. One of the outdoor activities during ground school was to try our hand at bailing out of the airplane. The naval base used as its bailout trainer a no-longer-flyable F6F but with a usable engine bolted to a cement base so it couldn't move. The instructor fired up the engine, and then one by one we climbed into the cockpit with a dummy parachute strapped on my body. When it was my turn I climbed into the cockpit and strapped myself in the cockpit using the shoulder strap and seatbelt just like I would in an actual plane. When all was ready I looked up at the instructor and he signaled me to advance the throttle to 30 inches of manifold pressure. When the engine was up to speed, and I was all set, I was given the signal by the instructor to bail out. Unbuckling the seat belt allowing the release of the shoulder harness I went head first from the cockpit over the left side aiming for the wing still wearing the mocked parachute. It was not that easy, but once clear of the cockpit the slip stream created by the propeller blew me backwards and downwards so that I landed in a net with out hitting the wing, even though I dove for it. It was a scary event, and fortunately I never had to use this while flying.

The Hellcat was a much bigger airplane, and it had many new features that were not found on the simpler SNJ. Engine management was much more complicated as well as the layout of the cockpit. This was the famous Navy WW II fighter airplane and certainly commanded any pilot's respect. The flight got an overview of the flight training schedule and it consisted of a number of different types of flights. The flights started out with several familiarization flights that included bounce-drill flights to practice our landing and takeoff under the watchful eye of our instructor. Then we went into formation flying, very basic WW II fighter tactics, night familiarization, instruments, and dead-recognition navigation for cross-country flights, air-to-air gunnery, bombing and rocket firing. It was a full schedule, and there would not be much time between flights. The training command was being pushed to get the students through to argument the fleet squadrons now that there was a war on. It was an exciting time for me, and I wanted to master this aircraft.

On September 12th I walked out to the flight line and walked around the Hellcat doing my pre flight. Gads, it was big. I could only look into the lower part of this massive engine. The parachute was all ready in the cockpit, and the plane captain help strap me in. A careful cockpit check gave me time to get my excitement under control, and I was set. I glanced up, and the ground crew was ready with the fire bottle in case the engine didn't start and gasoline was spilled. I primed the engine and hit the started switch. The big propeller spun, and with a belch of blue smoke it started, and I pushed the mixture control to rich and the rpm climbed to idle. I had successfully fired up the F6F in the chocks for the first time. All set, I took a deep breath, pushed down on both brakes, and signaled the plane captain to pull the chocks from the main landing gear. The standard signal was with both my hands clenched and the thumbs pointing away from me. They pulled them. When the taxiway was clear I got the signal to move forward far enough to have the wings spread. To save parking space the aircraft at Cabaniss were usually parked with their wings folded. This sure was a new experience for me, and I felt the tingle of excitement of flying a first-line fighter plane. Making sure that my hands were inside of the cockpit (the unfolding wings passed very close by the cockpit) I watched the ground crew as they unlocked the wing-fold lever located in the wheel well, and the wing started unfolding down and out, and with a big push from the crew the wing snapped into place. When both wings were spread, I reached back on the right side of the cockpit moving the wing locking lever to the lock position and checking that the two round metal flags or "beer cans" had disappeared into the wing indicating the wings were locked. Just like all tail dragger, unlocking the tail wheel was next and getting the standard hand signal from the ground crewman, I started moving forward. By pressing the left brake on his signal to turn the aircraft 90 degrees to move along the taxiway. Once clear of the flight line, I made the standard "S" turns while taxiing because there was no way to see directly forward around the larger nose of this airplane. This was a new high for me. I felt on top of the world, but humbled by the thought I was going to actually fly this machine.

After reaching the engine warm up area, there were many more engine checks to go through before I could give a radio call to the flight instructor that I was ready. The first check was to have the engine cylinder-head temperature reach the minimum level. Once up to temperature, I needed to check the two magnetos for proper operation. From there it was to check the engine oil, cylinder-head temperature gauges for normal temperatures; oil, fuel, and hydraulic-pressure gauges in the normal range. These were all the required engine checks that had to be made. I also had to run the two-stage supercharger of the engine through a full cycle. When all six students were ready, we moved into a line and taxied towards the duty runway always keeping the aircraft ahead in sight. No one wanted to taxi into the aircraft ahead.

As each student ahead of me was cleared by the flight instructor manning the runway portable to take the duty runway, each moved his aircraft out into position for takeoff. When the plane ahead of me rolled down the runway and lifted off I moved into position for my take-off. Locking the tail wheel and completing the takeoff check list one more time set the stage for my first takeoff. Clearance for takeoff was given I pushed the throttle smoothly to 30 inches of manifold pressure, while applying pressure to both brakes and holding the control stick pulled back to keep the tail of the airplane firmly on the ground. With all of the engine instruments still in the normal range I looked up at the instructor and got the green light for takeoff. Releasing the brakes and at the same time advancing the throttle to full power, I exclaimed, "Whoopee!" as I began the takeoff. I moved the control stick to a neutral position and used either the right brake or right rudder keeping the aircraft headed down the runway. This airplane, like all high-powered propeller-driven aircraft, had a strong pull to the left when full power was applied. Therefore, right braking was sometimes needed until enough air speed was gained to be able to use right rudder as the takeoff speed was reached and the plane lifted off the ground. Once airborne, my heart rate was going like crazy as I raised the wheels and made the standard clearing turn to the right to keep my prop-wash off the runway for the following aircraft. With all the horsepower this airplane had, it accelerated much more quickly than the SNJ and liftoff was quicker. After becoming airborne the aircraft would have been "cleaned up" further by raising the landing gear and closing the canopy. I reduced the engine power to 30 inches of manifold pressure, adjusted the engine cowl flaps and oil cooler flaps to maintain proper oil and cylinder head temperature. Just remembering all those steps for was demanding. Everything under control, I climbed to 1,000 feet and entered the landing pattern with the other members in the flight. I flew away from the field until the plane ahead was opposite me going down wind, and I started my left turn. On the downwind leg I went through the landing check off list. Wheels down, flaps down propeller in low pitch and engine cowl flaps open. Takeoff from the field did not require the use of wing flaps, but landing sure did.

My first several flights in the F6F were designed to give me the experience of taking off in this more powerful aircraft and to sharpen my landing skills. I made twenty touch-and-go landings during these three bounce-drill flights. The F6F was a sweet flying machine at landing speed, and it had a nice whistle when the plane was in the correct attitude: wings level, nose up for a smooth touchdown. Being a bigger and heavier machine than the SNJ it stayed firmly on the ground upon touchdown using the same full-stall three-point landing technique. With a wheelbase of about 13 feet, ground looping was not a problem even in a crosswind. When full power was applied, however, the torque of the engine was so strong it required a lot of right rudder to keep the aircraft rolling straight down the runway. The joke going around was you could always tell a Navy carrier pilot because his right leg was so much stronger than his left.

After these beginning flights the six of us started moving rapidly into the learning process of flying the F6F in formation and basic tactics. I flew every day until September 25. On that morning as I walked to the training hanger I began to feel a sharp pain in my lower stomach area. I just reached the student's ready room when a really strong sharp pain hit me and I passed out. I was quickly taken by ambulance to the base sickbay where I was diagnosed with an inflamed appendix. In the afternoon of that same day I was operated on at the Naval Hospital located at NAS Corpus Christi a few miles away. The operation went well, and by the next day I was "forced" to get out of bed for a short time. That was not an easy task because my gut hurt like someone had put a hot poker in me, and the pain was very strong. By the third day I was able to move around a lot easier, but I still had one tender gut. The Navy sure didn't baby me, and I was released from the hospital on the fourth days to go back to NAAS Cabaniss Field. I was told by my doctor at the hospital to take it easy, and so I stayed in the cadet barracks until ten o'clock when the officers' club swimming pool opened. I spent the time at the pool until lunchtime and returned for food. Later, about 3:30, after spending a couple of hours at the pool in the afternoon I walked slowly back to the cadet's barracks. It was an easy life, but I wanted to get back to flying. The training unit found out about what I was doing, and I was ordered to report to the officer in charge. He wanted to know what the hell I was doing all day. I told him what the doctor said. He had a strong difference of opinion of what "taking it easy" was, so I was made the full-time Student Duty Officer (SDO) until I was well enough to fly. My freedom was cut short. No more bathing beauties would I see for a while! I didn't suffer from my escapade, though I think he realized I pulled a fast one.

During the time I was standing the duty, one of the students in my first flight was killed. According to the others in the flight he made a poor join up during a tactical formation flight. He ended up ahead of the others and to let them catch up he cut his power to slow the plane down. He was so busy watching the flight he did not notice that his airspeed was dropping fast, and the plane suddenly stalled. It went into a spin to the left. He began his recovery, but by the time he had stopped the spin he was getting dangerously low. He must have panicked, because he tried to pull out too fast and got into a high-speed stall that put him into another spin. He was unable to recover from the second spin, and the plane hit the ground in a dive and exploded. There are big signs all around the hanger area that read in big letters, "Don't stall." His death was a grim reminder that one mistake can cost you your life.

I was grounded until October 16 when I was cleared for flight duty and assigned to another flight to continue my training. After the three-week layoff I flew a check ride on October 17 in an SNJ with a flight instructor and was given clearance to return to flying duty. I was back into the F6F cockpit on the 20th flying with this new flight. This flight had only five students, so I fitted in with no problem. The most senior student was Bill Homes, a full lieutenant. He was getting his fixed-wing training, having been a blimp pilot for some time. I was fortunate once again having good dedicated instructors all the way through training and able to get back into the swing of things very quickly. I flew two bounce-drill flights to get back into the groove of taking off, flying, and landing the F6F after the lay off. Given an okay I joined the others and flew two tactical formation flights before starting our ordnance training on October 27. We started out making two flights practicing dive-bomb runs without ordnance on the bombing target located on Padre Island south of Corpus Christi. After each dive a member of the range crew radioed back our dive angle and pull-out altitude. The next flights we dropped miniature bombs. These bombs were small enough to be carried in a case attached to a bomb rack under the wing. Each bomb contained a small explosive cartridge inside the bomb that sent out a puff of white smoke to show where the bomb hit. Our flight made four bombing flights of eight runs each, dropping these small bombs. The range crew now added the impact point using the clock-position numbers and the number of feet from the center of the target. Diving at a steep angle meant that I had to pull hard on the control stick during recovery. Pulling close to six Gs put me on the threshold of blacking out. So for a short time I had limited vision and flew by instinct, pulling smoothly through the recovery. After eight of these dives I really felt the impact of the high G pullouts on my body. I was concerned that I might rupture my scar, but the "G" suite I wore squeezed me enough that this didn't happen.

Then we switched over to two rocket-firing flights. The rockets were small sub-caliber aircraft rockets (SCAR). The dive angles for this type of ordnance delivery were either thirty or sixty degrees. The sixty-degree dive required another strong pullout that often caused me to "gray out" when pulling five to six "Gs." The student was again required to pull out 1,000 feet above the ground. Anything below that was an automatic down (failure) for that flight. Getting the bomb or rocket into the six-foot bull's eye was the ultimate success. These flights were physically and mentally tiring, and after two in one day my body felt a little beat up from the multiple dives. The one thing that was missing was being fired at by the enemy's automatic machine guns and flak cannons. I could not imagine what that would be like. I soon learned all too well what flak looked like and what it smelled like. I also found out what I smelled like after sweating through repeated attacks. The nervous sweat generated quickly left a white salt deposit and a generous smell. The flight suit had to be laundered frequently.

When the aircraft was loaded with rockets the preparation process had an added step before takeoff. The flight taxied to an arming area after warming up and checking the engine where we pointed the aircraft towards an empty area with no buildings or roads. The rockets had been loaded on the flight line, but their "pigtails" were hanging down, not plugged in. (The pigtail was an electrical wire that connected the aircraft firing system to the rocket motor igniter.) Sitting in the arming area, an ordnance crewman tested each plug for any possible stray electric charge. If there was none, the pigtail was plugged in to the aircraft's firing system. This took extra time for the flight to be armed before takeoff. During this time, the pilot kept his arms outside of the cockpit for the ordnance crewman to see. This technique was standard ordnance practice and was repeated every time in training flights. In advance training we were getting our first look and feel of actual fleet training activity.

Besides the air-to-ground ordnance training, we spent sixteen flights practicing air-to-air gunnery. These flights repeated the same techniques we were exposed to in basic training, but with the major difference being a larger, heavier aircraft with airspeed almost three times higher than the SNJ. Attacking a banner instead of a sleeve, the banner was rigged so it could be towed either vertically or horizontally, depending upon the type of gunnery run to be made. The flat side run, that is less than 30 degrees above the horizon, was done on the vertical banner. High-side runs, using a steeper dive angle, were made on a horizontal banner. Some times the banner was neither, so we just flew what ever was scheduled for that flight. With the higher airspeed in the approach there was far less time to maneuver the F6F into a good deflection firing position. Lining up on the banner by looking through the gun sight I was ready when the aircraft reached 1,200 feet from the banner. There was only time enough to fire a short burst before a breakaway and a pull-up to clear the banner. These firing tactics taught the student to be able to hit a target using deflection up to 45 degrees from the target's flight line. We were not to close on the target to within 15 degrees because of the danger of collision with the banner or having the banner tow line cut with a 50-caliber bullet that we were firing. I found it was no easy task to hit this small banner. Once again each member of the flight had the ammunition dipped in different colored paint. When I climbed into the cockpit of a loaded aircraft, there was always a red cloth flag showing to indicate the aircraft guns were loaded. We charged the guns that armed our machine guns for firing only after we reached the gunnery range out in the Gulf of Mexico east of Padre Island. We were also on the lookout for the possible small fishing boats that violated the gunnery range. They shouldn't be there, but no one wanted to fire when one was spotted.

The banner was always towed by one of the students in the flight, so we all took turns doing this job. The process for the tow plane and escort was to taxi to an unused runway to be hooked up to the towline and banner. The banner was placed down the runway with the towline laid back along the edge of the runway to the aircraft's position. An ordnance man directed you to the position on the runway for the hook up. After he had attached the towline to the aircraft he backed away and signaled you to check that the line could be dropped. If it did, he reattached it and you were ready for takeoff. Calling the control tower requesting takeoff clearance was next. Once clearance was given by the control tower, full power was used along with full flap for takeoff to get the aircraft and banner airborne as soon as possible. During the takeoff roll the towline was dragged along and then after passing the banner it started dragging along as well. I could feel when the banner was being pulled because of the noticeable tug when it happened. At liftoff a steeper climb was made to get the banner airborne as soon as possible. The control tower radioed telling you what kind of banner position you had. The escort took off right after the tow-plane to fly formation with the banner alerting other aircraft away from the banner and towline. The horizontal banner was particularly difficult to see from the side. Together the two aircraft climbed to altitude while flying to the spot over Padre Island to start the gunnery exercise.

The tow plane flew on a 90-degree compass heading for a set amount of time, then a wide turn was made, and the tow plane headed back towards land on a 270-degree compass heading. Dragging a banner was dull, far different than making firing runs, but we all had to do it. On one of my tow plane flights I almost ran into trouble. There was one possible problem that could occur while going through the hook up process. The F6F high-powered engine had a tendency to "load up"—deposit carbon on the sparkplugs. This could happen if the engine was left to idle too long at full rich fuel mixture. These carbon deposits would heat up and cause pre-ignition of the fuel air mixture at a high-power setting. When this happened, the engine could begin to detonate or backfire during the takeoff roll and would not produce full power. In the worst case, the engine could fail. On this one tow flight, the towline and banner had not been laid out, so I had to wait while the ordnance crew went through the process. I was finally hooked up, and everything tested okay and was ready for clearance. During this waiting time, I had reduced my mixture control to idle the engine with a leaner mixture to prevent the engine from loading up. I called the tower for clearance, but was told to "hold," as there were other flights in the takeoff process using the duty runway. Finally I was told I had my takeoff clearance and to takeoff immediately. Guess what. I had not gone back over my takeoff check-off list and I started my takeoff roll with the mixture control in the wrong position. I had just reached my liftoff when the engine started detonating because the mixture was too lean. A quick glance at the instrument panel showed I was losing power, but out of the corner of my left eye I caught sight of the mixture control not on full rich and slammed it forward with my left hand. The engine immediately smoothed out, and I started to breathe again. Lesson learned—always go back over the check-off list, no matter what.

Fortunately the weather in south Texas during the fall season was very good for flying, and we moved rapidly through the training course. There were many days when I made two flights in the same day. Flying this frequently certainly sharpened my flying skills. I built up 40 hours in November alone. During November I was also introduced to instrument flying. Over a two-month period I flew seven such flights. The F6F was a good instrument aircraft, and it was a delight to fly on the "gauges." The technique was to climb away from the airfield being chased by an instructor. Upon reaching the area for instrument flying, I put a big visor over my helmet that obscured the horizon and practiced flying on the gauges. I made sure that I did not peek out because I wanted to be as proficient in instrument flying as possible.

One of the things the flights of the four training units tried to do was show off at the expense of the others. The F8F flights were particularly prone to this. The F8F was the next generation of Grumman fighter planes and was much faster and more maneuverable than the older F6F. The procedure for the returning flight was to pass over Baffin Bay that was south of the airfield at 2,500 feet in parade formation. From there it was a steady descent to reach the field at 1,000 feet while formed up in a right echelon. During this descent, the F8F flights frequently passed us up with their higher speed. They did this to get into the traffic pattern ahead of us, causing my flight to circle around before we could fly over the duty runway for our own formation break up and landing. The cadets flying in the F8Fs sure loved to give us a bad time in the barracks over our slower aircraft.

In November, inside one of the letters I received from home was a postcard notice from my draft board. I had been reclassified to 1A and would be drafted. It was a complete surprise to me until I realized I might not have notified the draft board that I had joined the Navy. Not sure of what to do, I went to the administration building on the base to seek help. The yeoman on duty laughed and told me that this was such a common event that they had a form letter that he would send out. Problem solved!

When all members of the flight completed the instrument flight stage, we were scheduled for our first cross-country flight on December 1. The course was to fly using landmarks and terrain recognition to a specific railroad bridge northeast of San Antonio and make a simulated bombing attack and return. Each student had to keep up with the flight's position because the flight instructor radioed another one to take over the lead. You'd better know where the flight was at any given time, because the lead changed about every half-hour. After this successful short cross-country flight we were ready for a longer one. On December 9, with the instructor monitoring, we flew to NAS Dallas for an extended cross-country flight returning on December 10. All that was left to fly of the required syllabus were three night flights. The first two were to practice takeoffs and landing. The third one was a round-robin flight in the local area. In this part of Texas, the oil wells burned off the natural gas that came out along with the crude oil, so it was interesting to fly around and see this happening.

Our flight pushed ahead to finish the ground-school course work and the flying schedule before the Christmas leave started. We finished up with two night flights on the next to last flying day of December. As it turned out, Larry and I both completed our advance training flying course at NAAS Cabaniss at the same time. Instead of leave and having to return to Texas, we received our transfer orders to report to NAAS Corry Field for the final stage in advance training, carrier qualification (CQ) after Christmas leave. I had flown the F6F for 53 flights and built up 109.4 hours in this aircraft. I also added 12.0 hours to my SNJ time as well. I now had 216.2 solo flight hours and a total of 313.9 hours in the air. I had only one more training stage to complete to earn my Navy wings.

To add to my exciting life, in early November I lucked out when an officer student pilot wanted to sell his car because he needed a different type of car for his growing family. "Convertibles are for single males, not for a family man," his wife told him. So besides completing advance training I now owned a car and drove back to New England in high spirits and style. The car was a blue 1948 DeSoto convertible. One unique feature was a removable windscreen to shelter the back seat riders from the wind when the top was down. It was one great car. It sure did attract the girls. Not too many cadets had cars, so I was never driving in an empty car. The price for the cadets was simple; they paid for the gas. The price for the girls was of a different kind.

With orders in hand, I packed up my gear and loaded up the car. I had three other riders to accompany me on my trip north and to help with the driving. For the ride, they paid for the gas. It sure did help with the expenses because my small pay didn't go very far. Leaving the relatively warmer south Texas and driving north it got colder by the mile!

My ten days of leave passed quickly after visiting all my old haunts. One of the family friend's sons was on home leave from the USAF, and I offered him a ride him back to his air base. It was only a few miles out of the way so it was just another way to save my scarce monetary resources. After the Christmas holiday, Larry and I both reported to NAAS Corry Field for FCLP in our respective aircraft types. Larry came in from California, and I came in from New England. In the cold of January 1951 at NAF Barin Field, west of Pensacola, we practiced making the carrier approach, taking the "cut" and landing, adding power after the landing and did it again until the Landing Signal Officer (LSO) instructor was satisfied with our performance. I knew from my flying in Texas that the Hellcat was a great airplane to fly, but I soon learned that it was even a better airplane for carrier landings. It was steady and stable during the approach and in the groove. Landing after the Landing Signal Officer's (LSO) cut was great. A slight relaxing of the control stick pressure started the nose down and then a little back pressure to make a flare-out for a nice three-point landing. It was easy because this airplane once again whistled at you when everything was set up right. Making 64 FCLP approaches during 27 flights in 13 days got me ready on by the afternoon of January 20. The only part that was bad was the cold weather that came from a cold front that blew in at the beginning of this time period. Flying with the canopy open sure was breezy and cold. The instructor gave me a "complete" on my FCLP flights, and I was ready for my carrier landings.

On January 25, 1951 Larry and I both qualified on the USS *Monterey* CVL-26 with 12 landings, 11 deck take runs, and one catapult assisted takeoff. I had to make an additional landing because I made twelve carrier landings and the same number of deck takeoffs before the carrier air boss realized I did not have the required one catapult takeoff. Therefore, after being catapulted, I had to return to the ship and landed for my thirtieth landing. I now had a total of 19 carrier landings to my credit—more than other student pilots usually had. Landing the bigger F6F on this small carrier was even more challenging than landing the SNJ. The landing area was again the same short 300 feet, so it was very important to catch the early arresting wire. I didn't want to end up in the barrier. Catching a late wire still meant you could hit the barrier because this aircraft pulled out almost 50 feet of arresting wire. I also made sure I was right on airspeed as well as altitude so I never let myself get low and slow. With the big engine, it was necessary to make sure that there was a minimum of straight away in the groove. A well-planned approach meant that I was set up before reaching the ninety-degree mark. From that point on I needed only a very small throttle corrections. I also had the aircraft at the right air speed so I could trim the aircraft for almost zero back pressure on the control stick. Just as I rolled into the groove I squeezed off on the throttle so I didn't climb when I leveled my wings. All those FCLP flights paid off when I landed aboard. On each approach my mind was running at top speed to always stay ahead of the aircraft. I figured that if I could land on this small carrier, the bigger carrier would be one heck of a lot easier. It all paid off with all good graded landings and no wave offs.

During my time on the ship, a Corsair pilot got low and slow in his final approach and received a wave off. When he went to full throttle, the torque rolled the aircraft quickly over to the left to almost an upside down position. He looked as if he would crash into the sea upside down, but he was quick-witted. Pushing the stick forward while upside down and raising the nose he was able to continue the roll and righted the aircraft to a level attitude and pull up to safety. It was just too close! There were a considerable number of students to be qualified, so it was not unusual after finishing my qualifying landings to leave the aircraft with the engine running on the flight deck for the next pilot. I climbed out and was running on pure excitement. Larry and I rode the carrier back to NAS Pensacola in great spirits. There were four types of aircraft, F6F, F8F, F4U, and AD. The graduation from flight school held on January 31, 1951 had about 50 newly designated Naval Aviators. The group was a mixture of Naval Academy graduate officers, direct commissioned officers, Naval Aviation Cadets and a small number of Flying Midshipmen. I received my Navy Wings just before my 22nd birthday. I would not receive my ensign's commission until August 1951, back dated to June 19, 1951. I was proud to receive my wings. I had worked hard for the last 18 months to reach my goal. I learned that I graduated from flight training with the second highest grade of all students for the past year. That record propelled me into the next important step in my naval flying career. It was one of the best birthday presents I ever received. I had accumulated 335.1 flight hours with 237.4 being solo time. In three and a half years I had accomplished what I had set out to do. Now I was ready for the next big pilot test—to join an operating squadron flying off of a large fleet aircraft carrier in war time.

Being presented my Navy Wings by RADM Francis Hughes, USN Chief of Naval Air Training at Pensacola Florida on January 31, 1951.

Chapter 4
Orders to the Fleet

After our graduation, Larry and I hit it big time the next day when we went to the Pensacola base main training office for our assignment. We learned that we were to receive transfer orders to the Jet Transitional Unit (JTU) at NAAS North Whiting Field to learn the technique of flying the Navy version of the P-80, Lockheed Shooting Star. It was designated by the Navy as the TO-1 and later as TV-1. After completion the JTU course, we were to be transferred to NAS San Diego awaiting assignment to a fleet squadron. Larry and I loaded up our gear and together drove in my car from NAAS Corry to NAAS Whiting. We first checked out with the base OD at Corry, and after the short drive we presented our orders to our new duty station OD. All checked in we headed off to the Bachelor Officers' Quarters (BOQ). The usual activity of getting settled in our new quarters and finding the various places on the base was next. It was strange that just a little over a year ago we were just starting our primary training. What a difference a year made. Larry had received his commission as an Ensign, but I was still a midshipman. The big difference was I now wore the Navy wings which allowed me to be treated as an officer. What a difference the wings made. I had officers club privileges, ate with the other officers, and best of all got my share of stares from the Naval Cadets just starting out in primary training. I was the only designated Naval Aviator Midshipman on the base. I felt on top of the world.

On the first Monday of February the new class assembled, and we received our welcome briefing from LCDR V. P. O'Neil, the Office in Charge of the JTU. He outlined what we would be doing while we were at North Whiting field. It was going to be an intensive course and there would be very little time for us to do anything else. That was fine with me. The ground-school course work at JTU included jet engine design and function, fuel management control, cockpit layout, and fight safety. We also went through the low-pressure chamber because we would be flying up to 35,000 feet and needed the knowledge of oxygen management and how to recognize the onset of oxygen starvation. During the simulation of being at altitude in the low pressure chamber, we were shown what happens to a pilot when he suffers from oxygen starvation. The volunteer officer removed his mask and started to pitch playing cards into a hat. He just slowed down and then would have passed out if the corpsman hadn't put his oxygen mask back on. As soon as he became aware of his surroundings he continued tossing cards. He had no remembrance of what had happened. It was a little bit scary to realize that it could happen if I didn't include the oxygen blinker instrument in my cockpit scan. To get ready for my first flight I spent a few hours sitting in an unused jet learning the position of all of the dials, gauges, switches, handles and other devices. I had the aircraft manual on my lap and I wanted to be able to find anything in the cockpit with my eyes closed. Larry and I traded places and we grilled each other on finding any name switch or instrument. It was serious fun, because we needed to know without looking. The JTU rules were that when you left the cockpit everything was left in the correct position. Failure to do this was reported by the next pilot, and you got a black mark against your record. That sure was one thing I didn't want. Just before flying for the first time the class gathered for a picture.

Reporting to the flight hanger for my first flight I found a welcome surprise. My instructor was LT Parr, the same one who taught me during my primary flight training. I soloed in the SNJ on the 18th of February 1950 and I flew my first solo jet flight on the Friday, February 13, 1951. I think that the only reason I was one of the first in the class to fly was that it was the 13th and the side number on the airplane was 13. I guess everyone else might have been a little superstitious. After all, the only reason I could figure out being the most junior pilot in the class was there were some superstitious classmates.

The first time I taxied out to the duty runway in the TO-1 was exciting to say the least. After almost a week and a half of ground school I was really ready to go. The image of this first flight is still with me. After climbing into the cockpit and getting strapped in with the help of the ground crew I checked everything in the cockpit to be sure it was in the correct position. All set, I gave a thumb's up to the line crewman and the ladder was removed. The starter jeep rolled up behind my wing, and the crewman plugged in the electrical starter cable. I gave the jeep crewman a thumbs-up and with electrical power from the starter jeep all the lights came on in the cockpit. With everything ready I hit the Starter Fuel Sequence Switch (SFSS) and the tachometer started to increase as the starter motor spun the jet engine. As soon as the rpm reached 9% I felt and then heard the rumble as the engine had a light off and the tail pipe temperature gauge needle moved rapidly around. It stopped at the proper temperature level and just as quickly my rpm was at 35 percent. The TO-1 engine had an unusually high idling speed. With all the cockpit indicator lights in the green I was all set. Taking a deep breath, I pushed the brakes full down and gave the signal to the ground crewmen to pull the wheel chocks. One of the ground crewmen checked down the flight line for any moving aircraft. All clear, and he gave me the release brakes signal and motioned me forward using the standard "come on." I was told in ground school that this aircraft should be turned carefully because too sharp a turn could "cock" the nose wheel and it would prevent forward motion. It was not dangerous but you got a good ribbing by the others for doing it. The canopy was almost closed as I taxied out of the parking area. Getting in line with the other aircraft on the taxiway paralleling the duty runway to wait my turn for take off I was in seventh heaven. It sure was nice not to have to do "S" turns. I moved forward a plane length at a time as each one head of me took off. When the aircraft ahead of me rolled out onto the duty runway, I closed and locked my canopy. My takeoff checklist was checked one more time. I was ready. I tried very hard to be professional, and it was fortunate that the oxygen mask covered my big smile.

Then it was my turn. Taxing smartly out on to the duty runway to line the jet up on the runway between the white lines and came to a stop. When I was ready after one last look around in the cockpit and checked all the engine instruments, I gave a thumbs-up to the instructor at the runway portable controlling the takeoff and landings. The jet ahead had cleared the runway, and I received the green light from him for take-off. In the next moment I was to be launched into another of the highlights of my flying career. Pressing the toe brakes even harder I slowly eased the throttle forward to 100% power. The jet tucked it nose down slightly as the thrust reached the maximum level. With one big gulp of air into my lungs I released the brakes, and the jet leaped forward and quickly rolled down the runway gaining speed. After the noise of the F6F at full power, the jet was a dream machine. It rolled down the runway straight and true and at 90 knots easing back on the control stick raising the nose of the aircraft just enough to lift the nose wheel from the deck. The jet danced on the main gear for a few moments, and suddenly the noise of the wheels ended and I was airborne. As the jet continued to accelerate, the wheels and then the wing flaps were raised. The technique was to stay low until reaching climbing speed of about 300 knots. This was a fantastic experience. I am sure my heart rate was going like crazy. Without any tip tanks, this jet plane climbed without apparent effort like a homesick angel. Now this was flying!

Like almost every pilot on his first jet flight I was over-controlling the plane. I wiggled my wings until I settled down to fly with a light touch. This jet needed very little movement of the control stick to make the aircraft go where I wanted. The instructor chased me around as I went through the regular schedule work. Reaching the landing weight I headed back to the field to practices touch-and-go landings. What a dream to land! Unfortunately, reaching the minimum fuel level, I stayed on the ground on my next landing. Taxiing back to the ramp I felt on top of the world. From here I had frequent flights to sharpen my flying skills. The air work was to give us an over view of formation flying, high-altitude navigation, and fuel management in this new type of aircraft. This jet and all the jets that followed had hydraulic aileron boosters that certainly made it easy to fly. After pushing the F6F around in the sky, flying the jet sure was different. It required only a light easy touch to fly. Flying formation was a lot easier once the wing wiggling was overcome. It took a few fights to overcome the habits that were developed from flying a propeller aircraft. It was an amazing sight to be flying around at 25,000 feet over an area that I had flown in the SNJ. What a way to fly!

I was at the hanger one morning about halfway through the training course when the crash alarm went off. Almost everyone ran out just as the crash trucks headed towards the east side of the field. One member of the class had called into the tower stating he had an engine failure. With enough altitude and airspeed he attempted to bring the airplane back to the field. He could have landed on the south field except there were too many SNJ aircraft landing and taking off so he elected to try to stretch his glide to the north field. Outside the hanger we watched him in his approach. It was very strange watching the airplane as it silently descended. Just when we thought he would make it, he ran out of altitude and airspeed and hit short of the runway. The aircraft skidded along on the ground and then went into drainage ditch. The nose of the aircraft collapsed into the cockpit killing him instantly. It once again pointed out to each of us that danger was ever present. The toughest decision for the pilot was what to do. Do I stay with the aircraft or eject before getting too low? There were no rules; it was the pilot's choice.

The days went by quickly as we continued our jet flying schedule. On one of my last flights my instructor briefed me that we would do some dog fighting. He took off with me in formation and together we climbed to 25,000 feet. I took up a heading and he headed 180 degrees away. We then made a 180 degree turn and headed for each other. He was 1,000 feet below me, and when we crossed in opposite direction the fight began. It wasn't long before he was turning after me, and in a few more seconds he won the fight. My greenhorn ability showed me I had a lot to learn about flying a jet. The course was great training, and the experience gave me a sound grounding of the best practice for flying this new type of aircraft. I completed the flying course with 24.0 jet flight hours during 24 flights. Although the TO-1 could carry tip tanks, we never used them. I left the training command on March 9, 1951 with a total of 359.1 flight hours, of which 261.4 hours were solo time. I was now ready for the next important step in my exciting flying career, to learn as much as possible about jet combat flying because I was headed for the west coast and eventually to Korea.

It was during this time that the seven of us in the class learned that we would be ordered to VF-831, as part of Air Group 15, stationed in California at NAS Alameda on east side of San Francisco Bay. No one pilot in our group knew all the others, but many had been friends with some member of the group before then. At that time we did not know that we would be spending the next two and a half years together. The picture of the class shows seven members of this group. The group consisted of LTJGs George M. Benas, Charlie J. Clarkson, Richard C. (Dick) Clinite, Herman W (Bill) Jones, and Robert R. King. Added to this group was the newly designated Ensign Larry L. Quiel. I brought up the rear still as a Flying Midshipman. I was the youngest of the group. George, Bill, and Dick all knew each other from their time at the Naval Academy in the class of 1949. Each member of our group completed the flying course with about 22-24 jet flight hours.

Before driving to San Diego, I drove north to my hometown of Newport, Rhode Island, for my last goodbye before going overseas. I would not return again until June of 1952. After a week making the rounds, I headed for Chicago by myself to pick up another jet school classmate. Leaving Newport in the morning and driving all day and into the night I made many miles. Close to midnight I felt fatigue coming on so just before Columbus, Ohio, I pulled off the road for a few hours of solid sleep. After an early breakfast I was on my way to Chicago. Staying overnight with my jet school classmate, we left Chicago driving the old US 66 from beginning to almost the end. It was some trip. As we approached Joplin, Missouri, the storm clouds became thick, and the heavy rain came down in sheets. I knew that this was spring and tornadoes can come from these kinds of storm. So like good aviators, we pulled into a motel and slept the night away. At breakfast, we learned that there had been a tornado southwest of the town. That was just on our road. Sure enough, few miles out of town, the area was littered with broken trees and junk tossed all over the place. I was sure glad we pulled off when we did.

From Joplin, we crossed through one state after another. Oklahoma, Texas, New Mexico, and Arizona would soon be left behind. We took turns driving every four hours to keep us in reasonably alert status. We were getting into desert area by the next day as nightfall arrived, and it was time for a pit stop. The next gas station was in the Painted Desert, but when we arrived it was closed for the night. That will show you how much traffic we had on the highway. We seldom saw another car and only a few trucks in an hour. We parked at the gas pump, and I stuck a note under the windshield wipers of my 1948 Desoto convertible so the attendants would wake us when they opened for business. It seemed like only a few minutes when one of the attendants was knocking on the window as dawn was breaking. The car gassed up, and with a big cup of freshly made coffee plus a couple of donuts we were off for California. Growing up in New England, the wide-open spaces of Middle America and the West were a new experience for me. The car purred along as we reduced the miles to San Diego. When we arrived at NAS North Island outside of San Diego I had driven almost 3,600 miles from one end to the other of this great country.

After checking in with the officer of the day (OD) at the NAS North Island air station administration building and getting our orders stamped we were assigned to the pilot pool at NAS North Island to await our transfer orders to NAS Alameda. It was a boring time with nothing much to do except meet muster at 0800 each workday. Unless one was lucky, there was no flying, so we were free to do what we wanted. I was finally scheduled to fly, but it was back into the SNJ for two flights of two hours each, flying my minimum flight time of four hours that was required for flight pay. I flew up into the hills and then up and down the coast checking out the countryside. It was pretty, but that was not what I wanted to be doing.

One by one we were notified to report for a deployment physical at the base "sickbay." I got the full treatment plus a battery of shots. In one day I got five all at once. I wasn't much good for the rest of that day. I felt like I had a fever and as well as a little lightheaded. I repaired to the BOQ and slept the afternoon away. I felt better by evening, but I was in no condition to do much of anything. The next part of the physical was to have my teeth checked. After a normal examination they took a full mouth set of x-rays. A couple of days later I was called back to the dental office and was told I had four impacted wisdom teeth and they wanted to take them out. It wasn't that they were concerned about me. They just wanted to fix me up so I would not have a problem and be unable to fly while I was overseas. Oh well, might as well get it over with, and I set up the appointment. I didn't realize it, but they were going to take all four of them out in one sitting. I got a nose full of gas, and when I woke up I had the sorest mouth in the world. That sure laid me low for a number of days. I was not very heavy, and the liquid diet did not help my weight problem. I probably lost a few pounds before I could start eating solid food. I was soon eating everything I could get my hands on. Still, being a flying midshipman, there wasn't very much money to go hog wild. So I had others take some extra stuff from the officers' mess for me to eat back at my room.

One thing of interest that happened while I was in the pilot pool, was to take advantage of the training slots available for a two-week course at the Navy's fire-fighting school. A bunch of bored pilots thought this would be fun and an interesting activity. The chief petty officer (CPO) in charge of the classroom saw a chance to get things really jumping. He divided the class into enlisted and officers. We competed against each other for the next two weeks. It was a hot, smelly business, and I learned a lot about shipboard fires and how to handle them. But the most important lesson was there was no way to escape a shipboard fire unless you wanted to swim.

One day, Larry Quiel was on the nozzle and four of us backing him up were putting out a fire in a dark, smelly, small compartment. We had been taught in class not to corner the fire because it could flash back to your face. The nozzle man was to push the fire away from the corner, but Larry made that mistake, and sure enough it flashed back. When we came out, he had a bright red face, no eyebrows, and about an inch of his hair burned off. He took a lot of ribbing over that one. After the class had finished, the CPO in charge told several of us that it had been one of the best classes he had run through the school. He attributed it to having the two groups compete against each other. The enlisted men really tried to beat the officers at everything. We rose to the occasion, and it was a blast.

For the seven of us, our transfer orders assigning us to VF-831 finally came in early May, and we were off for NAS Alameda. At this time we learned that another fellow, Ensign Joe Perry, who graduated just before us, was also assigned to VF-831. Larry and I drove our cars north, and because he knew the way he took the lead. I was glad to follow him through the twists and turns from San Diego through Los Angles and up through the Central Valley of California to the San Francisco Bay area and finally to NAS Alameda.

Chapter 5
Fleet Training, First Deployment

Arriving at NAS Alameda, Larry and I checked in with the base officer of the day (OD) and then went to the Bachelor Officer Quarters (BOQ) to arrange for quarters. While I was checking in a lieutenant eyed me critically. He finally walked over to me and demanded I justify my wearing pilot's wings. I pulled out my card and showed it to him. He was still not satisfied but left me alone. I guess he never heard of this Navy program, where midshipmen could earn his wings but not be commissioned. Beside that little run in, on Monday morning Larry and I joined the others six to formally report to the new squadron. The members of VF-831 were all recalled reservists from NAS Floyd Bennett Field on Long Island, New York. After meeting the group, the next task was to assign us to the flight division we would fly with as well as our associated collateral duties. At first, the reservist didn't know what to do with me. I was not an officer nor enlisted man. They finally figured out the most thankless job and gave it to me. I was assigned as the squadron's first lieutenant, and we all went immediately to work. What the heck was my job as first lieutenant? I did not have the foggiest idea what that meant, but I learned long ago to keep my mouth shut, listen, and watch. I soon learned that I would be responsible for overseeing any moves the squadron would make from our home station. I also made sure I made friends with the squadron's chief petty officers. They had been in the Navy long enough to know the way things really worked. I would get a great amount of information and help from them. Maybe it was because I was so young and really not an officer. Heck, there were a few who were almost old enough to be my father. There was not very much time before the jet squadrons would be sent first to NAAS El Centro in southern California for ordnance training, then for carrier qualification out of San Diego and finally be deployed in early September. There was a lot to get done in only a few months.

For my flying assignment I was placed in the four-plane division headed up by LT Billy Jo Sanders. The section leader with whom I flew wing was LT Robert A. Clark, putting me as the fourth man or the tail end aircraft of the division. LT George De Pollo completed the four-plane division, flying wing on the division leader or the number-two slot. Being the most junior pilot and the youngest in the squadron, it was a natural assignment. I was still a flight midshipman and remained one until my commissioning orders arrived on August 19. The commissioning date was backdated to June 19, 1951. (Of note, prior to my commission the flight-line petty officer was paid more money that I was. I sure wasn't into this flying business for the money.) The other new pilots from the training command jet school were assigned to fly with other divisions. George Benas received a special slot, flying wing on the squadron command, LCDR Anthony J. (Tony) Denman. There were a total of six divisions of four pilots each. One pilot from the Carrier Air Group 15 staff also flew with the squadron to make up for the squadron only having 23 pilots. One of the recalled pilots failed the eye test during a routine physical.

The reserve squadron had been recalled on February 1, 1951 and had transferred its operations to NAS Alameda, California soon afterwards arriving on April 18, 1951. Air Group 15 was officially commissioned on April 5, 1951. VF-831 was scheduled to receive new F9F-2s soon after it arrived at NAS Alameda. But by the time the eight of us arrived in May the squadron had received just three of the new F9F-2s. It was not until June that more F9F-2s were received. The records showed eleven aircraft were received. That brought the total to almost a full complement, which for a jet fighter squadron was 16 aircraft. The remaining two aircraft were received in July, filling out the complement. In July an additional aircraft was received to replace one that was damaged in a ground accident and had to be turned over to the air base to be repaired.

Prior to being recalled to active duty, the squadron had flown F6F-5s at NAS Floyd Bennett Field as well as having some flight time in the MacDonald FH-1. The Grumman F6F-5 was a WW II propeller fighter extensively used in the pacific during WW II. Beginning in late June and into July of 1951 there was extensive flying by all of the pilots to become proficient with this new type of aircraft. The junior pilots, fresh out of jet school and educated in the technique of flying jet aircraft, had to keep a low profile so as not to get into arguments about the best way to handle the jets. For example, the older pilots were used to starting their climb to altitude soon after raising the landing gear and flaps. But in a jet you first needed to build up your airspeed to over 300 knots before starting your climb. Also, they wanted to use the defensive tactical weave taught to them and used in the WW II flying days. There was only one problem with this type of maneuver when the flight was at 25,000 feet or above. The turning radius of the jet at that altitude meant the two sections were so far apart that you had difficulty seeing each other. There were no other defensive tactics known by the older pilots to replace this WW II approach, so we were not trained in any other way. We were ignorant about the best way or any way to attack or defend against enemy jets that had superior performance in airspeed, maneuverability, and rate of climb. From the action report produced by the USS *Valley Forge*, dated August 25, 1950 through September 6, 1950 the following was written:

It is noted with grave concern the reported superior performance of the MiG-15 as compared to the F9F-3. It is believed that if they had been manned by pilots as aggressive and well trained as ours that our pilot and plane losses would have been great.

This was a similar situation faced by the fighter pilots at the beginning of WW II on how to handle the superior Japanese fighter airplane. Out of this WW II problem, visionary Navy aerial tacticians developed a new approach based upon the concept of "dissimilar air combat tactics." It would be a while, however, before a solution of this new problem would be developed for Navy jets in the Korean War. The F9F was definitely no match against the MiG-15. In our case, ignorance was bliss!

My first flight in the F9F-2 was on May 17, 1951. It was superior to the TO-1 flown in jet school as long as there was no external ordnance carried on the wing racks. That fact became apparent when the squadron's aircraft were equipped with wing racks to carry either bombs or rockets. These racks were added when we went for ordnance training. In just five months the October 17th would be burned into my memory. To keep up my flying time maybe I could take advantage of other aircraft available at Alameda. So a few days before my jet ride, May 11, 1951, I also had my first check-out flight in the F4U-4 Corsair that was on loan to the squadron from the Fleet Air Support Squadron (FASRON) 7. I picked up 16.8 flying hours during 11 flights in this aircraft.

Flying the Corsair was fun, but it gave me a great appreciation to be flying the F9F. Many of these flights were devoted to towing a target banner or acting as a target for the squadron's jet divisions. Every now and then, after the scheduled flight had been completed, we mixed it up in a dogfight over the Central Valley, east of the San Francisco Bay area. The F4U, at slower airspeed and at low altitude, could easily out turn the jets every time. It certainly showed me that any air-to-air attacks should be more of the hit-and-run type. Also, dog fighting should never be done against propeller aircraft. Keeping the air speed up was one of the major lessons I learned from this experience.

Several of the F4U flights made were in aircraft that came out of the air base Overhaul and Repair (O&R) facility. Most had been given major repairs or engine changes. Most of the maintenance flights flown were in aircraft that had major engine changes. Why volunteer? Just so I could add to my flying experience. Given a clipboard and a long checklist of engine checks to be performed off I went. After completing this long checklist, there was still enough fuel to be adventurous. These aircraft had no identification painted on them. With all of northern California open to my investigation, I took full advantage to fly up and down the valley and rivers. Sometimes I might have been a little lower than the flight rules permitted. But what fun and freedom to explore the area!

During July the squadron needed the use of the twin engine SNB aircraft for instrument practice to bring the pilots up to Navy requirements. The SNB was manufactured by Beachcraft Corporation. Unfortunately, the only place they were available was from FASRON 8 that was stationed at NAS Moffett Field at the south end of San Francisco Bay. The difference between the two types of aircraft was like night and day. The SNB cruised at 130 knots, whereas the jet flew at 300 knots or above. The entire procedure for instrument flight was different, yet that is the way it was to be done. Several pilots drove down the East Side of San Francisco Bay together to NAS Moffett Field outside of Mountain View and returned to NAS Alameda the same day. We completed the course and knew we probably would not use what we practiced in the near future. This was just one of many old ways that disappeared in the coming years.

During August, the last flight of the day frequently encountered the fog bank moving in from the ocean into the bay either coming in the bay entrance or over the low coastal mountain range. The civilian air traffic control did not want any of the jets descending through this fog on instruments with commercial airliner landing and taking off from the commercial fields near by. They viewed us as a "deferred emergency" if we had to make an instrument let down. The only way was to fly out to sea towards the Farallon Island a few miles off shore and then descend through the fog on instruments to 300 to 500 feet. After the flight was below the fog layer, the division made an 180-degree turn and flew back to the opening of the San Francisco Bay. We flew under the Golden Gate Bridge halfway between the water and the bottom of the bridge. Sometimes the road bed was obscured in fog. After clearing the bridge we made a slight right turn and went under the Oakland Bay Bridge at the same altitude to NAS Alameda. As we approached the field we did a standard formation carrier break up at 300 feet just below the bottom of the fog and make a full circle for a landing. The division I flew with made four such approaches. Supposedly, flying under the bridge was forbidden, except when the fog dictated it.

At no other time was there any attempt to fly our jets on instrument or practice the instrument descents that we would use flying with the task force. The procedures to do this technique were not covered in our training even though there was a significant body of information from the task force carriers operating in the Korean War. The Carrier and Air Group Action Reports covered many of these specific issues. They were not, however, made available to the pilots who would soon be facing these exact same conditions during the squadron's very short 90-day training period.

It was during the summer at NAS Alameda that the squadron had its first non-fatal accident. Ensign Joe Perry was taking off on runway 270 L (left) one morning when halfway down the 6,000-foot runway his engine began to surge, generating high tail pipe temperatures. He pulled back his throttle to the idle position and then shut down his engine. He applied full brakes, but with the engine shut down his hydraulic pressure dropped to zero, reducing his braking power. He immediately pulled the emergency brake air bottle handle, locking his wheels. This action, as expected, immediately blew both his main tires, but the airplane continued sliding down the runway on the wheel rims and into San Francisco Bay. The airplane hit the water off the end of the runway and had just enough speed to plow along and finally stopped about a hundred feet from shore. He quickly unfastened his shoulder straps and seat belt, climbing out of the cockpit of the sinking airplane on to the wing with the parachute still attached. He pulled his life raft from the parachute seat and inflated both his Mae West and life raft. He climbed into the life raft as the airplane sank beneath him, sliding off the wing into the water of the bay completely dry. In the meantime, the Alameda control tower personnel who had witnessed this event had sounded the crash alarm. The crash boat quickly got under way and sped full speed to rescue the downed pilot. There was only one problem. The crash boat rushing across the smooth bay waters generated a large bow wave, and in their eagerness to get to the pilot approached him too fast. The bow wave upset the life raft and dumped Joe into the bay's water. He was really mad because he had on a brand new pair of expensive flight boots. The bay waters around the airfield were none too clean, as well as being salty. Later, he had to work hard for several hours to get his boots back into good shape after drying them out. Oh, the airplane? It was raised by a floating crane and sent to the Naval Overhaul and Repair (O&R) facility for repair and refurbishing.

Starting in early July, the squadron began Field Carrier Landing Practice (FCLP) at the Naval Auxiliary Field (NAF) Crows Landing, an outlying field in the Central Valley. After burning off enough fuel flying to the airfield to reach 2,500 pounds, the maximum for starting landing practice. The flight of four flew up the right side of the runway at 250 feet for a few hundred feet. Then each airplane left the formation one after another in thirty-second internals, making a left 180-degree turn to parallel the runway going down wind. During this turn, the aircraft's speed was reduced to 165 knots to be able to lower the landing gear and reduced to 150 knots to lower the wing flaps as well as opening the canopy. The altitude was decreased to 125 feet on the downwind leg. At a point abeam of the end of the downwind runway, a shallow descending left-hand turn was started. This turn was made such that the airplane ended lined up in the center of the runway's heading about 200 to 300 feet from the end and about 20 to 25 feet in altitude. During the latter part of the turn, the pilot looked for the Landing Signal Officer (LSO) who stood on the side of the runway visible out of the left panel of the forward windscreen. The LSO, either LTJG J. C. Dunn or LT Dave Rose handled all the duties. One or the other monitored the aircraft's approach and by the use of his two "paddles" signaled to the approaching aircraft's pilot instructions assisting the pilot in the line up on the centerline of the runway with proper altitude and air speed. The other one made notes on each approach to be able to debrief us later on how we were doing. This required a lot of concentration by the pilot to keep all the factors in balance and to make a good approach. The air speed was only a few knots above stall air speed and the height above ground was about 20 to 25 feet. If all was well, I receive a "cut" signal. Upon seeing this signal pulling the throttle back to idle to reduce the engine power as well as letting the nose of the aircraft drop slightly to start a descent, then immediately stopping the descent with some back pressure on the control stick to effect a soft landing. As soon as plane was on the ground, the throttle was smoothly advanced to full power, and the aircraft became airborne to start the process all over again. Airborne, a series of shallow turns to the right and then the left was made to clear the runway of jet exhaust from interfering with the following airplane. Our landing interval between aircraft was about 30 seconds. After becoming airborne again I climbed to 125 feet with landing gear and flaps still down. A regular flight allowed enough time for about five to seven approaches depending on how many aircraft were in the landing pattern.

The practice hopefully would pay off when the squadron went aboard the aircraft carrier, and each pilot had to land 15 times to become carrier qualified. All the FCLP landings were touch and go. All landings on the carrier were straight up the deck and were all arrested or full stop. The angled fight deck of the present day carrier, which allowed for touch-and-go landings, was still at least three years away. After the last touchdown on the airfield, the throttle was left on full power, allowing the air speed to build up while raising the wheels, the flaps, and closing the canopy. With the aircraft "cleaned up" the air speed increased very fast. Reaching 300 knots, I raised the nose and the airplane started to climb about 6,000 feet a minute. The flight leader was at a slightly lower power setting so we could make a running rendezvous and head back to the home air base in formation.

Late in July the squadron switched emphasis from training flights for carrier landing technique and was ordered to NAAS El Centro in the Imperial Valley of California close to the Mexican border for ordnance training. This was a real change from the cool San Francisco Bay area weather to the summer heat of the desert. It was seldom cooler than 100 degrees in the shade or at night the entire time we were at NAAS El Centro. My collateral duty being the squadron's First Lieutenant meant now I was going to be very active. This title was a fancy name to oversee the movement of the crew and maintenance gear. The crew had to load all the gear on to the giant "Mars" seaplane that operated out of the air base. The more senior pilots either flew the airplanes to El Centro or drove down in their private cars. Then we were flown from San Francisco Bay to the Salton Sea. When the aircraft's hatch was opened, the heat of midday hit me right in the face. The Chief Petty Officers (CPO) organized the crew into four work parties to unload the aircraft. Each work party spent only 15 minutes before the heat got to them. The crew finally got the aircraft unloaded onto the Navy trucks and buses supplied by the air base, and we headed off to the El Centro air base. Not far down the road from the landing dock where we unloaded, there appeared a small roadside gas station and general store. I had the driver pull in and I gave the crew the opportunity to get a cold drink. If they chose a beer, I didn't notice. After all, in a few short months my life would depend upon them. I wanted them to be on my side.

After settling in the Bachelor Officers Quarters (BOQ) for the day we attended a briefing by the base operation officer and then by the medical officer. The base operation officer briefing covered the various ordnance areas, range safety procedures and general operations around the air base. Air-to-air gunnery was held over the Chocolate Mountain range to the east of the air base. Our kick-off point was a strange looking mountain that looked just like a Hershey Chocolate kiss rising up from the desert floor. The medical officer briefed us on the heat and how to recognize the danger signs. The one thing he covered was what to be aware of from the wildlife found in and around the buildings. In the quarters, we were warned to turn our shoes upside down and bang them together in the morning. Just in case a scorpion was hiding in one of the shoes. We thought he was pulling our leg, but a few days later it happened to one of the pilots. He woke up and went to put his shoe on. He saw the scorpion before he put his foot in and let out a yell. Everyone came running to see this big bug. The other thing was to be alert for snakes. They loved to get in the shade and we were told to watch out for them. The quarters we slept in were air conditioned, but only to about 85 degrees. Any colder, we were told, would not be good because of too much temperature differential could cause someone to pass out from the shock. The temperature outside never got below 100 degrees the entire time we were at El Centro. Gads, this was a hell hole. We flew from dawn until about 11:00 A.M., when it became too hot to touch the aircraft. It was a real ordeal, even early in the morning, to sit in the aircraft cockpit with the engine running while the ordnance crew checked the aircraft for stray electrical current before plugging the rocket pigtails into the wing receptacles. I thought I lost about a quart of sweat every time I had a rocket-firing flight. The rockets were sub-caliber aircraft rockets (SCAR) and looked more like a fourth of July rocket that threaten only the snakes on the ground. Each of us had one flight where we carried a full load of six 5-in. rockets. We would carry these rockets often in the future during ground attacks after we reached Korea. The rocket warheads we fired now were filled with a white powder instead of explosives so as to mark the point of impact. Larry Quiel was the squadron's sharp shooter. He put all six of his rockets into the six-foot bull's eye. I couldn't even come close to his score without a few more practice flights. The flying was done in a classic approach, nothing like what we would do when we reached the combat zone. Altogether, I only managed to get in a few rocket-firing flights. In these few flights there was no way to develop effective skills to hit small targets like a truck or military tank. Because the flights were flown with one aircraft making a run at a time, no real concepts of division attacks were tried. The real war would be nothing like the few training flights the pilots were able to receive. In the Carrier Air Group, CVG-5 action report dated November 10, 1950-November 31, 1950 the following was written:

> Pre-combat training in strafing and bombing under varying conditions should not be neglected. Low level and shallow attacks should be included. Targets located in varying terrain and altitude should be utilized with the aircraft flying in a fully loaded condition of either bombs or rockets, and fuel.

Here were specific recommendations for training in shallow rocket attacks. The report was never seen, and we did nothing like that during our two weeks at NAAS El Centro.

The bombing practice was done again just as before in advance training with miniature bombs about eight inches long that contained a similar white powder. When the bomb hit the ground it showed a white smoke marker. The airbase staff manned the target areas and they radioed to each plane upon the completion of the bomb drop the dive angle, release altitude, and where the bomb landed. The flight did 30-degree and 60-degree dives. The latter dive angle required at least a six-G pull out. We all wore a G-suit to keep from blacking out during the recovery from these bombing runs. These few flights were tiring, but they were good practice. We would use these methods many times in the future. Unfortunately, we did not have the opportunity to practice this type of attack with any of the larger bombs that we would carry on our combat missions. The training was very basic. There was nothing more than what had been done in the advance training command. I would learn later that there was a big difference in how the aircraft performed with six 250-pound general purpose or 260-pound fragmentation bombs on the wing stations. The additional weight of 1,500 or 1,560 pounds made the first bomb run far different than without the bombs being on board. The pullout from a bombing run when only one bomb was released was more difficult, and a higher altitude was needed at the release point to make a good pullout. Low pullouts were very dangerous because of the possibility of being hit with your own bomb blast and being too low to avoid small-arms fire. It would have been better to practice this in the training phrase than in combat. My first drop of any bomb that exploded had to wait until I could put a dent in the Korean countryside. I felt as if I was going off to war without knowing much.

We engaged in several air-to-air gunnery firing flights as part of the training. These flights were done using the same technique I used in basic and advance flight training. It was fun, but it didn't fill the bill. The problem was it wasn't the type of defensive tactic being used in the Korean War. It was totally different than what was done in WW II. This was covered in great detail in an enclosure to the USS *Philippine Sea's* action report for the period 1 January to 1 February 1951.

In jet engagements, the F9F-2 would almost always be on the defensive. The search radar on the ships of the task force had great difficulty in picking up jets at altitudes above 30,000 feet and often could give no information on the "bogey's" altitude.

The action reports covering the few times the MiG-15 engaged the F9F-2 describes the technique used to best advantage. The MiG-15 could out climb the F9F and often had altitude and speed advantage. Turning into the attacker for a quick heads-on firing pass often broke up their attack, causing the MiG to break away and climb quickly away. One significant point was to maintain air speed at all times and whenever possible, get altitude and up-sun position. It was unfortunate that this document and others were never made available to the squadron. It would have been extremely useful in the event that our flight was attacked.

71

My entire period of ordnance training at El Centro consisted of 11 flights spending 10.5 hours in the cockpit. This total was broken down as follows: four bombing, two rocket, two strafing and three air-to-air gunnery flights. Needless to say, I was not going to hit the bridges or tanks very often until practicing a lot on the enemy. All the practice in Korea paid off in later flights, but we were sure not ready in any sense of the word. There was no effort to try the types of attacks recommended in the reports rather than what the division was doing. Multiple aircraft attacking at the same time was the way to stay alive. Attacking one after the other was an invitation to get hit by flak. The Koreans, by the time this air group arrived, had plenty of practice. The green pilots of the air group squadrons would pay the price.

To break the routine, my division flew five cross-country navigation flights. None of these flights were in any relationship to the conditions we found later in the combat zone. It is all well and good to fly with all the radio directional finders operating, but the North Koreans did not help us that way. They did not turn on their homing radios to aid us in finding our way. Flying a planned flight to simulate the flight pattern that would be constantly used by the division in Korea was just not done. Flights over the mountains of California to seek a specific area about 120 miles from the airbase and perform dead-reckoning navigation over a set of roads or railroad lines would have been far more useful than flying at 35,000 feet at night. In the CVG-5 action report, dated November 10, 1950-November 31, 1950 the following was written:

> A course in enemy camouflaging and how to detect it should be given pilots going to the Korean area. There are known instances of armed-reconnaissance aircraft from newly arrived carriers passing over several camouflaged vehicles which were spotted and destroyed less than an hour later by more seasoned pilots.

At the time that the squadron was in the bay area, the Army had a very large base, Fort Ord, south of Monterey, California. It would have been a major training aid to fly over this area to see from the air what the tanks and trucks looked like from 1,000 to 3,000 feet. Some arrangement with the Army would have been very beneficial for our training. Also, if the Army tried to camouflage or conceal their vehicle it would have helped measurably to train us in how to spot such vehicles. It also may have benefitted the Army troops to know whether their camouflage efforts were effective or not. Even a few flights would have been a significant training experience. Using current maps of the area would have given additional training in map reading coupled with actual visual examination of the same ground. Unfortunately, none of this was done until the Air Group learned it the hard way in Korea.

Reading from an action report from the USS *Philippine Sea* CV-47, dated October 11, 1950-December 31, 1950, this comes through very clearly. It reads in part:

In visual reconnaissance the pilot is faced with the problem of what to look for and how to look for it. Intelligence must tell the pilots what to look for but only through experience and training can a pilot be taught how to see. The visual reconnaissance missions assigned during this operating period, the pilots were looking for enemy troops, supply dumps, military equipment and all types of transportation equipment. Through experience it has been found that it is difficult to see this type of target when concealed or camouflaged, from an altitude above 1,500 feet. In like manner, it has been determined that most of our aircraft have been hit by anti-aircraft fire when below 1,500 feet. As a compromise, one or two aircraft were sent low—50 to 1,500 feet— while the remainder of the flight stayed 3,000 feet above the low planes. Even with such an arrangement the results achieved, in many cases, depended upon the visual acuity of the individual.

During one cross-country flight flown at night from El Centro we got more than we bargained for. The flight plan was to fly from NAAS El Centro to the San Francisco Bay area and back at 35,000 feet. We took off at dusk and the outbound leg everything was okay, but on the return leg, the section leader reported that he was short of fuel because of a fuel transfer problem from his tip tanks. For some unknown reason one of his tip tanks didn't pass all of the fuel to the main tank. The flight leader calculated that there wasn't enough fuel in that one aircraft to make it to NAAS El Centro, and we had to land some where in the LA basin. There was only one problem. The fog that forms this time of year over the ocean had started to move inland, and there was only Los Angeles International airport reporting enough visibility for landing. The flight of four headed down with dive brakes fully extended at eight thousand feet a minute. The flight had been flying at 35,000 feet, which meant the aircraft were very cold. At this altitude, the outside air temperature was about a minus 55 degrees. I had to turn up the cabin temperature to full hot so that when the canopy was opened I did not get completely fogged up when the warm moist air hit the inside of the cold plexiglass canopy and wind screen. With clearance from the LA tower, we made a high-speed breakup over the field at 800 feet, just below the fog that was moving in over the field. After landing and guidance from the control tower we taxied to the North American Aircraft Corporation hanger area hoping that we could get more fuel. At this time, the commercial airliners were all prop driven, so all they had was aviation gasoline. Their jets were years away from becoming operational. After some time we were able to arrange for our airplanes to be refueled. We did not take on any fuel for the tip tanks. The full main tanks would be enough to get us to El Centro. We climbed into our aircraft, and one by one we were started.

After getting operational clearance from the tower, we were able to taxi out to the duty runway to takeoff headed due west. We were in the second takeoff position behind a commercial airliner, a DC-6. The flight leader requested to go around the DC-6 to be able to takeoff ahead of him. There was only one small problem. There wasn't enough room on the taxiway to go completely behind the DC-6. So we just taxied under the tail of the aircraft and made it to the duty runway. I sure wondered what the passengers thought to themselves of our action. Takeoff clearance was given, and all four planes took off in formation. We had to stay low until climb speed was reached and then start the climb through the fog on a westerly heading. Once above the fog we turned east southeast and we were on our way. We landed back at El Centro early that next morning. The first leg of this flight was 2.3 hours long. The second leg was only 0.8 hours. It had been one very long night. Once again it showed us that careful planning and cruise control was essential for successful jet flying. It was more so, when there were no friendly fields for refueling in North Korea. Such was our training to be ready to fly in combat.

As noted before, there were many detailed carrier and air group action reports available from the carriers and air groups attached to these carriers highlighting their experiences. In these reports was a wealth of information about air tactics developed for the air war in Korea. These tactics covered large strikes with a mix of F9F-2 (jets), F4U and ADs (props), Jet reconnaissance flights, photo escort and Combat Air Patrols (CAP). There was only one major problem. They were not addressed to the air group I was assigned to nor forwarded to us. We did not see nor read them. Sure made a lot of sense?

For an example, from the USS *Philippine Sea* action report dated, October 11, 1950-December 31, 1950, come these words:

> In order to safely escort the conventional planes a new procedure was adopted by all jet squadrons of this Task Force. This consisted of establishing an approach and retirement corridor through which all conventional planes passed going to and returning from the target area. The initial point, designated Point Able, was set up over some well-defined landmark 30 to 40 miles from the object area. Point Baker and Point Charlie were established as 1/3 and 2/3 of the distance toward the target. The strike leader informs the jet cover as he passes each of these points, to facilitate keeping track of the flight without having to constantly watch their progress. Usually four jet divisions were employed, with divisions stationed at 20,000, 25,000, 30,000 and 35,000 feet.

After our days in the desert, NAS Alameda seemed really cold even though it was mid-August. Upon my return I was called into the squadron commander's office and was handed my commissioning orders. My days as a flying midshipman came to an end. To celebrate this occasion we repaired to the officers club and drank a few toasts to my release from the low-paying job. I could now rattle more money in the pocket. I also had to have my picture taken for the official squadron roster after having my uniforms updated.

We were soon into FCLP flying again, because we were getting close to the time for carrier qualifications. The clock was running, and soon the planes were loaded aboard at Alameda and the ship left port on the 19th to begin carrier qualifications for the two jet squadrons. The props were flown down to San Diego to be loaded aboard after the jets finished their work. On August 20, the first day of carrier qualifications on the USS *Antietam* off of San Diego did not start off very well. Even though the day was clear and the sea surface calm, this area of the California coast was noted for large swells that traveled from the far North Pacific storms. These swells meant that the pilots were faced with a pitching deck. It wasn't bad pitch, but it seemed to be enough to create an image problem. To add to this problem there were a large number of poor approaches that either caused a wave off or when signaled for landing ended up with the aircraft being damaged by hitting the barrier after a late touchdown.

There were also too many times that the pilot dove for the deck, resulting in a bounce, which almost always got you into the barrier. The faster air speed of the jets cut down on the time from the cut to touchdown, so too many were reacting too slowly and landing to far up the deck. The air speed difference between the F6F and the F9F was about 40 knots. That meant you not only received the "cut" further from the flight deck but also had less time to land. This slow reaction might have been caused because of the earlier cut, but whatever the case there were too many touchdowns up the deck, picking up a late arresting wire and the possibility of engaged the barrier. There were some great saves when the barrier operator dropped the first barrier after the plane had caught a wire; otherwise it would have hit the barrier. The flying was stopped early because too many pilots were getting too tense. None of the eight who had come from the training command flew the first day. I think we would have done a better job because we had recently completed carrier landings. The recalled reserve pilots hadn't done carrier landings in years.

The next day was better, but a significant number of the jet pilots still showed that they were not doing very well. The other "bunkroom boys" and I flew on the second day, and although once again these landings can be a very demanding task, I made my approaches and landings without difficulties. I found that the bigger carrier made it a lot easier to land the jet than landing the F6F on the smaller escort carrier. On August 21, 1951 I made my first four of 15 carrier landings in the F9F-2 including four catapult launches. I was launched again on the 21st and made four more landing and catapult launches. I did not fly on the 22nd but flew again on the 23rd and added three more landings. I finished carrier qualification on the 24th adding four more landings and an equal number of catapult launches to my logbook. After qualifications were complete, the two jet squadron flyable aircraft were catapulted and were flown on the 24th to San Diego while the ship returned to the Naval Shipyard at Hunters point, San Francisco. Too many of the squadron's aircraft had to be offloaded in San Francisco because they were not flyable after being damaged from hitting the barriers. Most of these were repaired by the air-base maintenance crew and returned to the squadron.

We left San Diego by divisions and flew back to NAS Alameda. I was pleased that I made my carrier qualification without a problem. Landing in this jet straight up the deck on this carrier did not seem to be any more difficult than landing the F6F. The only thing I noticed was the process was faster and that meant less time to make corrections in the final stage of the approach. Once again, getting all set up by the ninety-degree mark in the approach turn made it easier to arrive at the "cut" point in a good comfortable position. The jet, just like the prop, climbed if the power setting was not reduced slightly when rolling the wings level in the groove for the final stage. Fast reaction to cut power and drop the nose slightly when the cut signal was received meant a much higher probability of catching the number-two or-three wire.

By August 30, the full squadron was back at NAS Alameda to finish the final preparations for our deployment aboard the USS *Antietam* (CV-36). I traded in my old car for a new one but left the delivery date open. The dealer also agreed in writing that in the event of my death, the down payment money would be sent to my parents. That was my only possession I could not take with me. There were several new aircraft transferred to the squadron to make up for the ones that had been too damaged during carrier qualification to be repaired in time for our departure.

The last week in Alameda was busy getting packed up and moving all our personal effects aboard. The eight of us were assigned to a twelve-man bunkroom on the hanger-deck level. It gave us extra room, and we made good use of the space. I slept aboard the night of the 7th to be ready for the departure. There were no family members or outside friends to see me off, so I helped the others wherever I could. The morning that arrived was a beautiful, clear one. By 9:00 o'clock the orders came for all hands to come aboard and all non-crewmembers to leave the ship. The painful goodbyes were said by those with family and friends in the area, and at 9:30 the mooring lines were cast-off and the tugs pulled the ship away from the pier. With a mighty blast of the ship's whistle, the ship began to move backwards out into the bay. Far enough out, the ship's screws were reversed, and we began to move forward, and the ship steamed out of San Francisco Bay. So on September 8, 1951 I was headed for the unknown job ahead. But first, we would get the treat of liberty in Hawaii. The ship and air group began the big task of becoming good at carrier operation. This was a very big challenge for all hands. The ship had been in the reserve fleet and was really not ready to fight in the Korean War. It had been cleaned up and outfitted at the Hunter Point Naval Shipyard after being activated on January 17, 1951. Being placed in active service didn't mean it was ready, however. When the ship left on September 8, 1951 there were still shipyard workers aboard finishing up the last of the changes needed for operations. Ready or not, the air group was headed for combat flying.

Chapter 6
Carrier Training, First Tour

During the crossing we slowly got settled into our new quarters as best we could. It was a tight squeeze to fit every thing in. The *Antietam* arrived in Hawaiian waters on September 12, 1951 and entered the channel leading to Pearl Harbor. Aided by a couple of tugs the carrier docked at Ford Island. The dock was just a few hundred feet from the sunken hull of the USS *Arizona*. Standing on the forward part of flight deck I could make out the outlines of the hull under water. The sight of that hull brought back a flood of memories of that Sunday afternoon when the family gathered around the radio to hear the news of the Pearl Harbor attack. Little did I know at twelve years old that one day ten years later I would be going to war. The following day the ship and air group still aboard left Pearl Harbor for a short operational period. It sure was short because there were too many landing accidents. I did not fly but watched from "vultures' row" the wild approaches and landings. A number of landing aircraft ended up as barrier crashes. Not a good start, so we returned to Pearl Harbor for the weekend.

During the next air operations in the Hawaii area, the squadron (VF-831) lost its first pilot, LT William J. Callahan. His aircraft left the catapult in either the wrong attitude or he raised the nose of the aircraft too much, resulting in a stall. Whatever was the reason the jet crashed just ahead of the ship, and his aircraft broke up on impact, sinking immediately. The *Antietam* helicopter as well as plane guard destroyer made a full search of the crash site, but there was no sign he escaped the aircraft, and his body was not recovered. This event was a sobering reminder that carrier air operation was a dangerous business and very unforgiving of mistakes. We all hoped it was the last one, but I knew that it could happen again to anyone at anytime. We were to face not only the operational hazards of carrier air operation but also the bullets and shells of the enemy's anti-aircraft artillery (AAA) guns in the very near future. What we didn't realize was there was another significant danger, the cold winter weather. Korean weather was under the influence of the vast Asian landmass. That would mean the cold weather was something to deal with every flight day in the upcoming months. It would be colder than I had ever experienced during my years in New England. What the future combat was going to be like frequently crossed my mind, but I had no answers. The carrier operation skills gulf between the recalled reservist and the new pilots was considerable. The older pilots hadn't been active in carrier work for years and were all new to jet carrier aviation. The eight of us had done our carrier work only eight months ago.

During this very short stay in the Hawaiian area, the air group never flew together, just as in the states. It is still amazing to me that during the short three-month training period in the states, the squadron never flew a flight with any other squadron. We usually flew as a division of four, never with any larger flight of aircraft. There was no way to practice fighter escort, flak suppression, Combat Air Patrol (CAP) or coordinated attacks. It was all going to be on-the-job training. After the weekend the carrier left port and we were at sea for four days for flight operations. I flew once on the 13th and landed back aboard the ship. On the 14th, I flew a short flight with my division to NAS Barbers' Point. On the 16th and the 17th we flew around the island with no purpose other than sight seeing. Then later on the 17th we headed back to the ship to land aboard. That was the sum total of my flying from the carrier to get ready for war.

I added three more carrier landings and catapult launches to the logbook, as well as some more F9F flight time. I was going to war with 92.2 flight hours, accumulated during 81 flights along with 18 carrier landings in the F9F. There wasn't any pretense to do significant training. I still had to wait until my combat flights to drop any bomb bigger than the small practice ones. I did not carry or drop live ordnance until we entered the war zone. The rumor that floated around the wardroom that the ship and air group could not have passed an Operational Readiness Inspection (ORI), so there wasn't much done. The ORI consisted of a short operational period at sea on the 20th. But at least during almost two weeks in the Hawaiian waters the ship and air group seemed to begin to work together as a team aboard ship. There were still too many rough spots to our operation that showed up when we got to the task force and started full-scale operation. The air group as a unit was not ready to face the enemy, but we were going anyhow. Now I learned another meaning of what the words, "ninety-day wonders" really meant. I had lots of questions, but no place to find the answers. I was headed out to fly in combat in an aircraft that I was just beginning to fly other than straight and level. My expertise in ordnance delivery was at the beginner's stage, and I had no idea of what lay ahead. Apprehension dominated; maybe the fear was something I could handle. I wanted to do the job assigned to the best of my ability but was well aware I had a lot to learn. I figured that if I could make it through the first thirty days I had a good chance to go all the way. I knew I could handle the aircraft around the carrier. My carrier landings were still a little rough but I concentrated on making them better. I was determined to stay out of the barrier.

Ready for Combat

The Air Group left the Hawaiian Islands for Yokosuka, Japan, just after lunch on September 26th with the following number of aircraft and pilots:

Unit Type A/C Operational Pilots
Aircraft
CAG-15 3
VF-713 F4U-4 17 26
VA-728 AD4, AD4L 18 28
AD4Q
VF-831 F9F-2 15 22
VF-837 F9F-2 16 22
VC-3 F4U-5NL 4 6
VC-11 AD4W 3 5
VC-35 AD4NL 4 6
VC-61 F9F-2P 3 4
Total 80 122

With the lush tropical world of Hawaii fading in our minds our small task force of the carrier and the four destroyers that made up the carrier's screen steamed on to Yokosuka, Japan. The entire air group was not trained for the combat missions ahead. Everything practiced was from the last war. This was especially true of the jet pilots. If we couldn't hit them with our ordnance, maybe we could scare the hell out of them with our aggressiveness.

From another carrier action report, these words took on significance once we were in the combat zone.

The F9F is an extremely effective flak-suppression weapon. The four 20-mm cannons make the F9F valuable for any coordinated strike. The F9F should be made available for flak-suppression for the propeller aircraft strike on a well-defended target. As the propeller aircraft begin their attack, the jets dive from above and pass them to be able to drop their 260-pound fragmentation bombs. After the bomb release the jets made their pull out and then climbed for altitude. At the top of the climb, a hard 90-degree banking turn was made, reversing direction so as to come back around for a diving firing run. In this run the 20 mm cannons were used to strafe the AAA gun emplacements as the AD and F4U bomber were completing their drop and initiating a recovery to retire from the target area.

This might help keep most of the enemy gunners off their AAA guns. With eight jet aircraft in a loose formation, this was demanding flying requiring skill and sharp visual awareness of all the jets around you. Properly done, a coordinated attack was highly effective and reduced the damage to the attackers. As far as Air Group 15 was concerned, it was never done during the training in the states. As with other aspects of training I would learn this technique in actual combat. It would have been a big help to have some practice to work out the bugs or problems.

On the way to Japan, the air group pilots regularly gathered in the officers' wardroom to become acquainted with the maps of Korea. Each pilot was given a complete set of maps covering all the eastern half of North Korea. There were names of cities that I never heard of nor could pronounce until these briefings. I would soon know them all too well. We made our map books in such a way that it could be unfolded like turning the pages of a book. Later on, this became too bulky, and I took only the map of the area to be attacked along with the route in and out. I also checked out my winter flying gear. I added wool pants, a wool shirt, and best of all a set of long johns. I was also issued a 38-caliber pistol with regular and tracer ammo along with a survival vest. With all this gear, I could only move around more like a duck than a human. This trip, however, there were not enough exposure suits to go around in my size. I was well aware of the danger of landing in the cold water off the coast of Korea. I had learned to swim in the cold waters around Newport, Rhode Island, so I knew the effects on the body. I was not a happy pilot, but that was the breaks of the game. Maybe I would get one later. The air intelligence briefings were not very encouraging because the Koreans had been adding more and more antiaircraft artillery (AAA) guns. Getting shot at would be a brand new experience for me.

Upon arrival at the mouth of Tokyo Bay, Japan on the October 4, I got my first impressions of this new and strange land. There were many activities to take care of while anchored in the bay outside the Naval Operating Base (NOB) Yokosuka, Japan. On one occasion I went with some other officers to attend a meeting and briefing aboard another carrier, the USS *Boxer*. The

Antietam was relieving the *Boxer* and we wanted to get everything of value from them. We took the officer's launch to their gangway and climbed up the ladder to the hanger deck. After saluting the colors I stepped aboard to the quarterdeck, and what a surprise I had. Standing there as the junior officer of the Deck (JOD) was Ensign Bill Boyd with whom I had worked at the Newport Creamery in our hometown. He had been a class ahead of me in high school and had gone on to the Naval Academy a year later, graduating with the class of 1951. This was his first duty station. It sure was a small world.

Christmas would come very early this year for us. We were told when we first arrived that we had to do our Christmas shopping this week in order that the packages arrived back in the states for the holiday. Everything was to be shipped via slow freighter, then over land via railroad. My packages had to go more than half way around the world to New England. So a group of the bunkroom guys went off to Tokyo to see what could be found as gifts for the family and friends back home that could withstand a long sea voyage. It was strange to be doing Christmas shopping in the second week of October, but that was the way it was. To my delight the large Post Exchange run by the US Army in Tokyo was decked out with all the trimmings to get us in the mood. I managed to complete my mission in one try, and so I was all set—packages wrapped, boxed, and shipped because there was so little time.

One week after we arrived on October 11th the USS *Antietam* steamed out of Tokyo Bay with its escorts and headed for the task force several days of steaming away. On the 11th and 13th a few sorties were flown by the air group. The weather was marginal and only 27 sorties were flown on the 11th and 56 sorties on the on the 13th. I did not fly either day. The tension was running high throughout the ship as we rounded southern Japan and headed north to meet the task force. We would soon be deeply involved in the action that awaited us. A few of the older reservists had been in combat before and had gone through this sensation. It was all so new to me. The entire concept of carrier air operation was alien to me and so it was watch, listen, and comprehend as best I could. I felt fortunate that I was able to sleep no matter what the excitement level was aboard ship. I wanted to be as rested and alert as possible. I was now going to find out how well I dealt with fear.

The trip around southern Japan turned out to be rather exciting. Quoting from the *Antietam* first action report about Typhoon Ruth:

Upon leaving Yokosuka for the operating area, the *Antietam* was given a typical Western Pacific meteorological welcome. A severe 120-knot typhoon named "Ruth" was heading north from Okinawa. Recurvature to the east of Japan was indicated for "Ruth," but after passing close to Okinawa on a northerly course, it appeared that the storm would enter the Sea of Japan while recurving. At this stage a modified typhoon Condition Two was set on the *Antietam*. The center of the storm passed over central Kyusyu Island, and entered the Sea of Japan on a northeasterly track. Had the recurvature been delayed any longer, typhoon Condition One would have undoubtedly been set. Between 12 and 15 October, the *Antietam* sailed across the northern edge of the storm with low stratus (clouds), rain, and moderate to strong northeasterly winds prevailing.

The storm meant a lot of hard work for the air group and ship's crew to secure the aircraft on the flight deck and below on the hanger deck. All the aircraft had the air pressure in their landing gear oleo reduced, and each aircraft was bolted to the deck with nine steel cables. Once done, all the weather decks were off limits. As night approached the wind continued to rise with the waves becoming larger. At the first sitting that evening the junior officers were treated to an unusual event. We had just sat down at our table when the mess attendants brought out the first course, soup. Just as we started to spoon the soup, the ship changed course, and it started to heal over because of the turn. The wind caught the ship as it turned broadside to the wind line and it was pushed even further over. All of a sudden all the crockery and silver on the tables began to slide to the down side. The officers at the foot of each of the tables got far more soup than they could possible have drunk in a year. The crockery and silver crashed over the end and into each officer's lap. What a mess, but it was so unexpected that we just watched it and then all burst out laughing. Except for the few at the end, it was funny. That night we had the pleasure of trying to sleep hanging on. Officer's country was in the bow of the ship and it was going up and down a good forty feet each way. During the night the ship took green water down the flight deck. It was one wild ride! The next day was another load of extra work to change the tie down from cables to normal ones and re-inflate the aircraft's oleos. So before we reached the task force the ship was back in operational shape. It was still raining and windy, which made it a much more difficult and dangerous job.

Chapter 7
Korea, First Deployment

Just like the character, "Snoopy," in the *Peanuts* comic strip showing him on top of his dog house starting his book with, "It was a dark and stormy..." For me it was the beginning of my introduction to combat. On October 14th, as the USS *Antietam* with Air Group 15 (CVG-15) aboard entered the war zone as it rounded the southern Japanese Islands into the Sea of Japan. The tensions were running high in the bunkroom as we gathered after dinner. It was all new to us, and each was trying to put on a good front. The first day was going to be rough because we were facing bad weather as well as the potential of combat. I think I was more worried about landing than about the enemy. Landing back aboard was real; the enemy was somewhere out there, but it wasn't real enough to me to get all worked up. With only 18 jet landings, I was still very wet behind the ears. On the following morning the ship joined Task Force 77 that was operating in an area about 100 miles off of the East Coast of North Korea. The stormy weather began to break up during the morning and became marginal enough just before noon for the air group squadrons to begin some flight operations against the North Koreans. There were only 35 sorties flown before the cloudy weather closed in again. Our division was not among the first to fly. To prolong my torture of the unknown, the Task Force went south to replenish on the 15th so there was again no flying.

Early the following day the task force had moved north again, and now the *Antietam* was the early carrier meaning operations was started before dawn. The weather was bright, cool and sunny with completely clear sky. The 16th was a full day of flying for the air group. Dick Clinite and I flew our first defensive mission, a Combat Air Patrol (CAP). It was more of a training flight because we just tagged along with another division from VF-51 part of Air Group 5 aboard the USS *Essex* (CV-9). There was nothing unusual about the flight itself other than to pay close attention to the radio transmissions between the flight leader and the *Essex*'s Combat Information Center (CIC) to start learning the lingo. It sure was all new to me. Flying off of and then back onto the carrier was my main concern. Getting catapulted with a good wind over the deck with only a slight pitching of the ship relieved my various emotions. The CAP mission was over. Dick and I were relieved from the other flight, and we came up the starboard side to start the approach. Now I was to make my 19th jet landing. It had been a long time since I had flown, almost a month. I was just a little apprehensive to say the least, but all went well as I approached the flight deck in my flat turn. The ship was steady as I rolled my wings level into my final straight away astern of the carrier and received the "cut" from the Landing Signal Officer (LSO). That landing almost up the center of the deck gave me a great feeling, and I was delighted to be part of an operating squadron doing what I had looked forward to do since I entered the Navy.

Jet landing in the combat zone

I was really keyed up walking into the ready room behind Dick Clinite, who had landed just 30 seconds before me. Dick and I just could not stop grinning at each other. It was a good thing no one was there to count my heart rate. It must have been out of sight.

Later in the afternoon on the same day a few of the other bunkroom boys and I who were not flying were up in that aft part of the carrier's island, called vulture's row, to watch the recovery. We were watching an AD from VA-728 in a normal approach turn when suddenly the landing gear started to retract as the aircraft slowly settled into the water with a big splash. We found out later that LT Geho's aircraft engine quit due to a fuel-pump failure. The picture of the sinking plane's tail sticking up from the sea did not make a pretty sight. We were all relieved when the pilot's head was seen floating on top of the water in his Mae West. He was quickly rescued by one of the task-force screen destroyers acting as plane guard. It sent a shiver through me watching this event, thinking, "That could have been me out there." Even though I was cold from the blast of wind over the deck while watching the ditching, I was sweating from the tension.

The rhythm of the task force's operation was to have air operations usually for three days and then the entire force moved south in the Sea of Japan to replenish at sea the depleted stores of fuel, ordnance, and food stuff. It soon became the way we counted off the days in this new world. Not by weeks, but by the cycle of flying until the next replenishment day. Instead of a normal seven-day week, it was compressed into a four-day "week." The day of the month meant nothing to me. The only way I knew what date it was to put on my letters home was to look at the flight schedule that we received every evening in the bunkroom after our five o'clock dinner. This was the document we lived by while in the combat zone. My own personal schedule completely revolved around briefing, flying, eating, sleeping, and writing my letters home and to Beverly. I also made notes about the events of the day. Sleeping was sometimes more difficult because when there was no flight quarter; the junior officer had to stand a four-hour fire watch that covered the flight and hanger decks. An enlisted man and I roamed the two decks checking on the aircraft tie downs and general condition of the aircraft. On the hanger deck, the maintenance crews were busy working on the aircraft. The flight deck was blacked out, and with only red lenses on our flashlights it was difficult to walk among the aircraft with out running into something. The aircraft tie-down wires were the biggest hazard because they were very difficult to see with the low light emitted from the red-lens flash light. The tie downs were attached at the top of the F9F main landing gear and then radiated out at 45 degree angle and hooked to the flight deck. I barked my shins more than once moving around on the flight deck. Being the most junior officer in the air group as well as the ship's company, I got a variety of non-flying duties on a very regular basis. It seems I always got the midnight to four o'clock duty. Not only did I get this fire-watch duty when we were at sea, but also as "boat officer" on the enlisted liberty boat whenever the ship was tied up to a buoy in Tokyo Bay. The small-landing craft docked at a float against the side of the ship, and the crew climbed down the ladder to board the boat. As long as there was not rain or wind it was not all that bad. But in the winter time that was rarely the case.

The tour of duty was usually about four hours. As usual, my plight was getting the last boat run late at night. The toughest part of the boat-officer duty was handling the sailors coming back from an evening of heavy drinking. Often the last liberty boat departed the fleet landing about 12:30 A.M. This load was usually made up of a lot of drunken sailors. Getting them loaded on board without having any fall into the water was always a chore. The boat left the shelter of the inner harbor, and we were soon rocking and pitching because of the wind-driven waves in the bay. The carrier was usually about two miles off shore so it took some time to make the trip. The rocking of the boat and the smell of the diesel engine exhaust was enough to upset almost anyone, but that is when the sailors started getting sick. Ugh, what a mess in the bottom of the boat! Reaching the carrier side, the boat was tied up to the float, and those that could climb the gangway up to the hanger deck were off loaded. Those who were too sick or had passed out had to be hauled aboard in a cargo net. The boat crew rolled several men into the cargo net at a time, and away they went as the boat crane carried them up to the hanger deck level where they were deposited none too gently. The duty hospital corpsman checked them over, and if there appeared to be no injury the duty petty officer of the various ship's divisions or air group squadrons claimed their crewmembers and carried them off to sleep off their excessive drinking. What a delightful experience!

The officers had a much better way of getting ashore. Ours was an enclosed-cabin power boat, which and in made it a more comfortable ride. It still required a careful jump from the stable ship to a bobbing float and then on to the boat. This was especially interesting when the bay waters had wind-driven waves. It also wasn't much fun when it was raining because everything was slick.

After all, my low place in the official pecking order was because my commission date was only a few months before. This affected my place in the wardroom seating. I was the last chair. There were 256 officers on board, and my napkin ring had 256 on it. There was one good thing about this condition; at least I could not be demoted.

After the first three full days of flight operation, the task force moved south to replenish. This was my first of many observations of replenishing at sea, and I watched the entire process with fascination. The only large ship I had ever been on prior to the carrier was the paddle wheeler I took as a kid from Newport, Rhode Island to New York City. Later on it was not always a curiosity that sent me topside to watch. Often during a replenishment day, the junior pilots of the jet squadrons had to stand Combat Air Patrol (CAP) alert duty. Sometimes it was in the squadron's ready room, but more often it was sitting in the aircraft on the flight deck. Sometimes we could take turns walking around to flex our legs if the weather wasn't too nasty. We did this alert duty supposedly in the event that an unidentified aircraft was detected by the task force's radar. If this should ever happen, the CAP would be launched on short notice to intercept the aircraft. It was shades of World War II. The task force was so far from any North Korea operational airfield that it was out of range of any of the enemy jet fighter aircraft. The only bombers known to be in the area were Russian, and we were many hundreds of miles from these Russian airfields. Sitting in the cockpit wasn't much fun. When the weather was good, this wasn't too much of a problem to stay warm, but later on during the latter part of the deployment in the deep cold winter months, I got really cold sitting in the cockpit without any cockpit heat generated from the engine's air conditioner. The air was taken from the running jet engine for the heating. To make up for this lack of heat I wore lots of cold weather gear just to try to keep warm. The four jet pilots had the catapult crew hooked up the aircraft's batteries as well as having the carrier's external power supply plugged in. One of the benefits of having electrical power was we could at least close the canopy to stay out of the cold wind. During the winter months, it was also helpful if the ships were running downwind instead of into the wind. Electrical power from the ship meant that all the flight instruments and radio gear were up and running. In an event we had to be launched, it would take only about two minutes to start the engines and to build up pressure in the catapults. Then the aircraft were ready for launch. Often the first aircraft was spotted on the catapults with the other three parked behind the blast shield. The other side of the forward flight deck was full of aircraft.

After replenishing I flew my first armed-reconnaissance mission along the Korean East Coast northeastwards from Pukchong to Songjin. My exterior calm in the ready room did not reflect the knot in my stomach. To add to my apprehension the weather was poor with low clouds predicted over our assigned route. No one liked the idea of flying under the overcast.

It was easy for the enemy gunners to know altitude. They could easily measure the height of the base of the clouds. We received our briefing from the Air Intelligence Officer (AIO) LT Von Southern, and I finished dressing in my flight gear after he had done his job. The voice from primary fly came out of the squawk box in the ready room announcing, "Pilots, man your planes." We filed out and climbed to the flight deck. Finding my aircraft aft of the number-two elevator, I made a quick visual pre-flight of my aircraft. It was loaded with six 5-in. rockets mounted on the wing stations with the rockets electrical connection, pigtails still hanging loose. They would be plugged in as soon as my engine was running. The plane captain helped me get strapped in, and I settled into the cramped cockpit as best I could.

Hooking up to the catapult

As the carrier came towards the wind line, the first jets that had already been started and locked up on the catapult now received the two-finger turn-up signal from the catapult officer. The pilot advanced the throttle to full power, grabbing the catapult post and throttle with his left hand, put his head against the head rest, and reviewed all the engine instruments one last time for normal takeoff condition. With everything okay, the pilot saluted the catapult officer with his right hand and just as the ship reached the wind line, with everything in readiness, the catapult officer dropped his arm pointing forward. The crewman in the catwalk pressed the firing button firing the catapult, and the plane was hurtled down the track from a stand still to 125 knots in two seconds, becoming airborne. As soon as this took place the jet blast deflector was lowered, and the plane directors started to feed the following jets in order for launch. Soon it was my turn, and just before taxiing forward a nose-wheel tiller bar was attached to allow the catapult crew to spot my jet exactly to the spot on the catapult. I had only to use the throttle for forward movement and brakes for slowing or stopping under the plane director's signal. Spotted correctly on the catapult the crewman attached the hold-back mechanism to the rear ring on the belly of the aircraft. The bridle was attached to a hook just aft of the nose wheel. I could feel the shuttle move forward taking up the slack in the bridle, and the plane was firmly attached to the catapult. During this process, the catapult director gave me the brakes-off hand signal to drop my feet from the toe brakes onto the flying position on the rudder pedals. All was ready! The catapult crewmember located in the catwalk gave the thumbs-up signal to the catapult officer that there was a full head of pressure for launch. I got the two-finger signal to go to full power. With the engine at full power I made a quick complete scan of all engine instruments and with everything okay, I looked up and saluted the catapult officer. Putting my head back quickly against the head-rest, right elbow in my stomach with my hand on the control stick, left hand wrapped around the throttle and catapult post, I was ready for one of the greatest thrills a human can experience. I was shot off the carrier's flight deck by a catapult in sixty feet reaching flying speed of 125 knots all in about two seconds. Free of the bridle, with the airplane's nose slightly up, I was flying.

The four of us joined up in a running rendezvous and headed north from the task force for the coast to begin our mission. Reaching the Korean coast, a diving right hand turn set us up to fly along the coast be fore we entered the clouds. The heavy cloudy weather made it tough to see the road and railroad. If there were any targets we sure didn't see them. I don't think we had the foggiest idea what we were looking for. As far as I could tell, there was no enemy reaction to our flight. I sure did look, however. I had no idea what enemy anti-aircraft artillery (AAA) fire looked like. I only had the pictures in my mind of big bombers flying through large puffs of black smoke. I learned all about flak very soon in the next few flights. After cruising along the coast for about twenty minutes our fuel level was reaching the "Bingo" or departure amount without us firing our rockets, so we finally fired all six rockets one at a time at the railroad roadbed. We flew the mission, but we really didn't add anything to the war effort. After the last run, we headed out to sea taking up a southerly compass heading to return to the Task Force. I sure wasn't very proud of my war effort. The amazing part was that it was first time I had ever fired an armed 5-in. rocket.

On the way back to the task force we slowly climbed to 20,000 feet and after finally breaking out of the heavy overcast we flew above the clouds almost the entire time. The pilots of the three planes flying in a loose formation behind Sandy heard him as he checked in with the strike controller. "Blue 1 inbound 180."

"Roger, Blue 1, squawk one." As ordered, he turned on his Identification Friend or Foe (IFF) transmitter. "Roger, Blue 1, read your squawk, contact Eskimo on channel 3. Over."

Switching channels, Sandy contacted the *Antietam* CIC controller with our fuel state and aircraft status. "Eskimo, this is Blue 1 with four, low fuel state, 1,300 pounds, no damage."

Orbiting over the task force we were finally given our orders to descend to enter the landing pattern. "Blue 1, this is Eskimo, signal Charlie, over."

"Wilco, our signal Charlie, starting descent." We closed up in a tight formation and started down. Flying tight meant that you had to keep your head out of the cockpit, and you flew on the leader or the plane ahead. Being fourth man, I was flying wing on Bob Clarke. As we made a formation decent through the clouds it was normal to get vertigo. Your senses told you that you were in a turn, but you were really flying with wings level. As we passed through 1,000 feet we broke out below the cloud cover not far from the task force.

We were given the radio command to enter the landing pattern of the USS *Essex*, not the *Antietam*. I thought, *What has happened on the Antietam?* As it turned out, the *Antietam* had not re-spotted the aircraft from the aft part of the flight deck to the forward flight deck, so we could not land on our carrier. The *Antietam* returning two jet divisions were instructed to land aboard the USS *Essex*, which had a ready deck. We all landed on the first pass, which certainly made us look good to the more experienced jet pilots of VF-51 on the *Essex*. After taxiing forward, and shutting down the engine, the weather closed in solid with rain and low clouds. We had gotten in just in time. Shortly thereafter, all flight operations for the task force were cancelled. That meant we ended up staying overnight on the *Essex*. It was not much fun to have to eat in one's smelly flight suit. The next morning after an early breakfast on the 21st, I had the opportunity to find out what the difference was between the WW II *Antietam* H-4B catapult and the newer H-8 catapult recently installed on the *Essex* during modification. The catapult shot from the H-8 catapult was a lot smoother, lasted longer, and the aircraft left the flight deck with far more airspeed than the catapult shot from the H-4B the day before. Flying to our low orbiting altitude assigned prior to takeoff to await our landing orders. It was a short flight, and there was no reason to put fuel in the tip tanks. After the USS *Antietam* finished its morning launch and did a re-spot forward of the remaining aircraft we made our approach in a right echelon formation to the ship on the starboard side after circling for twenty minutes to burn down our fuel to maximum landing weight of 2,500 pounds. Once again I came aboard with no problem.

Later on this same day, LT A. Stan Kalas of VC-61 while flying on a jet photo mission was wounded by enemy antiaircraft fire when his aircraft was hit taking photos over Hamhung. He was able to fly the damaged airplane to friendly territory and successfully landed at K-18 on the East Coast of Korea. K-18 was a forward airfield used by a US Marine squadron on one side and a South Korean Air Force squadron on the other side flying WW II P-51s. Arriving back to the ship via a Carrier Onboard Delivery (COD) flight before dinner, we gathered in the wardroom, and he gave us his tale about the mission and the startling event when he was hit. The warhead came up from the bottom and part of it hit him in the inside of his upper left thigh. The fragment opened a wound and he felt a sharp burning sensation in his lower body. He said, "I reached down with my left hand and it came way with blood on my flying glove." He thought to himself that his manhood had been hit, and he might as well just pushover and dive the plane into the ground. This broke the tension and we all had a good laugh over this aspect of his tale. To all of us present, however, it was another wake-up call that this was going to be a very dangerous business. The possibility of injury or death was always with me every time I crossed the coastline and flew over North Korea. I think I rationalized that I could dodge their gunfire with constant changing of direction and altitude.

On the following day, the 22nd, we flew a CAP mission in the afternoon without any interesting activity during the flight. Near the end of the flight, the

Fighter Director Officer (FDO) in the *Antietam* CIC vectored us to intercept an income flight of prop aircraft that turned out to be fun and easy. Returning to the carrier was a different story. The newness of carrier landings was still there and to make a good approach with a close interval behind the plane ahead was "the name of the game." Once set up, the next step was to arrive at the 200-300 foot straight away lined up on the center strip ready for the cut by the LSO. After the cut, a slight dip of the nose, a flare-out and touchdown was the finality. After the tail hook caught the wire, the arresting cable rapidly de-accelerated the aircraft slamming my body against the shoulder harness. The arrested landing was one fast stop! With all forward motion stopped, keeping my feet off of the brakes, the airplane rolled back a few feet. This allowed the arresting wire to fall free of the plane's tail hook. I pushed the button in the cockpit raising the tail hook to horizontal when the yellow-shirted plane director's gave me the signal. Clear of the wire, the next signaled to me was to move the airplane forward as fast as possible with a burst of power from the jet engine to get rolling and move past the barriers so the deck was ready for another aircraft to land.

From cut to clearance of the barrier was to be only 30 seconds. Moving forward I was passed to another plane director stationed by the ship's island. He usually gave me the wing-fold signal. That meant I unlocked the shoulder harness and reached back on the right side to first move my wing-fold lock to the unlock position and then move a second lever to start the wings folding. All this time I had to keep my eyes on the plane director to learn whether I was to taxi forward (one finger) or head for the number-two elevator (two fingers). Learning the layout of the cockpit was essential so I could find anything without having to look. I had practiced this many times before deployment. If I was directed to taxi forward on the flight deck, I was passed to another plane director, and this third director took charge. He often parked me in a spot with only a few inches between the other aircraft and mine. Right after his lock-brakes signal, and he had chocks on my main gear, he gave me the cut signal, and I shut down the engine. With the plane tied down, I got out of the cockpit as fast as possible. No pilot lingered on the flight deck. If you had no business there, get off! This entire process took about the same amount of time to do as to read this. Everything on the flight deck was time critical. Leaving the aircraft, the flight-deck crews were already starting the process to refuel and rearm for the next launch.

So the four-day rhythm continued. As it turned out, the weather was good for the rest of October, interrupted with replenishing activity almost every fourth day. During the remainder of the month I flew three armed-reconnaissance missions with only one of them having a significant incident of consequence. The first mission on the 24th our division was assigned a more difficult area and we settled in the back of the ready room to learn all about our route from the Air Intelligence Officer (AIO) LT Von Southern. We were to be launched at dawn and were to start out on the northeast side near the bomb line and then follow the road and railroad northeastward to Wonsan, a distance of about 70 miles. The launch and join up were somewhat of a hazy memory as we climbed slowly to altitude.

The real concern for me was the amount of flak we could expect. As we approached the coast we leveled off at 20,000 feet from our climb. Crossing the coast, "feet dry," we planned to be well away from the bomb line as well as to avoid the large number of antiaircraft guns reported around the city of Pyonggang (not the capital). The most recent aerial photos of the city showed just how many antiaircraft guns were there. Approaching our pushover point, we took up our positions for the work ahead. The deep valley was just becoming light because the sun wasn't very high in the sky. The flight started off as planned with one exception. We did not fly far enough north of Pyonggang and the larger flax guns fired at us. Those big black bursts were not pretty against the blue morning sky. We were learning a basic rule of combat—expect the unexpected.

Reaching our pushover point, we set up our tactical formation and went down into the valley. The flight leader was low man flying at 500 to 800 feet above the valley floor looking for targets. He soon spotted some troops marching in columns on either side of the road well ahead and called them out for us to strafe them. This was the real thing. Following the other three I dropped my nose and jammed the throttle forward to 100% power. With the airspeed increased rapidly, I banked the plane to line my gun sight on the last man in the column. The flight leader and his wing man started firing and in a moment dust kicked up as his shell smashed into the troops. As the other two cleared from their runs it was our sections turn to press home the attack. Squeezing the trigger I was startled by the sound of my guns and the smell of the cordite smoke picked up by the air conditioning system of the airplane. I had only time for a quick burst and then a fast pullout in a high G-level climbing turn trying to stay with the section leader. Glancing back in my rear view mirror I could see we had hit them hard. They did not hear us coming, and the strafing left many lying in the road. We kept moving on without finding any additional targets. On the way we flew over the city Kosan or what was left of it. Approaching the Wonsan Bay area near the town of Anbyon we fired our rockets at a suspected storage area without creating any secondary explosions. By then we had hit our time and fuel level numbers to leave the area and head eastward back to the ship. We had seen some tracers along the way, but they were not even close. It is the ones you don't see that can worry you. That was the first but not the last time I shot someone. I found it to be a very difficult thing to do. Shooting at objects can be impersonal, but when I actually saw the troops go down in the hail of my 20-mm gunfire I knew I was right in the middle of the fighting.

The Air Group did not fly many flights the next three days because of bad weather and replenishment for the task force. The few flights flown, however, by the other squadrons were not so lucky. On the 22nd the Anti-Submarine Warfare (ASW) group, VC-11, lost an AD aircraft when it lost power after a wave off from an attempted night landing. The destroyer, USS *Hansen*, acting as plane guard, quickly recovered LTJG Masek and his two-crew men from the water. Then on the 25th LTJG Dorsey of the F4U squadron, VF-713 was forced to ditch his plane in Wonsan Bay after being hit in his engine by enemy flak, knocking out his oil system. He made a good ditching, and he was quickly rescued by the USS *Helena's* whaleboat.

The next mission after replenishment, on the 28th, we flew over the roads and railroads leading from Wonsan to the south in the opposite direction from our first mission. We reached our time and fuel levels at Kumsong without much activity. On the 30th we did the same activity to the southeast along the coastal road. The only targets found were a few ox carts and an occasional truck. The flight leader called them out and the three of us dove down and fired our rockets or strafed depending upon what ordnance we were carrying. I rolled the aircraft over into a vertical bank and dropped the nose to enter into my dive from 3,000 feet; the two planes ahead were already firing. On this mission the ox cart blew up in a fireball when Bob Clark's 20-mm shells hit it. It must have been carrying gasoline or some other kind of fuel. No one in the division was hit by antiaircraft fire during these flights even though we did see some tracers fired in our direction. It seemed unreal, but I knew that it could all change in a blink of an eye. At first I had to make an effort to keep changing direction and altitude to try to spoil the enemy gunners' aim. Later on it became second nature to fly that way. The division was flying well together, and we were beginning to see targets and attack them effectively. At first, this kind of attack did not go all that well because we had not tried them in the states. The attacking game was to get your nose down, push the throttle to 100 percent power to up the airspeed, go in fast, line up the target in the gun sight, and fire when about 2,500 feet slant range from the target. For a rocket attack, the ordnance switches were set to the rocket position, which allowed the gun sight to become a rocket sight. With the center of the gun sight on the target the gyros in the gun sight began to fly the rocket trajectory. Flying the airplane to keep the center of the sight on the target, until reaching about 3,500 feet slant range I pressed the firing button, and off the rocket went. To drop off a bomb, the sight was used with the gyros locked, and the center dot was placed above the target by the proper number of mils to plant the bomb on target. If it was a strafing attack with the 20-mm cannons the gun sight piper was used and placed on the target. In any case once a drop or strafing was completed a break off was done and then it was to get the hell out of there. Each attack sure raised the adrenal flow to a higher level as well as elevated the pulse rate. By the time the flight reached the coastline on the way back to the ship I was damp with sweat and often had a dry mouth from tension as well as breathing dry oxygen. One of the first things I did when I got off the flight deck was drink my fill from the scuttlebutt (water fountain.) Breathing dry oxygen and sweating from the tension really dehydrated my body.

On the last flying day of the month, LT Kramer of VC-3 ditched after a night catapult launch when his engine failed. He had to fire his pistol with tracer ammo and light a flare off so he could be located. The destroyer, USS *Ebersole*, acting as plane guard, found and rescued him from the ocean. Each one of these ditchings was a grim reminder to me that carrier aviation is doubly dangerous in wartime.

November began with good flying weather for the 1st, but it did not hold, and the weather closed in on the next day. I flew another CAP this day without anything unusual about the flight to stay with me. It was just a typical CAP flight. The sky was a beautiful dark blue with low cumulus clouds. The cloud cover was heavier to the northwest.

The four of us briefed in the ready room, and I copied down all the needed information for the flight on my kneepad. We were first off and last aboard because the CAP almost always had plenty of fuel. The division was making its landings on schedule, showing that we were beginning to get into the swing of smooth operations around the carrier. On the third, my job was the SDO.

November fourth was a day that I will long remember. The division I flew with was sent off in the first morning launch to the area north of Wonsan Bay near the town of Yonghung. We were to fly up the coastal road and railroad line from Yonghung passing by Kowan towards Hamhung looking for targets as well as to check on the conditions of the road along the way. Reaching the coast we headed down in a high speed dive to our assigned route checking for targets. Just as we started our spread out formation to begin the reconnaissance part of the flight, the flight leader, LT Sanders' aircraft was hit in the left horizontal stabilizer by an explosive antiaircraft shell. I was flying 1,000 feet above and to his left when it happened. Being the fourth man in the four-plane division, it was my job to keep everyone in sight. Suddenly I saw a bright flash as the left side of his tail exploded. The aircraft continued flying as it held together, even though badly damaged. He radioed that he was okay and planned to stay with the aircraft if it continued to hold together. We immediately broke off the mission and started climbing higher as we headed east towards the coast a short distance away. Once out of anti-aircraft gun range we joined up and headed down the coast to K-18. We fired off our rockets because we did not want to land with them. LT Sanders was able to keep the airplane under control even though it was vibrating badly from the big hole in his stabilizer, as well as many holes in the rudder and aft end of the fuselage. Upon arrival at K-18 the three of us landed first in case he had a problem and might foul the only runway. As we taxied towards the ramp we watched him make a successful landing. Together we taxied to the visiting aircraft parking area and shut down. After lunch at the Marine Corp Officer's mess with his aircraft fixed with a completely new tail section, we headed back to the task force. While we were landing at K-18 instead of on the ship, one of the returning jets of our sister squadron was involved in a deadly flight-deck crash during landing.

From the USS *Antietam* action report:

Then at 0945I LT George S. Brainard, USNR, of VF-837, made a normal approach to the ship in his F9F but made a hard landing. The plane bounced without engaging a wire and the pilot pushed over to get down to the deck again, landing nose wheel first. The nose tire blew immediately, and the nose wheel began to disintegrate at once. The plane went through all Davis barriers without actuating them and continued on up the deck, crashing into the parked planes forward. The pilot and a deck crewman were killed instantly; two other crewmembers died later in the day. One pilot (LT George De Polo, VF-831) received serious injuries and nine crewmen lesser injuries.

LT George De Polo was transferred to the Yokosuka Naval Hospital for further treatment and hospitalization. He did not return to duty with the squadron for the remainder of the deployment.

When our division returned to the ship later in the day from K-18, it was to a very somber crew. Not only were there four deaths, but there were also ten injured officers and crewmembers. The possibility of a deck crash made me realize that a carrier flight deck is one of the most dangerous places to work. Each pilot had to evaluate his own role in landing his aircraft in such a limited space. The margin for error is very small, and with the higher landing speed of the jet. One small mistake by a pilot can cause serious harm to himself, to other pilots, and the flight-deck crew. After our flight had been recovered and tied down all flight operations on the *Antietam* were cancelled for the remainder of the day. The badly damaged aircraft from the accident were either jettisoned over the side of the ship or struck below on the hanger deck to be oft loaded the next time the ship was in port.

The 5th was a replenishing day. After replenishment had been completed in the middle of the afternoon it was time for the burial service. Standing at attention on the hanger deck with the other members of the air group squadrons I witnessed the very dramatic, emotional, and difficult experience of attending the burial-at-sea services of those killed in the deck crash. The four flag-draped, canvas-shrouded bodies of our shipmates were committed to the deep in a painfully moving ceremony on the lowered deck edge elevator. The chaplain read the service, and the order was given to uplift the stretchers as taps sounded. All you could hear was the sound of the sea, the bugle, and then the splashes. There wasn't a dry eye among those in attendance as the playing of taps really hit home. To this day, I cannot hear taps played without remembering with wet eyes those shipmates being buried at sea on that cold, gray, rainy day so far from home.

The next two days there were no flight operations because of the foul weather over North Korea as well the Sea of Japan. It had begun to get noticeably colder as the winter season progressed. On the 8th the weather cleared, bright and cold, allowing full flight operations to return in earnest, flying three CAP and two armed-reconnaissance missions during the next three days. On the first CAP the air was so clear I could see the snow-capped mountains of North Korea to the north and northeast. These mountains would remain snow covered for almost the rest of the deployment. Both of the reconnaissance missions started at Yonghung and went in different directions. On the first one on the 8th, we headed from Yonghung to Yongwon into the mountains. We didn't find anything along the route, so we left our ordnance calling cards on a few small bridges. The second mission on the 9th we went to Pukchong. This was along the coastal road and railroad checking out the status of the many bridges. We didn't expect to find anything when suddenly the flight leader spotted five boxcars sitting on a siding. What an opportunity! Dropping my wing and letting the nose fall through until I was headed down in a 30-degree dive towards them I was determined that I going to nail a box car with one of my five-in. rockets before the others did all the damage. Looking through the gun sight, I placed the center of the gun sight on a boxcar and un-caged the gyro with a twist of my left wrist. With the armament switch set on "rocket" all I needed to do was keep the piper lined up on the boxcar. I was now flying the aircraft on the rocket trajectory. At about 3,500 feet slant range I pressed the button on the top of control stick to fire the rocket. That five-in. rocket took off with a big swish straight for the boxcar. I waited for a moment and then pulled back on the stick to recover from the dive and to climb for altitude to make another pass. As I passed over the railroad I saw my rocket explode—on the opposite side of the railroad tracks. "Damn, did I miss?" No I didn't miss the boxcar. I managed to have the rocket go through the pair of opened doors and hit the earth on the other side. Doing a high-speed 180-degree wing over to make my next run, I made sure that this did not happen again, and on my second run, firing a pair of rockets this time smashed into the boxcar, blowing it apart. The others in the flight finished off the other boxcars. Five for five was a good score.

Each week the North Koreans seemed to be moving more AAA guns in and the area was beginning to become better defended. On the second mission, my airplane was hit in the port wing by small-arms fire during one of my rocket runs. I had not seen any tracers or gun flashes, but that didn't mean the North Koreans were not shooting at me. I was unaware at the time that the airplane had been hit until the maintenance crew checked the airplane over for battle damage. There was minimal damage only to the wing skin, and the aircraft was quickly repaired and put back in to operation. With the cooler air and stronger winds of the oncoming winter, our external ordnance loading was changing. Instead of just 5-in. rockets we switched to carrying six one-hundred-pound bombs. We used them to try to hit the road bridges along the way as well as the railroad bridges and roadbed that snaked down the coast from the northeast. Military supplies destined for east coast forces were either brought by ship or overland from Russia and China to Chongjin. Then the supplies were shipped either down the coastal railroad where the Navy air arm tried to destroy them or by small boats where the Navy ships of TF 95 tried to intercept and destroy them. This was the first time I dropped a live bomb from any aircraft. In areas where there were no known enemy guns, we made the classic dive-bombing runs. After six of these runs I got the hang of aiming and hitting (most of the time) the narrow road bridges and railroad bed. It had been awhile since I did any of this type of dive-bombing. These dives required a high-G pullout after the bomb release that often almost blacked me out for a short time.

On the following day, our division had the pleasure of another boring CAP flight. It was not so for Dick Clinite flying with another division. He was on an armed-reconnaissance mission when his aircraft was hit in the nose section and a piece of flak penetrated the canopy and struck him above the right eye. He was not seriously injured and was able to return to the task force to make a normal carrier landing. We kidded him that he actually had hit his head on the top of a hatch so he could get his Purple Heart medal. Dick was six feet four inches tall and had to duck his head every time he went through a hatch.

The next day was replenishment for the task force with no flying or any other air group activity. On the plus side, I did not have to stand the CAP-alert duty. The following day the weather was marginal for flying with a cold front due to move through the area and the return of foul weather. During the launch of the pre-dawn hecklers, LTJG L. O. Warfield was forced to ditch when his Corsair engine lost power right after his catapult shot. He was picked up by the USS *Boyd*, the *Antietam* plane guard. The two detachments, VC-3 flying the F4U-5NL and VC-35 flying the AD-4NL made up the group referred as "Night Hecklers" or "Morning Hecklers." When the ship was the morning carrier, two aircraft of each kind were launched three hours before dawn and recovered at dawn after the first launch of the daylight flights. For the late carrier schedule, these two units would be launched at dusk and be recovered three hours later, making night carrier landings.

I had not been scheduled to fly so I didn't even suit up in flight gear. On the thirteenth, I was the squadron duty officer (SDO) overseeing the routine business of the squadron's activities on a full flying day. Standing the duty makes for a long day. After flight quarters had been secured and we had eaten dinner, sleeping was in order. On board ship, I learned to sleep whenever I could.

On the 14th, our last day in the task force, before this ship's period was to end, our division flew a Target Combat Air Patrol (TARCAP) cover for the propeller strike at Yangdok. This town was an important road and railroad link between Wonsan and Pyongyang, the North Korean capital. The problem for the strike was the several bridges were in a steep-walled valley. It was a very well protected by many AAA guns, making it a very dangerous target to attack. Our division was not involved in the actual attack, but stayed at altitude in case of an enemy fighter plane attack. This area was close enough to the MiG bases that there was a possibility they could make a firing pass at the slower prop aircraft. After the strike was over our division then finished the mission off by making a high-speed sweep over the bombed out airfields between Wonsan and Hamhung. These airfields were all empty and there appeared to be no sign of repairs being made to either the empty buildings or the bombed out runways.

After all the air groups aircraft had been recovered from the last strike, the USS *Antietam* and its destroyer escorts left the task force and set a course for Yokosuka, Japan, arriving on the 16th. My first combat experience period came to a close. All the other bunkroom boys except Dick made it through without any problems. We were one very happy bunch of guys. Our combat baptism had been difficult because of the losses and injuries that were sustained to the air--roup pilots and flight-deck crew. The apprehensions and fears I started out with still stayed with me every time I flew into North Korea. But with the experience gained I felt I could handle these emotional feelings and do my job with a high level of professionalism.

During the period in the Korean operating area, the air group's performance began slowly to improve, but it was not up to standard by any measurement. Aircraft losses due to enemy antiaircraft fire were two, but operational-aircraft losses were still too significant. There were eight aircraft damaged beyond repair on the ship and nine lost in operational accidents. Two aircraft lost were the result of the November 4th deck crash along with four of the eight damaged losses. These two jet aircraft involved in the deadly deck crash were so badly damaged that they were jettisoned. The remaining four of the eight damaged were because of hard landings or barrier engagements. There were two aircraft lost from either weak catapult shots or more likely because of engine failures. Two planes were lost before recovery when their engines failed, and one was lost on a night wave off when the plane collided with the catwalk before gaining altitude. It was not a very good operational record. It was especially noticeable for the two jet squadrons. The lack of training and flight time in the aircraft really showed how inexperienced we were.

The enemy's antiaircraft fire was very active and accurate during the period, and the enemy hit twenty-six of the air group's aircraft. The AD squadron headed the list with twelve hits; the two jet squadrons were next with nine. The F4Us were hit four times, while one photo plane was hit. All were repaired aboard ship or off loaded to be repaired at O&R. On the plus side, the air group flew 1,418 sorties and expended 1,054.41 tons of various types of ordnance during 22 flying days. I flew 15 flights both offensive and defensive while building up 22.5 hours in the air. Best of all I felt good about handling the fear factor on my missions over North Korea. I also felt good about my flying around the ship, especially my landings. I was still not satisfied with them because I didn't consistently hit the center white strip. Talking with the LSO gave me several things to concentrate on in my final approach.

During the 30 days the USS *Antietam* was with the task force, there were numerous problems for the ship's flight-deck crew, the air group crew, and the pilots that came to light with startling clarity. No part of the flight operation was without difficulties. With the jets, it began immediately after recovery when the jets needed to be refueled. The fueling crew had to overcome two significant problems. First one was that the carriers could not carry jet fuel, so that to refuel the jets required that lubricating oil had to be added to the jet's rear main fuel tank while the two tanks were being filled with aviation gasoline. These statements taken from the USS *Antietam* action report for the first period shows this problem with startling clarity. First:

The main problem encountered in servicing aircraft with fuel has been refueling of jet aircraft with their wings folded. This necessitates the use of wing ladders and experiments to date have not resulted in a satisfactory ladder. The ladder must be light in weight and yet strong enough to withstand constant heavy usage. New ladders of thin-walled steel tubing are on order and it is hoped they will provide the answer.

Second:

The present arrangement for use of oil proportioners [sic] for mixing jet fuel is not satisfactory for flight deck use in cold weather. The oil will not flow properly during cold weather and it is necessary to use regular gasoline cans to pour warm oil in the after main tanks of jet aircraft.

It is difficult to understand how the Navy could accept the design of a jet aircraft that would not effectively function on the operating carrier of this period. Or why wasn't the carrier modified to carry jet fuel? Refueling of the F9F jet's tip tanks between launches was difficult and dangerous. Why wasn't there a way to pump the fuel up to the tanks using the same fuel lines used to transfer the fuel from the tanks to the main tank? Just visualize this picture: the F9F is parked on the port (left) side of the flight deck with its port wheel a few inches from the edge. A crewmember drags a gasoline hose to the jet's port side. He then returns with a ladder that has a curved hook on the top. He climbs up onto the wing from the front, moving the ladder in a way that the curved piece hooks over the tip tank. Then he proceeds to climb the ladder dragging the fueling hose with him. At the top of the ladder he unscrews the tip tank's cap and puts the hose into the tank. Sound easy? Well just don't look down because the wing angles out away from the fuselage at about 20 degrees.

The man on the ladder will have a great view because all he can see is if he looks down is the water below him. The tank is 17 feet above the flight deck and the flight deck is 65 feet above the still-water line. So he is hanging on to the ladder and hose while he fills the tank with 120 gallons of gasoline 82 feet above the water. Now if that is not enough, add to this picture a ship that is pitching and possibly rolling as it moves through the sea waves. Let's hope that the ship is going down wind so as not to add to the danger of being buffered by the wind. Not a very pretty picture, yet the best was yet to come. As that one tip tank is being filled, the main wheel oleos were extended because the plane was nearly empty of fuel after landing. As the tank is filled, adding weight to the aircraft, the oleo will suddenly sink, and the aircraft will shift, moving the port wing tip even further out board. Just hang on tightly until the tank has been filled. Then all you had to do once the tank was filled was to reverse the steps and move down the wing without falling off. It becomes apparent that the designer of this configuration was never aboard an operating carrier on the high seas.

If that was the only problem with fueling that would be bad enough, but it wasn't. The Navy, knowing that the jets were going to be deployed on the WW II, carriers didn't make any provision to be able to carry jet fuel. The Turbo Jet Control (TJC) unit was specifically designed to operate with a JP-type fuel because the small working parts needed lubrication by this type of fuel passing through the unit. Aviation gasoline is considered to be "dry" and as such could cause damage to the control mechanism. So instead of fixing the problem by carrying jet fuel, the Navy dreamed up a "fix" for this problem by the addition of lubrication oil in the aft main tank to make up for the dry gas. This "fix" was not always successful, and TJC units failed on an all-too-frequent basis. The results were losses of aircraft and pilots due to the TJC failure when the small working parts "froze" and the engine flamed out. It was bad enough to face the enemy, but it sure would have been nice not to have to face a menace of the Navy's own making. Putting the jets aboard the Essex-class carriers was not a good marriage. The Navy's carriers weren't ready for them, and many of the Korean War aircraft operating problems were never solved during the three-plus years of carrier operation in the Korean War. In some cases, this fuel problem got much worse with the advent of the next version of the aircraft manufactured by Grumman. That will be discussed later.

The four 20-mm cannons located in the nose section of the F9F presented a number of problems that caused stoppages. The worst offender (67%) was caused by the hydraulic system used to charge the cannons for firing. A briefing discussion is necessary to explain how this system worked. When the squadron's ordnance crew finished loading the 20-mm cannons the weapons were put in the safe condition for catapult launch. This meant that the breechblock was all the way forward against the firing chamber with no live round in the chamber. Once airborne with the wheels retracted and clear of the task force, the pilot moved the gun switches down to the charge position. When this was done, the hydraulic gun charger moved the breechblock all the way aft allowing it to engage the sear pin while compressing the drive spring. The fluid then drained away, and the gun was charged. To set the guns for firing, the pilot moved the switches up from the charge position through off to the fire position. Now the cannons were ready to fire. When the trigger on the top front of the control stick was squeezed, the electrical solenoid pulled the sear pin out, allowing the breechblock to move forward driven by the coiled drive spring. As the breechblock moved forward it picked up a live round and pushed it forward. The round entered the firing chamber. When seated, it and the breechblock were abruptly stopped. The firing pin inside the breechblock, however, was free to move further forward, striking the cartridge primer resulting in firing the round.

Some of the gas from the exploding powder was used to drive the breechblock backwards. As it moved aft, it extracted the spent round, which dropped clear. If the trigger was still held down the cycle continued, and the gun fired again. If the trigger was released, the sear pin caught the breechblock when it was all the way aft, and the firing stopped. The 20-mm cannon fired 10 rounds per second. The ammo belt contained three types of ammunition in continuous order. The three types were High Explosive Incendiary (HEI), Armor Piercing (AP) and Tracer. The HEI was very effective in starting fires, while the AP was excellent in destroying transportation vehicles or damaging tank treads.

One trick we used was to put a dummy round as the first round in one of the guns in each set, upper and lower. The gun operated in pairs so that by turning on only one pair of the gun switches to the firing position, the pilot could strafe using one gun at a time. If you couldn't hit with one gun, why use more guns? After the one gun was empty, recharging pulled the dummy round out of the firing chamber of the second gun, and now when the trigger was squeezed the gun would pick up a live round. The F9F with the APG-30 gun sight was an excellent gun platform, and strafing ground targets was not difficult. Using this management technique, more targets could be attacked during the reconnaissance mission and still have ammo remaining.

A quote from the action report says it all.

The hydraulic system of charging the 20 mm caused two-thirds of the stoppages or malfunctions experienced in the F9F type aircraft during this period. The low side of the pressure switch (Aero 1-A) gets out of calibration leaving a residual pressure in the hydraulic charger (MK5, Mod 1) cylinder, thereby cushioning the travel of the breech-block to the battery position. This causes a light primer strike or no primer hit at all.

To the jet pilots, this meant that the gun or guns might not fire just when they were needed the most. It sure helped our confidence level in being able to complete the mission and not just go along for the ride. These were new aircraft from the factory, not some old war bird with multi tours. It was interesting that the two jet squadrons during the first operating period only fired 38,000 rounds, so we were not over stressing the gun system.

For our missions over North Korea, the external ordnance carried by the squadron was either six 5-in. air-to-ground High Velocity Aircraft Rockets (HVAR) or six 100-pound bombs in about equal number (543 and 546). The rockets were used against trucks and tanks, when they could be found. The gun sight also had a rocket setting that made this gun sight very good for rocket firing. When carrying rockets the pilot entered into a dive and placed the center of the gun sight on the target. Rotating the throttle handle counter clockwise released the gyros, and all the pilot had to do was fly the airplane so as to maintain the center of the gun sight on the target. By firing the rocket when reaching a slant range of about 3,500 feet while the airplane had been flying the rocket flight path for several seconds gave a very good chance for a direct hit or near enough to do considerable damage. The bombs as well as the HVARs were used to break rail along the railroad lines or to attack enemy buildings when suitable targets could be found. The North Koreans, however, quickly repaired these railroad breaks. For the jets, besides breaking up railroads, there were routine fighter sweeps over the airfields in the area from Wonsan to Hamhung to verify that no repairs were being done to the buildings or runways. The results were totally negative.

No matter how many times you climbed into your armed jet fighter-bomber sitting on the carrier's flight deck, the high level of tension was always there. The briefing format for a four-plane strike or armed-reconnaissance was often very much a standard boilerplate activity. It would cover altitude and bearing from the ship for rendezvous, course heading inbound to the start of the reconnaissance run, area to be covered, known flak concentrations, type of weapons, search and rescue forces availability, tactical radio frequency and Identification, Friend or Foe (IFF) to be used. Last, but most important, was the flight course back to the carrier. We checked the weather for the trip into the target area, weather during the time over the enemy territory, and the expected weather for the task force upon return. The important facts were written down on the kneepad for quick reference.

With everything crammed in the brain there were only two more things to do. First, hit the "head" to take care of all the coffee that had been consumed, and second, complete dressing for the flight. The latter meant we put on all the remaining bulky external flight gear needed for survival. In the wintertime, that meant climbing into a multiple layers of winter clothing and finally into the exposure suits used by most of the pilots. I was not one of the lucky ones to have one. Even with the suit it could be a very chilling experience if I had to ditch the aircraft or parachute from a crippled aircraft into the water. Then, whether it was winter or summer, the next item for me was my survival vest with all the goodies I might need for a landing in enemy territory: flares, extra ammo for the .38 caliber pistol I carried, water purification tablets, matches in a sealed container, and other important items. To all of that I added a 6-inch hunting knife, and my .38-caliber revolver loaded with five rounds of tracer ammo. I always checked to see that the sixth chamber was empty under the firing pin. There was no sense shooting oneself during a hard landing in the water or on the ground. Last of all was the famous "Mae West" for floatation after an aircraft ditching or making a parachute water landing. Before all this gear was put on, I wrapped my signal scarf around my neck. It was bright yellow on one side and bright orange on the other. (I still have this scarf). It was 36 inches long by 12 inches wide and could be folded in various ways to signal the rescue combat air patrol (RESCAP) what I might need or want then to know while I was on the ground. It also helped protect my neck from a flash fire in the cockpit.

Then we waited. That was the toughest part, waiting for the command, "Pilots, man your planes." When this came over the squawk box in the ready room from the air boss, I picked up my helmet, oxygen mask, maps, and kneepad and waddled out the hatch to the catwalk to the ladder to climb the eight feet up to the fight deck. Depending on the type of flight assigned, the jets were spotted in order of launch. The Combat Air Patrol (CAP) was forward with the reconnaissance fighter-bombers after them strung down the port side from just behind the catapults and mid-ship aft of the deck edge elevator. A quick pre-flight could be taken care of if it was daylight, and then it was up into the cockpit. With all this flight gear on, it was not an easy task to get settled in. The plane captains were a great aid in the process. I wiggled into the "best" position in a very cramped cockpit. My shoulders touched either side of the canopy railing. It would be my home for two-plus hours. After strapping on the parachute's two leg straps and hooking up the chest straps in the center, I then hooked the lanyard to the life raft in the parachute seat. Then the plane captain gave me the shoulder harness to connect with the seat belt. After these were secure I plugged in my oxygen hose, "G"-suit hose and finally my radio jack. The last thing was to adjust the headrest for catapult launch and raise the catapult rod in the front of the throttle quadrant. After working up a sweat getting settled, all was in readiness.

Again, the wait seemed forever. If I was spotted on the catapult for a CAP mission, the turning of the ship into the wind wasn't bad, but if I was spotted a mid-ship at a forty-five-degree angle to the ship's centerline it was different. When the ship turned into the wind I sometimes had that weird feeling of being toppled backward into the sea or skidding across the slick flight deck into another aircraft. Many times when in the turn, the plane settled back on to the tail skid. That movement was a very unsettling sensation. During the winter months, the icy wind was painful to take on the left side of my face. The canopy had to be left open, so there was no way to hide from the wind. Even with my oxygen mask in place, the left cheek became icy from the cold wind.

All was in readiness for the air boss's command; "Start jet engines." The three-wheeled starter jeep was already plugged into the first aircraft in line, and upon signal from the cockpit, the airman gunned the jeep's engine and the jet engine starting operation began. Once there was a good start, the pilot gave a thumbs-up and the jeep cable was unplugged from the aircraft and the jeep moved quickly to the next jet in the pack. The music for the fight-deck-launch dance had begun.

Under low wind conditions 65 feet over the water the stall indicator often vibrated the control stick, warning that the aircraft was struggling to stay airborne right after the catapult shot. As soon as possible I started to clean up the plane by raising the landing gear and start accelerating. A slight clearing turn was made to keep the jet exhaust away from the following aircraft. Depending upon which catapult was used; the clearing was always away from the centerline of the ship. The next plane would be about 30 seconds behind you. After raising the takeoff flaps upon reaching 150 knots, the normal fight pattern was to stay at about 100 feet above the water until you reached climb speed of 300 knots. Often my flight path took me past one of the destroyers in the task-force screen. I always waved or rocked my wings to those on deck. You never knew when you might need their services. At proper climb speed, I started my climb up to the designated altitude to quickly join up with the others in the flight heading off for the coast or to the CAP station. The fourth airplane always radioed the fight leader that he had all planes in sight, and a running rendezvous was made.

No matter what mission I flew, the return to the carrier was much the same procedure. From missions over Korea the flight tried to arrive about five minutes before the task force turned into the wind with about 1,200 pounds of fuel, which translates to about 200 gallons. If the mission was a defensive CAP, the flight stayed on station until the relief CAP had been launched and was on its way. Then the FDO in the *Antietam* CIC radioed to the flight leader a heading vector to return to the task force. When flying at altitude for the entire period, the CAP usually had much more fuel aboard, so it routinely scheduled to land last during jet recovery. All jet flights orbit at about 20,000 feet until each flight was called down to make the approach and enter the landing pattern. The prop aircraft's orbit was lower and they would land after the jets had been recovered. Before leaving the orbit, the flight leader gave the signal to drop the tail hook. Each of the pilots checked the tail hook of the other aircraft for a successful tail-hook deployment, and when all was well we were ready for recovery. The radio call to the division leader by the *Antietam* CIC kicked off a high-speed descent made with full diver brakes extended; diving to a point astern of the carrier so as to pass by the starboard side at 250 feet. Past the carriers bow the flight leader started the breakup of the formation when the aircraft already in the pattern was abeam of him. In turn, each member peeled off from the formation with a left turn, one by one, to set up about a thirty-second separation between aircraft. Finishing the turn to the downwind leg, the wheels were lowered when the air speed was below 165 knots, and the flaps went down after 150 knots was reached.

On the downwind leg, following once again the landing check-off list insured everything was done. Even though I did this many times, I always read the list each time. Depending upon the wind over the water, I started another left turn for the final approach either abeam of the island structure of the carrier or slightly ahead if the surface wind was stronger. During this 180-degree turn the speed was reduced further and more altitude was lost. The perfect approach was to arrive directly 200-300 feet astern of the ship, 25 feet above the flight deck at about 108-110 knots. During the turn, the aircraft had slightly less lift so a slightly higher power setting was needed to maintain altitude. The FCLP practice on land and actual carrier landings had drummed into my brain that the nose position controlled the airspeed; the power setting controlled the altitude.

As the aircraft rolled out of the turn to level flight, this small amount of extra power was reduced to prevent the aircraft from gaining altitude. Lining up with the centerline of the flight deck, on speed and about 20 feet above the flight deck, the LSO gave the cut signal with his paddles. Throttling back to cut the engine power to idle as the nose of the aircraft was lowered slightly to start the descent, then immediate back pressure for a flare-out and making a smooth landing (I hoped). There was always the potential for a pitching deck that could cause some extra problems. Later on when the air group and arresting crew had honed their skill with practice, the interval between landing aircraft got even shorter. It was a very satisfying recovery when this landing interval was close together with no wave off—a great picture of teamwork by all hands!

During WW II the carrier based Combat Air Patrol (CAP) was the primary defensive measure used against enemy multi engine land based bombers, carrier-based dive-bombers, and torpedo bombers. The raiding aircraft were discovered by either search aircraft or later in the war by radar on the ships of the task force. The incoming enemy raid could be flying at altitudes as high as 12,000 feet. The enemy bombers were protected by covering fighters who tried to engage the CAP so that their bombers could make their attacks. The cruising speed of the enemy was not that high until the aircraft reached the pushover point for their attack. Interception by the CAP could be made 30 to 40 miles from the task force. At speeds of 230 knots, there was a window of time (about six minutes) to make as many attacking runs against the bomber before the attacker came in range of the ships antiaircraft guns. The CAP tactics used by the Navy were developed into an effective defensive system for the fast carrier task forces.

The SPS-6B and SX radar that was used was very effective in detecting the incoming propeller aircraft as these aircraft gave an excellent radar return.

It was not unusual for the incoming raid to be discovered at ranges of 60 to 75 miles. The CAP positioned in an orbit 40 to 50 miles from the task force could be quickly vectored towards these incoming enemy aircraft. The CAP was controlled more often than not by the carrier's Combat Information Center (CIC). Thus, the CIC was developed into a highly structured aircraft-control system by the end of the war in 1945. It worked then, but it was out-of-date now.

Moving forward five years, these techniques had not been changed, yet the aircraft that were used as the defensive CAP had changed significantly. The radar return of even the Jet CAP was so poor or non-existent at higher altitudes when the flight was more than 40 miles from the task force. (The Jet CAP normally operated at altitudes above 25,000 feet.) The results of this change in the type of aircraft used and the altitude they flew at, dramatically altered the equation. This is shown in the following table taken from one of the USS *Antietam* action reports. This one is dated 10/15/1951-11/16/1951:

RADAR Type of Aircraft Altitude Range
Type in feet in miles
SX search props 8,000 75
Jet 12,000 25
SX height props 8,000 50
Jets 12,000 30
SPS-6B props 8,000 60
Jets 12,000 45
SK props 8,000 60
Jets 12,000 20

It should be noted here that jets returning from North Korea normally flew at 20,000 feet, conserving fuel to be able to meet the requirement of having 1,200 pounds of fuel (approximately 200 gallons) at recovery time. The detection of incoming jets by the task force became more difficult as the altitude increased. (See the next report.) It is also important to note that a jet fighter pointed directly at the radar station offers a very small cross-sectional target. The thinner wing and oval shaped fuselage combined to give a poor radar refection. If the jet is crossing at 90 degrees to the radar beam it will, however, have a larger return because the side profile was larger.

From an earlier report from the USS *Boxer*, dated 07/26/1951-08/24/1951 the problem become even more disquieting:

> Jet Aircraft not using IFF (Identification Friend or Foe) continue to present a very serious problem, particularly at altitudes in excess of 15,000 feet. While generally detected at an optimum range of 40 miles, it is not unusual for a section of jets (a section consists of two planes) to call in overhead without having been detected or reported once. The seriousness of the inability to detect jet aircraft at altitude can be more readily appreciated when one considers that these conditions prevail while the task force has been searching with an average of 12-15 SPS-6B and at least 2 SX Radar.

While the range of detection appears to be enough to alert the CAP to the presence of hostile aircraft, it should be pointed out that a jet flying at a ground speed of 450 knots, or 522 mph will cover the distance of 35 miles in about 4 minutes. That means an attacking jet aircraft would be within firing range of the task force in a very short time. Furthermore, the jet CAP had to close and overtake a diving enemy jet to engage it. In almost any scenario, it would not be possible.

In this period, I flew five CAP defensive missions out of the 52 that were flown by the air group. The difficulties experienced during these flights by our division were not unique to us, but were typical of those experienced by other pilots in other air groups. The *Antietam* air controllers were very green, and they had little understanding of the difficulties of finding another flight of jets when no altitude information was known. Flying at 30,000 feet, there were a lot of cubic miles of air space within eyesight. Finding even friendly jets was difficult when looking down at them against a dark blue sea. When vectored out for a practice intercept, it was difficult to get them to put us into a good attack position. The controllers all too frequently vectored us directly over the flight to be intercepted. The best positioning for the CAP was "up sun" about 5,000 feet above and at least 3,000 feet to the side of the boogies. This happened once in a while, rather than the standard. The controllers also didn't realize the turning radius of a jet fighter at these higher altitudes. Their training must have been done using slower prop aircraft. Interception of the ADs and F4Us was a lot easier, and we had a great time zooming past them as they returned from their missions. During these five CAP flights no enemy aircraft were ever detected. We would have been at a great disadvantage if we had to intercept enemy jets. The task force was fortunately operating too far away from any known active enemy airfields.

The *Antietam* and its escorts departed the task force in the late afternoon of the 14th after a full day of flight operations. That first night after operations ended and we were headed back to Japan I could feel the tension slowly ebb out of my mind. For a short time, I didn't have to concern myself with early morning wake-up calls nor struggling through darkness before dawn to find my assigned aircraft. I had a respite from the penetrating cold wind blowing in the open canopy while waiting for the dawn sky to light up. For a while I was relieved of that strange feeling in the stomach that came from my concern of what today's mission would bring. I had made it through my baptism. So much had happened that it was hard to comprehend I was all in one piece.

It took two full days to reach Yokosuka, Japan. The ship docked at Piedmont Pier, NOB Yokosuka on the 16th and with the exception of standing as SDO for one day, the others and I were free to explore the area around Tokyo. One of the best perks available were the Rest and Recuperation (R&R) hotels outside of Tokyo run by the military. Being adventurous and wanting to take advantage of seeing the country, I signed up for the one in the mountains, the Akakura Hotel. It was for six days of free leave. I tried to get some of the others interested, but no one wanted to go. I said the heck with them, packed my bag, and headed for the local train station with leave orders in hand. After arriving in Tokyo, I caught a cab for the Ueno train station, where most of the trains left for other cities. I spoke no Japanese, but I figured I could get around. I got my train ticket and with hand signs went to the specific track to await my train. I was told that the trains run on time in Japan, so don't get worried. Five minutes before the departure time: still no train. Then it appeared backing into the station. The conductor spotted me and in no time I was shown to my seat in the Pullman car. The train ride was to be an overnight one. It sure turned out to be an interesting night.

After dark, the sleeper was set up, and I figured I would get some sleep. The train must have stopped at every station along the line. As the train came to a stop, I bumped my head against the headboard, and I banged my legs against the footboard when we started again. Heck, the berth was only about 5 feet 5 inches long, and I am 6 feet tall. It wasn't the best sleeping condition.

I was sound asleep, however, when the conductor woke me in the morning. It seemed like it was in the middle of the night, but we were due at my stop in 15 minutes.

As dawn was breaking the train arrived at the station on time, and the conductor helped me off. I remembered not to try to shake his hand, but bowed slightly when he bowed before getting on the train. There I was in a completely strange world, sure that no one in this small town could speak a word of English. So now what do I do? I was trying to figure out what my next step would be when a voice behind me said. "Sir, are you going to the hotel?" I spun around, and there was a US Army sergeant walking up to me. He picked up my bag and led me to an Army track vehicle called a "snow weasel" that they used to climb the steep road over a mile up the mountainside to the hotel. He apologized that there wasn't any snow, but I didn't really care. The mountain air was terrific, but most terrific of all was the wonderful quiet of the place.

That was more than enough for me. The carrier was always noisy with crew activity, maintenance, and the constant sound of the air blowers moving air throughout the ship's spaces. Without snow, the hotel was only partially filled up. I spent the good days exploring the area around the hotel, and then returning for lunch. The food was good and plentiful with the cost per day being $1.08 for room and board. Before dinner, the few other military officers on R&R leave populated the bar. The war stories grew as the evening wore on until time for dinner. The martinis were $0.13 a drink or two for a quarter. For less than a $1.50 a day, life was good. It was a great rest both mentally and physically, and in no time the days went by until it was time to leave. I got my orders stamped by the officer in charge (OIC) of the hotel and was on my way back to the ship. The Army jeep drove me to the train station in time for the train back to Tokyo. After arrival at Ueno, a taxi ride to the local station to catch the local train to Yokosuka was next. The carrier was due to leave on the morning of November 26th. The old saying came to mind, "I did not want to miss the boat."

Chapter 8
Back for Another Round

The weather, which had been good in Japan, turned foul by the 26th, and the ship rolled and pitched as we sailed around southern Japan, first to the south, then turning west and finally north into the Sea of Japan. Late on the night of the 28th the carrier and its escorts joined up with the task force. The weather began to clear on the morning of the 29th, and the air group was back into full combat flight operations. I flew one armed-reconnaissance mission from Pyonggang to Wonsan carrying a much heavier load than the last tour on the line. The air had turned much colder with more wind over the water, so all the aircraft could carry more and heavier external ordnance. With six 250-pound bombs, the F9F was slow to accelerate after launch. Often the stick shaker vibrates as the aircraft struggles near stall speed before the air speed increases after the wheels came up. Our rate of climb to the coast, even with full power was also much slower. We were carrying 900 pounds more during these colder months than we did earlier. But these bigger bombs did a lot better job of smashing the railroad rails and roadbed plus the small bridges that dotted the North Korean countryside. As usual, flying in just north of the front lines, we dropped our bombs on a suspected storage area. This was followed by our run up the road from Pyonggang northward. The flight leader hunted for targets, but we were out of luck and found nothing,. Probably because the enemy stays off the roads by running their trucks either off the roads under the pine trees or covering them with white cloth to blend in with the snow. As usual, being fourth man, it was my job to keep everyone in sight, while watching for tracers aimed at the others. I also needed to look alternately over both shoulders for possible enemy flak explosion from gun fire aimed at me, at the same time jinxing back and forth to make sure I was not an easy target for the antiaircraft gunners. The others who were flying lower moved through the gunners' area faster than I did, so I was constantly changing my flight path to make a less inviting target. In addition, I also kept a sharp eye out for any signs of targets further out from the route we were traveling. The nagging fear that had all but disappeared while in port, came back to me on these flight. When we were getting close to the Wonsan area, our mission was completed, and we climbed eastward to head back to the task force to arrive in time for recovery. Either the North Korean gunners were using ammo without tracers, or they were lousy shots because I saw no flak. Clear of the coast I began to relax and looked forward to my landing in about thirty minutes. So chalk up another combat mission.

On the second scheduled flight on the 29th I had to abort the mission when one of my main landing gear wheel well doors did not retract. Anything over 165 knots could damage the door and possibly jam the landing gear from coming down. After notifying the ship about the problem by radio, I moved to set up my orbit as directed by the ship's controller outside the destroyer screen. Clear of the ships I jettisoned the bomb load on safe as well as dumping the fuel stored in my tip tank. The carrier completed the launch and re-spotted the flight deck with a ready deck. I was recalled to land back aboard. I was a little faster and heavier that normal, but all went well. It was a dull, cold half-hour flight after getting mentally ready for a mission.

The end of November was a replenishment day and rest for most of the pilots, but not for four of us. We had the enjoyable task of standing the CAP-alert duty for four hours in the afternoon. Not much to do, but that is the way it can often be. The weather remained clear, and the first three days of December saw lots of scheduled flying. I flew each day starting with a Target Combat Air Patrol (TARCAP) over the area where the props were attacking. This area was north of Wonsan and was close enough to the MiG-15 air bases just across the Yalu River to allow the MiG to make a firing pass at the slower prop aircraft. Flying spread out in loose, two plane sections kept the eyes scanning the skies for sunlight reflection off of the aircraft or their contrails. There were no signs of them, so after the props finished their attack we proceeded on our secondary job, looking for targets on the road and railroad while dodging the flak sent our way. Most of the flak was way off and didn't really worry me. That did not stop me from flying a constantly changing course and altitude. It didn't need to be a lot, just so I was not in the same airspace where they were firing.

The next day was a regular CAP without any activity other than boring a hole in the sky, and finally another TARCAP preceding the armed-reconnaissance part of the flight to finish the period. The TARCAP was again uneventful so we headed for our reconnaissance part of the mission. Our assigned area for our division was the hot area from Wonsan to Kowon. These two missions were flown without any incidents or aircraft damage even though this area had lots of enemy antiaircraft guns. As we were moving fast, the gunner often did not have a chance to get their guns on us before we had sped away. Our bombing ability was improving with all the practice we had during the last cruise with the task force, and the division was making more railroad-bed cuts. Hitting a narrow railroad bed from a speeding jet was no easy job. To hit the center, I had to take into account from which wing the bomb was to be dropped. The bomb racks were over twelve feet from the aircraft's centerline. So I aimed to the opposite side of the tracks I wanted to hit. The Navy didn't teach any of this in training, but after a lot of drops, it dawned on me to make this adjustment. I guess they thought we would be bombing only big things. During this three-day period the air group flew a total of 219 sorties with good results for their efforts and no aircraft losses.

After a day of replenishing on December 4th, the air group was back for another three days of flying. Flying one mission each day, including two armed-reconnaissance flights, plus my first photo-escort mission on the 5th, showed me that I was getting better. When I saw my name of the flight schedule for this one I new I had arrived. Then I realized I was going to be the only plane with loaded guns. The briefing was intense and to the point! Get the photo plane back even if it meant you had to trade shots with a MiG-15. The task of the photo escort is basically to watch for flak and enemy aircraft. If the flight was south of Wonsan, the flak was the big concern. North of Wonsan, the possibility of enemy MiG-15 jet fighter attacking was much higher. During the photo run, the escort weaved back and forth behind and above the photo plane constantly scanning the sky for aircraft as well as watching out for any flak bursts or indication of tracers. On this flight, thankfully there were neither. There might have been some 20- mm shells or smaller machine gun fired, but without tracers or timed explosive shells, it is difficult to know when either of us was under fire. Thirty minutes of this activity sure made the neck muscles work hard. The hardest part, however, of being a photo escort was managing the fuel supply. The photo plane had no external bomb racks, so it burned less fuel than the escort to maintain the same airspeed. Getting back to the task force with 1,200 lbs. of fuel requires careful flying. Taking advantage of free cruising allowed for a constant power setting whenever I could as well as flying higher than the photo planes' 10,000-foot altitude to save every pound of fuel possible. The mission was without any occurrences, yet no matter how I tried I came aboard with 800 pounds of fuel showing on the gauge with the red low-fuel warning light glowing brightly. It took about 250 pounds of fuel to take a wave off and make another approach. If the aircraft ahead had a deck accident, it would not be very long before I either landed on another ship or got my feet wet.

The first reconnaissance mission on the 6th was flown from Tanchon on the northeast coast to Pungsan north up in the mountains. The road was not much more than a dirt track, and it didn't show much use. It ended at the base of a tall mountain. On the other side was Pungsan where we picked up another road and followed it back to the coast. As we approached the coast we hit out fuel minimum to end the mission over the land. It was another dull fruitless flight. This was turning out to be a rather dull series of flights. At least we could report to the AIO that these roads appeared to be empty of traffic and little used.

Breaking off from our mission the division climbed to a higher altitude to conserve fuel and flew back to the task force using minimum power setting to maintain airspeed of 180 knots for maximum endurance. This was more of the boring time while flying back to the task force. The division went through the usual activity and we all got aboard without difficulty. The second mission was from Wonsan to Panchunjang. This mission was totally different. We received information at our pre-flight briefing that a locomotive had been reported in the area that we were to cover. Reaching the coast north of Wonsan we commenced to search for this juicy target. Just as were passing over a damaged railroad bridge, Sandy spotted the locomotive on the bridge. There was the juicy target. We wheeled around in a tight 90 degree bank to commence our attack. We spread out in two sections and made a simultaneous low level shallow diving attack on the locomotive and tender combination from different headings. The Koreans, as expected, had moved in some additional AAA to defend this locomotive, but their gunfire wasn't very good, and one 250 pound bomb hit the locomotive knocking it off the bridge into the river below. It was a wild few minutes for all of us. The flak followed us closely, but they never seemed to give us enough lead for our fast moving jets. I know that those red tracers came close enough to raise my "pucker factor" to a really high level. Somehow we managed to successfully complete our bombing runs without any flak hits on any of us. It sure did help to have more than one plane attacking at the same time to split the amount of gunfire any one plane received. As usual, I was constantly changing direction and making irregular turns until the last minute before aiming and dropping my bomb. This type of flying was becoming second nature. As soon as the reconnaissance part of the flight started, I was into my own chaotic type of flying. At the same time as we were hitting the target more often, the other pilots in the air group were becoming more effective in their attacks. The action report listed that the air group flew a total of 262 sorties without loss of any aircraft during this period.

After a day of replenishing on the 8th, the air group was again back for another three days of great flying weather. Flying one flight each day including two CAP flights and one armed-reconnaissance mission, I picked more experience. Again, they were straightforward flights with out any great excitement. The most exciting part of the CAP flight was getting back aboard the carrier. The reconnaissance mission was from Yongdaeri to Sangjigyong-ni. We did our route and were shot at the two river crossings by 20-mm antiaircraft guns set up to protect the bridges. They were shooting behind us, and no one was in any great danger from these gunners. I was learning to worry only when the flak came close and to concentrate on getting good hits with my external ordnance. Other than the one time that Sandy's plane had been hit we seemed to be living on borrowed time.

Our CAP flight had the same problems as before, but the controllers seemed to be getting better. They were setting us up in better attack position and had learned about the turning radius of the jets at altitude. The shipboard radar, however, hadn't improved that much. Sometimes the atmospheric conditions helped the radar to pick up returning jets 10-15 miles further out than on the first month on the line, but most of the time these returning jet aircraft were spotted because the flight leader had turned on his IFF. Not a particular happy thought for the ship crew. This rhythm was repeated for the next four days. On the 11th, the USS *Antietam* action report stated:

> The 21,000 landing aboard the *Antietam* was made today. Today marked the ninth consecutive flying day with perfect flying weather during which time the *Antietam* combined with the *Essex* accounted for 937 railroad cuts and destroyed many locomotives, railroad bridges and ox carts. It is believed that this long stretch of perfect clear cold weather is unprecedented in this area at this time of year.

The air group was hitting its stride and flew 277 sorties during the three days ending on the 11th. This was the highest number since being in the combat zone. The pilots were coming into their own with superior performance around the ship and landings. The operational accident rate had decreased significantly, but not completely. During this time, there was only one aircraft lost when an AD crashed ahead of the ship immediately after a deck take-off due to engine failure. There were 28 aircraft damaged, however, by either enemy small-arms fire or from their own bomb blasts during aggressive attacking by the AD and F4U aircraft. Fortunately there were no pilots seriously injured during this period of intense flying. Even though the daylight hours were very short, the air group flew an average of 92 sorties per day. In ten flying days, I flew a defensive or offensive mission every day. These missions were becoming routine, and that is when it get dangerous. Boredom leads to carelessness and either your airplane get a belly full of flak or you make a poor landing and end up in the barriers.

Once again on the 12th the task force sailed south to replenish. In three days of flying, the air group had expended approximately 163.3 tons of all types of ordnance and burned 157,500 gallons of aviation gasoline. Not a bad record for this new air group during their second period with Task Force 77.

Beginning on the 13th and through the 24th, the air group was able to operate almost every day except on the two replenishment days. The weather was exceptionally good for this time of year. The air group flew 769 sorties with an average of 75.7 flights per day. The weather was excellent for all but one day when the morning was spent finishing the replenishment that was curtailed on the 16th because of high wind causing rough seas.

During this long period, the air group on the 19th lost its first pilot, Ensign Glen Riley of VF-713, due to enemy action. His aircraft crashed into the ocean after he completed his attack. There was no radio transmission, so it was assumed he was hit and lost control of the aircraft. One other plane was lost to enemy antiaircraft fire, LT Seymour Marshall of VA-728 who was leading two divisions had to bail out because his AD was hit by flak and set on fire. He bailed out over enemy-held territory and fortunately landed on top of a mountain ridge. He was able to spread his parachute out on the ground to mark his location for the Rescue Combat Air Patrol (RESCAP). The Corsair division kept him in sight as they set up their RESCAP while one of the AD division's aircraft flew to the coast to rendezvous with the helicopter. The helicopter was then escorted to the downed pilot without being subject to ground fire along the way to the downed-pilot site. The helicopter pilot was successful in being able to land, pick up the downed pilot, and fly out of the enemy area. LT Marshall was returned to the carrier a few days later.

None of our flights had any problems or incidents with flak or small arm hits except on a flight around Kowan. I was concerned that I was becoming a little complacent about the enemy's ability to hit my fast-moving jet. I figured that moving fast with frequent turns helped keep me out of harm's way. That idea got knocked out of me on this flight. I got a real scare when I looked down when I was in a vertical bank and saw a battery of AAA guns firing at me. I could see the muzzle flashes and the tracers streaking up at me. Fortunately for me the gunners were not leading me just enough and the shells drifted aft as they closed in on my aircraft. That was too damn close for comfort. We had done our job and were fortunate that no one had been hit. Our division flew two CAP flights, one fighter sweep of the 12 airfields around Hamhung, and three reconnaissance missions. The steady schedule of flying showed that the air group had improved in all aspects. Our division was getting better at spotting targets and most of all, hitting them on a regular basis.

It was during this time that an interesting demonstration of the endurance and ruggedness of the F9F-2's J-42 engine occurred. One aircraft took flak hits in a forward combustion-chamber casting. The slug, together with a two-inch square piece of the chamber casting knocked off by the slug, went through the combustion chamber, the nozzle guide vanes and out through the turbine blades. The result was that the trailing edges of all of the nozzle-guide vanes were severely notched at the top, plus most of the turbine blades were curled into a "U" shape at their tips. The pilot continued on his mission operating his engine for over 3/4 of an hour at all power settings with no sign of malfunctioning. Even the carrier approach and landing were made without any apparent engine difficulty. It is a steadying thought to pilot that the engine can take this kind of battle damage and continue to operate to bring the pilot safely home.

With this stretch of clear weather, flying once every flying day either a CAP or an armed-reconnaissance mission, I added eight more sorties to the logbook. The more missions flown meant getting more familiar with the road and railroad system in the northeastern sector of North Korea. The division leader's knowledge of the hot spots helped to keep us from flying into too much flak. When we were to strike a bridge, we used our tactical technique to minimize the flak. On the 23rd it didn't work completely when we attacked a bridge near Kowan. This area was another hotbed of many AAA guns. Finishing my strafing on the first run covering the first section in their bombing run, I climb and flipped into a wing over and started down on a bombing run. The first section was either ahead of schedule, or I was late, because they were leaving the target area just as I entered my dive. Halfway down in my bombing run, the 20-mm or 37-mm flax guns opened up and lots of red tracers were headed my way. It was like flying through a flock of red birds. Most of them were off my flight path, but one that was coming up looked like it had my name on it. It missed, but I swear that I could smell that one as it went by. That one was all too damn close! This mission raised my "pucker factor" to a whole new level. Those tracers may look pretty, but they could very deadly if they hit the aircraft. Others had been hit; why I hadn't been was a mystery to me.

Flight operations were secured on the 24th as well as Christmas Day. With that much flying the ship needed to replenish all the ordnance and gasoline expended and to celebrate the holiday. The bunkroom boys had their own special Christmas celebration or put another way, given a tough project, the eight Junior Officers came up with a creative solution.

When it became apparent to the eight of us in late November 1951 that the USS *Antietam*, part of Task Force 77 in the Sea of Japan, would be at sea through December 25th we decided to do something about celebrating Christmas. The eight of us in the small Junior Officer Bunkroom on the 01 level got together to figure out how we could obtain a small Christmas tree for our space. There was just enough room for a very small tree, because the bunkroom was originally set up for twelve junior officers. There were only eight of us, which allowed us to remove four bunk beds for extra space to hang uniforms and store our luggage. It was decided that the first one who had to land at the emergency airfield (K-18) because of bad weather or battle damage to a member of his flight would try to find a small pine tree and bring it back to the ship. It had to be small because it had to fit into the lower nose area of the F9F-2 Panther. During early December, there had been no reason for any one from the bunkroom to land at K-18. We all held our breath, but then it happened. Ensign Joe Perry's flight had to land at K-18 because of bad weather.

When the flight was scheduled to return the next day, those of us who were not flying headed for vulture's row in the ship's island to watch the recovery. We had a clear view of the aft end of the flight deck. When Joe's plane landed and was taxiing forward out of the arresting gear we could see a small sprig of green sticking up from his flying helmet. Once all planes were aboard we headed for his airplane. Out of the nose section of his airplane came one of the greatest looking Christmas tree you ever saw.

It was about four feet tall all tied tightly up and stuffed carefully into his aircraft's nose section. When we got the tree back to the bunkroom we stood it up in a used coffee can that we then covered with brown paper. It sure looked beautiful in the bunkroom. In typical Navy fashion we had to solve the next problem on how we could decorate the tree. Well, we all had learned a lot in kindergarten on how to make garlands out of colored paper, using scissors and paste. The effort paid off when all material was found through some midnight small-stores raids. We sat down to make our tree the best on the ship. It certainly gave a festive air to our drab navy green and gray bunkroom far away from home.

Joe told us about his effort to get the tree and how he was able to get help from the US Marines stationed at K-18. It was an effort that lasted in each of our minds for the rest of our life. For most of us, this was the first time we were separated from our families on Christmas. LTJG Robert King got the most unusual Christmas gift of all of us. His wife, Mary, had baked him a big batch of his favorite cookies and packed them into a nicely decorated metal tin. It traveled via cargo ship from the states finally arriving on the USS *Antietam* just before Christmas. It was a long sea journey for the cookies. When he opened it on Christmas Day he was in for a big surprise. He shared the cookie crumbs with all of us. The only way to eat them was with a spoon. The constant motion of the cargo ship had reduced the once lovely cookies to nothing but a tin full of small crumbs.

Back to the war on the 26th, but the air group had only one more day of flying because of bad weather. We gladly flew a nice boring CAP while the air group flew a only 64 sorties on the 28th. After everyone was back aboard, the ship with its escorts turned south and headed for NOB Yokosuka for ship maintenance and for the pilots some R&R. We had a "small" celebration in the bunkroom because we had run low on our liquor supply. A nicely chilled martini sure tasted great.

A recap of the air group's efforts showed that the second period with the task force that the pilots had settled down. They became much more effective around the carrier, making good landings, and when over enemy territory hitting the targets. The aircraft launches and recoveries came up to professional standards with fewer delays in takeoff and often no wave-off during recovery. There were 21 flying days allowing for 1,651 sorties to be flown. I was not flying every flying day, but ended the period with 20 missions flown. They were six CAP flights, 13 armed-reconnaissance missions, and one photo-escort flight. I managed to stay clear of the antiaircraft fire on my 14 flights over the beach. The few other pilots of the air group were not so fortunate. One was killed in action, and five were wounded, fortunately none seriously. On the plus side, besides sorties flown, the air group dropped 1,632.6 tons of ordnance and fired 609,170 rounds of 20 mm and 50 caliber ammunition. There were 419 jet strikes using mostly 250-pound bombs. This was because the colder weather and higher wind over the sea allowed for the heavy load. Carrying six 250-pound bombs made the F9F-2 sluggish after takeoff and climbing to altitude. Until we burned down our fuel, the F9F wasn't much of a fighter plane. With 1,500 lbs. of bombs we were very close to the max catapult-takeoff weight.

Our missions over North Korea were of several types. We made fighter sweeps over enemy airfields insuring that the enemy was not using or preparing for use any of these fields. The primary targets of all the interdiction flights were changed from the reconnaissance routes to rail cut with the reconnaissance route being secondary. The ordnance load was also changed from rockets to 250-pound bombs exclusively. The total rail cuts increased with the use of the 250-pound bombs. Hitting the narrow railroad consistently came from lots of practice. We got that and a whole lot more. Heck, unless I was really on target, I did not drop. I just pulled up for another run. As long as we were not being shot at, it was no different than a training flight.

Now that we were carrying more and larger ordnance there were several problems with different aspects of the F9F aircraft that made it tough on the flight-deck crew. Of the 1,472 bombs carried by the jets, 12 could not be dropped. All were brought aboard without exploding even though 10 of them came off and slid up the deck. On the beginning side of the mission, 22 bombs were left behind on catapult shots. Having a 250-pound bomb rolling around on the flight deck is asking for major trouble because the arming wire often stayed with the aircraft.

For the pilots, one significant problem occurred when either the arming wire came loose from the bomb rack or it pulled free of the fuse. For those who are not familiar with the way an external bomb rack operated on the F9F, I offer the following description. The F9F carried six Mod 55 bomb racks. The bomb attached to the rack at two points. The bomb had two mounting lugs that fitted into two slots on the rack. When depressing the button on the control stick with the arming switches set to drop live; the electrical solenoid pulled the rod holding the bomb to the rack. The bomb dropped free towards the target. To accomplish the start of the arming of either the nose fuse or the tail fuse, or both required that the arming wire stay attached to the bomb rack. To add to this process, the dropped bomb needed to be further armed. This arming of the fuse required a certain amount of air travel causing a small propeller on the fuse to spin turning a plate allowing the firing pin to strike the primer when striking the ground. If the arming wire remained on the bomb, it did not arm, and when it hit the ground, it was a dud. Without the pilot's knowledge, the arming wire some times broke, and even when all the switches were properly set the dropped bomb did not arm. All that work and danger to drop a dud! The most worrisome problem was when we were carrying 260-pound fragmentation bombs with VT fuses. The fragmentation bomb was created from a regular 250-pounder, but with 10 pounds of steel bands wrapped around the body. These fuses, when armed, detected the ground using a radio signal and exploded at a set altitude above the ground. They were great for antiaircraft gun suppression, but if the arming wire pulled out of the fuse while still attached to the aircraft in flight; the bomb armed and could detect the aircraft and explode. When carrying this type of bomb, I kept a careful eye on my bomb load. From the cockpit, it was possible to see all six bomb-nose fuses. We also kept a careful eye on the each other's aircraft in the flight. Often the wires broke because of the higher jet-flight speed. This arming system was a carry over from WW II when the aircraft flew at a lower air speed.

If the solenoid failed to operate or jammed, the bomb stayed with the aircraft. Bringing a bomb or rocket back aboard the carrier was dangerous for the pilot as well as for the deck crew. The arrested landing of the high-speed jet frequently caused the ordnance to break free of the bomb rack and slide or tumble up the flight deck. It was not a healthy event even if the ordnance did not explode. That much weight could kill or seriously injury any crewman it hit.

This was well stated in CVG-15 action report dated 11/26/1951-12/31/1951.

Out of a total of 1,755 100 lb. and 250 lb. bombs carried by both VF-831 and VF-837 on the Mark 55 Mod "0" Bomb Racks, 22 have accidentally dropped on catapult launches and 12 have been brought back to the ship after all means to release in the air have failed. Of these 12, 10 dropped off on arrested landings or while taxiing immediately after an arrested landing. Those dropping off on arrested landings often damaged the aircraft flaps.

Besides this problem with hung bombs, the jets bombing suffered because numerous bombs were duds. Again quoting from the same action report:

A number of dud bombs were encountered. On catapulting the F9F, the arming wires are pulled free of the Mark 55 racks. To eliminate this trouble more care has been exercised in arming the bombs. Two clips are placed in front of the arming vanes and two just behind the vanes. Finally, a rubber band cut from an inner-tube was placed around the rack in such a way as to prevent the arming wire from slipping out.

Good old American Navy know-how to make a shipboard fix that should have been done by the designers back in the states. The jet squadrons on this ship and other carriers faced many of these types of problem during the Korean War. The introduction of jets into the fleet pointed out the rapidly changing world for carrier aviation.

The firing mechanism for a High Velocity Aircraft Rocket (HVAR) was dependent upon electrical current sent from the cockpit through to the connection in the wing, then to the rocket. The connection between the wing and the rocket was called a pigtail. The pigtail was attached to the rocket motor on one end and an electrical plug on the underside of the wing on the other end. The higher air speeds of the jet could cause either the pigtail to pull free of the rocket or the wind wiped the wire and broke it. The ordnance crews tried numerous methods to prevent this from happening, but the results were bad no matter what was tried. The HVAR was an effective weapon, when it worked. It was useless when it did not work. The nose fuse of the rocket armed just like a bomb and had similar problems. It was WW II ordnance trying to be used for high-speed aircraft, and unfortunately it failed too many times. The jets brought back to the ship too many unfired rockets that always seemed to drop off on arrested landings.

There were 157 20-mm gun stoppages during the period. This was a continuing problem for all the jet pilots. One never knew whether or not all the guns would fire. The guns were plagued with several problems. The hydraulic gun charger failed to release the fluid, and the gun had a soft firing-pin hit. The 20-mm rounds also jammed in the feed chutes or the links broke. It was frustrating to make a strafing run and get nothing when you were lined up on a target and squeezed the trigger to fire the cannons. When they did fire the jet makes an ideal platform for strafing, and getting good hits on a small target was not difficult. Only a few rounds were needed to severely damage or destroy a truck or ox cart. To make sure that I had enough rounds, I only used two guns at a time. I would rather bring back some ammo than run out, especially when flying armed-reconnaissance missions north of Hamhung. This area was within flying range of the enemy's MiG-15 jet fighters.

To add to the jet pilot's concerns were the numerous cases of engine surge at altitude that resulted in two flameouts. Both pilots were able to dive to keep the engine windmilling and make an air start once they were below 20,000 feet using the manual setting. Investigation revealed the cause to be the seizing of the aneroid shaft of the Turbo Jet Control (TJC). During this period twelve control units were changed due to failure. The lubricating oil proportioned system was operative only on the hanger deck and regular fueling with the required percentage of oil was not possible on the flight deck because the low air temperature caused the oil to congeal.

For the flight-deck crew life was difficult. During this period the advent of cold weather began to take its toll, especially the flight-deck crew. The WW II mentality for fighting a war still in the minds of the Navy Department showed up in so many ways. The warm weather environment of the pacific war seemed to blind their thinking, and so when Korean operations began it had not even been recognized that this was different. The *Antietam* arrived in the fall 1951 almost 15 months after it started. When the second period with Task Force 77 started these cold problems became acute. For example, the flight-deck crew responsible for the handling of aircraft on the flight deck lacked proper outer jersey for identification. From the *Antietam* action report dated November 26, 1951 to December 31, 1951 the following was reported:

The present type of jerseys provided for identifying personnel at flight quarters is considered unsatisfactory for cold weather. The jerseys do not fit over cold weather clothing, they are difficult to remove or don when coming in or going out of shelters, attrition rate is high, and they do not contribute to the warmth and comfort of personnel. Colored cloth has been stitched on the cold weather clothing and seems to be much more satisfactory and is more economical.

The cold weather affected the arresting gear in several ways. Again quoting from the same action report:

A great deal of trouble has been experienced with air valves freezing during operations. It has been necessary to keep two gasoline torches in constant use in order to keep gear operating.

Further, it was reported:

Trouble with yielding elements is chronic and colder weather is increasing the seriousness of the problem. Drainage under present type elements is not effective, and jet recoveries often batter the entire housing to the point where water leaks into the spaces below due to gasket failure between housing and deck.

The coming of the jet aircraft into the fleet generated many problems for the unimproved WW II carriers. The Navy was unprepared for this new type of aircraft, and even after 15 months there was little change to help overcome these defects. These problems were present in the carrier's action reports from the beginning of the conflict to the end.

The *Antietam* with its escorts arrived in Tokyo Bay and moored at Piedmont Pier NOB Yokosuka at noon December 31, 1951. New Years Eve would be soon in full swing, so a group of us went over to the base officers club to check out what could be done for a party. As I climbed out of the base shuttle bus and started up the steps a pair of Naval officers came out the front door. Being a very junior ensign I quickly saluted them and then stopped in my track. The Wave officer also stopped with a surprised look on her face. It only took a second for us to recognize each other. She had been my seventh-grade

English teacher. Even after nine years she remembered me as well, because I was something of a cutup in her class. She had just started teaching school two years before I was in her class in 1941-1942. What a pleasant surprise to meet her halfway around the world. The year 1951 ended on an interesting high note. To meet two individuals from Newport in less than three months was amazing.

What to do on New Year's Eve when all the reservations have long been gone? Go or not to go? Pulling on my dress blues, I thought, *What the hell, at least I can have a couple of drinks at the bar.* Grabbing a ride on the base shuttle bus to the O club, I climbed the front stairs to sound of the band playing in the main dinner room. Slowly moving through the crowd to the main bar I searched for an empty chair. No such luck, but catching one of the bar tenders' eyes, I did get a martini on ice. It was a pleasant ,well-dressed crowd, and it was especially fun watching the ladies. They sure were dressed to kill. No matter where I looked, the really pretty ones all had escorts, so it looked like it might be a dull evening.

I killed the first drink and went back for another. I was standing behind a middle-aged man in civilian dress waiting for him to be served. The bar tenders were really busy, so as he looked around, he spoke to me. We made small talk, and when the bar tender answered is call, he asked me what I was drinking and added it to his order. He was drinking whiskey and his other drink was ginger ale. Handing me my drink, he asked if I was by myself. Answering that I was, he asked would I dance with his daughter? Sight unseen, I said, "Sure, I like to dance."

We thread our way back out to near the front of the club and to a small alcove. Seat was a young woman, dressed in a white formal. She rose when the man walked in, and he turned to me to introduce me to her. She was a beautiful young lady, but rather shy. I minded my manners giving a smile to ease the tension. We engaged in some small talk, trying to make some relaxing remarks. I was saved when the band starting playing a new set of dance music. With a slight bow, I ask her to dance. I got a nice shy smile back, and I offered her my arm. Now I might have been nervous climbing into a jet, but not as nervous as I was right now. It had happened so quickly. The dance floor was crowded, but I eased us on to the floor when an opening appeared. To my delight, she was a good dancer, and it was not to long before her shyness began to melt with the music.

We went back to her father after the set was over. At least I thought so. Maybe I floated! Her father was smiling, she was smiling, and I had a BIG smile. She was half English and half Japanese. The result was breathtaking! Her father took a picture of us together. It seemed like only a few minutes had passed, but the evening ended all too quickly. They thanked me, and with a light kiss from her, they were gone. I stood there and realized there was no way to see her again. I had no address, phone number, or any other facts to go on. I felt like prince charming after the ball.

Several days later, I was SDO when the ships PA system came on. "Ensign Schnitzer, you have guests at the OD station." I slid down the ladder leading from the squadron ready room to the hanger deck, and emerged to see the two standing by the OD. I saluted the OD and turned to my guest. Even in street clothes she was beautiful. Her father was beaming, and she was smiling. So now I had the wonderful job of entertaining them in my domain. I was saved by the father when he asked to see the flight deck. It might be hard for her to climb the steep ladder, but I lucked out when I spied that the deck edge elevator was manned. I excused myself for a minute and hailed the elevator operator asking him for a ride.

A quick glance to my guest and with a wicked grin answered, "Yes, sir." Away we went to the flight deck. I wasn't sure she would be interested, but she asked some good questions. We did the tour from bow to stern and all the aircraft in between.

With another ride to the hanger deck, I invited them to the wardroom for some refreshments. It was hard to keep my eyes off of her. She was a sight to behold. The officers who came in the wardroom gave her admiring glances. I was able to get some information so I could contact her again. *Hey,* I thought, *this war has taking a great new twist.* I followed down the gangway to their car. She reached in and took an envelope from the back seat. Inside was the picture taken of us at the New Year's night. Handshake for the father and a kiss for her, and off they went. She sure made the cool weather seem a lot warmer.

Chapter 9
Korea, the Bitter Cold

Like all good vacations, my R&R in Japan was over all too quickly. While the others and I were playing, the ship underwent almost two full weeks of maintenance work. The jet's tail hook had dug big pieces from the planking on the aft end of the flight deck under the first four arresting wires. There was major work that needed to be done, especially to replace a large section of the old scarred flight deck planking with new planking. Then the entire flight deck was given a complete going over with degreaser and other cleaners to remove the oil, hydraulic fluid, and gasoline leaked from the aircraft. It sure looked a lot better free of the oily surface that made it seem you were ice-skating when it got wet. When finally scrubbed clean of the residue, the flight deck was given a new coat of gray paint. The aft section of the flight deck, which had many linear feet of new planking, now blended in with the old. Being stuck aboard ship as SDO, I had an opportunity to watch the Japanese shipyard workers put the new decking in place.

With just hand tools, they did a fantastic job. With the addition of newly painted white lines, it was a sparkling sight. The last day before leaving the Yokosuka Naval Base, four of us replenished our liquor supply from the officers' club package store, so we did not have to depend upon the medicinal brandy that the fight surgeon gave out when any one had a particularly difficult flight. We brought it aboard in two parachute bags, with a wink of the OD's eye.

The carrier left at 0730 on January 16, 1952 for the last tour with Task Force 77. On the following day, passing through the straits around southern Japan the air group managed to fly 49 refresher sorties. During the launch, LT Aaron (Mo) Modansky, operational officer of VF-831, experienced a major control problem when his ailerons jammed right after the catapult launch. He crashed into the sea ahead and to the side of the ship on the starboard side, and the aircraft quickly sank out of sight. He was finally able to get clear of the cockpit about 30 feet below the surface of the ocean and inflated his Mae West, which brought him to surface by its buoyancy. Meanwhile, the helicopter, flown by LT Jenkins, had already started moving forward from its station 100 feet out board on the starboard side of the ship to where the plane crashed. He spotted him as he surfaced off to the side of the ship's path and was able to place the helicopter in a hover right over him. Mo saw the rescue sling just above his head even though as the down wash of the helicopter main blades sprayed into his eyes. He was only able to get his arms into the sling before they hoisted him out of the water, as the ship was approaching him and the helicopter. The crewman raised the sling to the edge on the cabin, but Mo was unable to climb into the helicopter because of his badly bruised legs. With this difficulty he was flown back to the carrier still outside of the helicopter. The crewman, Lester Hargood, held the pilot's arm down to keep him from falling out of the sling. By this time, the ship had passed the impact point so it chased the ship until it was over the flight deck. Mo was lowered to the waiting arms of the medical corpsmen who were ready to deposit him into a stretcher. Strapped in, he was taken to the aft elevator to rush him to sickbay for medical evaluation. Surprisingly, Mo suffered no major injuries from his crash, and after a number of days of rest he came back to flight status. Another close call! From the time he was launched to his arrival back on board was an amazing six minutes. It sure was not the best start for a tour. I did not fly on that day, as I was not included on the flight schedule. The ones who did fly had fun making simulated bomber attacks on the US Air Force Field at Itazuki and then flew back to the carrier and made low, fast passes at the carrier and her escorts. The latter event was to give the ship's gunners a chance to track fast moving jets. We called it legal "flat hating."

The following day the ship joined Task Force 77, and it was back to the attack or better known to us as, "Let's go fishing, and we will be the flak bait." On the 18th our division led by Sanders set out to bomb a bridge on our assigned railroad sector at Hongwon and then covered the route northeast along the coast for targets of opportunity. The rail strike was a bridge that the aerial photos supplied by the intelligence officer showed had a number of known active AAA gun positions protecting it (noted with a circle and a small marker). There were many other positions (noted with an upside down "U" outside of the circle in the photo) that were unoccupied as well. How many more guns had been moved in since the photo was taken was unknown.

135

Photo mosaic of a destroyed bridge and bypass on the Korean East Coast

We made our plan on how to make the strike to minimize the gunner's accuracy and intensity of their AAA gunfire with a flak-suppression technique. We discussed a couple of approaches but finally settled on the one that worked before. When we approached the coast, we split up into two sections, with the lead section splitting again so as to be able to attack the bridge from opposite directions. One dove from the northeast and the other from the southwest. As the two approached their pushover point at 20,000 feet, the second section where I was flying started into our dive just before they did. We dove a few miles short of the bridge coming in from the sea headed northwest to attack the AAA guns flying low (200-300 feet) and fast (450-480 knots). The river that the bridge spanned had the numerous AAA gun emplacements dug into the dikes along the river, some almost next to the bridge. (See above photo) The enemy gunners were looking for the bombers up in the sky with their guns aiming towards the direction where the two jets would have to dive down for their bombing run. The two of us in the second section, flying low and fast up the river on either side, totally surprised the gunners with our strafing, putting them out of action. The bombing was right on target, and after our pullout to clear the mountains, the four of us climbed back to altitude to repeat the process. The two sections switched positions and our section was able to make a classic 60-degree dive bomb attack without any AAA flak coming from the enemy's guns. The gunners were either dead or hiding from the 20-mm shells that were hitting all around them. It was an effective technique that we repeated again and again whenever the opportunity presented itself.

The next day was a photo-escort mission for me. This one had the potential of enemy air opposition because the mission was to start at the far northeastern city of Chongjin, not that far from the Chinese and Russian borders. The two of us were out of the radar range of the task force, so we were on our own. We were, however, in the radar range to the Russian Ground-Intercept Radar. That made me apprehensive to be a possible target for a flight of Russian MiG-15. Those aircraft would have all the advantages of altitude, speed, and numbers. The photo pilot and I discussed how we would defend ourselves from a MiG attack. In this case, the squadron AIO could offer us no information. The goal was to get back with the film and without damage. With this in mind we planned if attacked to put our nose down slightly, go to 100% engine power, and head 180 degrees south to put as much distance between us and the MiG air base. I planned to be on the opposite side of the photo plane from the formation of MiGs to be able to keep them as well as the photo plane in sight. If the MiGs attacked I could make a radio call to the photo plane to turn hard into them just as they came into firing range, causing them, hopefully, to over shoot so that they could not hit either of us. As they passed, I then could make another call to tell the photo pilot to return to the original heading. I might even get a shot at one of them as they flew away. I had absolutely no plans to chase them, but to continue our southerly course. We flew the mission as planed, and all went well smoothly, much to my delight. We had no problems, but I ended up having sore neck muscles from constantly moving my head back and forth scanning the sky above and behind us. I scanned to my right when I was moving left to right as I weaved slowly above and behind the photo plane, then checked the photo plane and repeated the process to the left on the return. It was a clear day, and the pilot of the photo plane and I had a great view of the entire coastline both going north to Chongjin at altitude and returning on the photo run. We fortunately had the air to ourselves and returned to the task force without sighting any enemy aircraft or known AAA fire. It was a long flight, however, and I returned to the task force with 700 pounds of fuel with the low-fuel warning light burning brightly. With this low fuel state I needed to get aboard on the first pass. I flew a "Roger" pass all the way without the LSO giving me any correction signals and received my "cut," making a smooth landing. After the photo pilot and I debriefed with the AIO, and I began to relax, I realized I was very tired from the tension. It had been a long flight of 1.7 hours in the air, with much of it in a high state of alertness. With the pre-mission briefing, waiting for takeoff, flying the mission, and debriefing, the entire mission had consumed almost three hours. I was sound asleep before the night hecklers landed. After flight quarters ended, the task force retired south to be ready for replenishment the following day.

The weather continued to be good, so starting on the 21st the next three days we were actively flying our assigned missions. Day one was another division strike done the same way as before on a bridge near Hungnam. The area around Hungnam was always a very dangerous place to attack. We were getting our timing down so that our flak suppressing strafing by one section finished just a moment before the other section released their bombs. After dropping our bombs, we headed up the coast from Hamhung to Tongmungori. We found nothing to strafe. Several tunnels along the coast showed telltale signs of either a parked locomotive hiding inside or maybe it was a fake. The

North Koreans often built fires inside the tunnels to throw us off. Even so, the flight leader passed the information along to the AIO when we debriefed after landing. The task force night fighter would be looking for the locomotive when and if it emerged from hiding after sundown.

The AD squadron wasn't as fortunate as the jet flights when enemy flak hit the aircraft piloted by LT James Walley of VA-728 aircraft. He made it to the ocean and successfully ditched his plane off of Wonsan Harbor. The battleship USS *Wisconsin's* helicopter quickly picked him up. The ability to recover downed pilots so quickly was a significant morale factor for the pilots. The second day for us was an easy defensive mission with the division flying a CAP. There were no unidentified boogies during the flight until the end. The FDO vectored us out so we once again had fun buzzing the returning strike flights as part of our continuing intercept practice. The CIC FDO controllers were getting much better in setting us up in a good position to discover the flights as well as commencing our simulated attacks.

The sky was clear, and the sea relatively calm, so landing back aboard was a lot easier to make another smooth landing. The picture shows the aircraft at the moment of receiving the "cut" from the LSO. Note the arresting wires in with a member of the arresting crew in the catwalk. I was finding my work around the carrier was becoming easier because of the 52 jet landings I had made on the earlier trips to Task Force 77. The only thing I had to watch out for was getting over confidant. I kept telling myself, *Use the checklist and stay alert.*

The third day's mission was a joint coordinated attack on the city of Kowan. Kowan is on the route between Hungnam and Wonsan. The area around this town has many places to hide the trucks that move on the main road. Our briefing with the AIO covered recent photos of the area with the gun emplacements plainly marked. Each section of the jet division was assigned specific sets of AAA to hit on the first dive in. This was the classic propeller-dive-bomber- and jet-flak-suppression attack. The props were launched first and the jets 15 minutes later. Crossing the coastline, the jets over took the props and flew high cover for the AD and F4U divisions until we all reached the target area. Sixty seconds before the props started their dives; the jets rolled over into their steep dive from 25,000 feet, popping the dive brakes wide open, and started down in a shallow "Vee" formation. The jets were armed with 260-pound fragmentation bombs to be dropped on the pre-selected known AAA gun positions. These bombs were fused such that they went off about 50 feet in the air. After our bomb drop, closing the dive brakes, making a 6-G pullout, and going to full power, we climbed for altitude. With all this excess speed generated from the dive and the full power we gained altitude quickly. As we approached 12,000 feet the entire eight-planes in a shallow "Vee" formation did a 180-degree high-speed 90-degree banking turn and dove again on the target area. We were in our dive just as the props completed their bomb drop and had started their retirement after their pullout. The diving jets fired the 20-mm guns to keep the North Korean gunners' heads down, which allowed the slower props a safer exit. It was formation flying at its best. It sure would have helped if this had been practiced a few times before the air group had left the states. So much for on-the-job training!

The air group flew 252 sorties in the three operating days, so on January 24 it was once again time to replenish the bombs, gasoline, and ammo we had expended. It was a quiet time for the pilots to relax and catch up on our other duties. The weather closed in when a cold front moved through, and there was no flying the following day, the 25th due to snow, high winds and heavy seas. The next day, right after the crew had removed the snow from the flight deck, air operations began again. The deck was still slippery, but the pilots made it to the aircraft anyhow. After being launched for a CAP mission my aircraft developed a mechanical engine problem, and I had to abort. I went into an orbit at 2,500 feet outside of the task force destroyer screen and waited to land back aboard once there was a ready deck. Landing under these conditions was a little different from the usual flights because I was carrying more than a half-ton of fuel than normal. The approach was at a higher airspeed, which meant that the cut for landing was further back from the carrier's flight deck. At a landing speed of 125 knots the jet was traveling about 161 feet per second relative to the carrier. To pick up the number-two or -three wire was going to be a little more difficult. I received my cut and dropped the nose slightly, just enough to start the descent, and then a little back pressure for a smooth touchdown. All went well, and I was safely aboard.

The last flight for this three-day period was another boring CAP with nothing going on. On this flight I had discovered that my low-frequency-radio direction finder could pick up two different Japanese radio stations when at the higher altitude. I couldn't understand the talking part, but the music was often very good, and it helped me stay alert and pass the time while listening to music. What a way to fight a war!

After replenishment on the 28th, the 29th turned out to be an unusual day for me. I flew an armed-reconnaissance from Yonghung to Yongwon in the morning without any incidents. We made our bomb drops and zigzagged up the road with not much action. On the way we buzzed the airfields north of the city. We returned with out any battle damage. That afternoon I went back to the LSO platform to learn more about their work and watch their technique assisting the air group pilots in their final carrier approaches and landings. I was standing behind the LSO when LT Stan Kalas of VC-61 made his landing approach in a F9F-2P photo plane.

He began to get slow as he entered the last part of his approach, and the LSO gave him a come-on signal. (This meant for him to increase his engine power) He was slow to respond, and his aircraft began to settle in a nose high attitude. At this point the LSO gave him a frantic wave off as the plane continued to settle. He finally added full power to take the wave-off just as he arrived at the flight deck. Unfortunately his left main landing gear struck the lip of the flight deck, tearing it off. Both LT Dave Rose and I were already off the platform having dived into the safety net to escape the crashing aircraft. The plane skidded up the deck on the remaining two wheels without picking up any arresting wires and went over the port side just as the right wing struck the barrier support, taking the right wing off. The aircraft landed in the water tail first, upside down. Watching from my position face down in the safety net I could see the fuselage slowly rotating as the heavy left wing sank. The pilot was visible but not moving. As soon as the wreckage cleared the ship's stern, the *Antietam* helicopter flown by LT Wilson moved in for the possible rescue. The helicopter pilot hovered his aircraft over the sinking photo aircraft and was able to lower the crew member, L. J. Harwood, AL3, to the fuselage in the sling. He landed on the side of the aircraft and was able to get to the cockpit and reach Stan. Harwood was able to free him from the shoulder straps and lap belt and pulled him out of the cockpit just as the plane sank below the surface. Fortunately it took some time for the aircraft to sink because the two internal main fuel tanks were almost empty and were still sealed. Stan was hanging in the safety sling 20 feet below the helicopter as the helicopter rose and flew to the ship's flight deck. The helicopter pilot slowly dropped down towards the flight deck and was able to lower him to the waiting arms of the medical corpsmen already in position on the flight deck. Stan was sure lucky! He woke up in sickbay. The crewman who accomplished this daring rescue was picked up by a sister ship's helicopter and brought back aboard the *Antietam*. I appreciated even more the tough and dangerous job of the air group's LSO. The helicopter pilot and crewmember performed an amazing feat rescuing the pilot from the sea. After that wild event, I sure wasn't going to get low and slow on the final approach to the ship.

The division flew the next two days doing what we were getting good at, breaking enemy transportation equipment in all its forms. Even the infamous ox carts were targets for our strafing attacks. We covered the route between Sinchon and Orori on the first one and the area around Sinchon on the second one. We found some boxcars on a siding and blew them up with our bombs. Our switch from 100-pound to 250-pound bombs allowed us to make a lot bigger hole in the railroad bed. The enemy antiaircraft fire was again either poorly aimed, or we were getting good at jinxing around spoiling their aim. As usual, spotting enemy tracers certainly raised my adrenaline level and made me fly the aircraft even more erratic as if I was a drunken pilot. In all, these three days' sorties added up for the air group to 236. On the first day of this period the Corsair squadron's Ensign William W. Marwood's aircraft was hit by flak in the right wing, severing the wing from the aircraft. The stricken aircraft crashed into the sea without his attempting to bail out and he was declared Killed in Action (KIA). No matter how well you flew, there is always the chance of getting hit. That was always in the back of my mind on every offensive mission anywhere in North Korea. I knew my ejection procedure down cold. It was called: Pre-Pos-Ox-Pull. It stood for: **Preparation** by tightening all straps and jettisoning the canopy, **Position** the body straight up in the seat, Pull the toggle on the bail out **Oxygen** bottle carried in the parachute seat, and then **Pull** the face curtain by the handles over the helmet and down in front of my face, firing the ejection seat. If I had to use it, I would not sit there and debate. An uncontrollable aircraft is no place to be.

Also on the 29th the pre-dawn fighter of VC-3 lost an aircraft when LT Murphy's Corsair was hit by enemy fire northwest of Hamhung. He successfully crash-landed his plane in the rice paddies almost due west of the city just as dawn was breaking. He climbed out of his aircraft and looked around him to find a place to hide to await rescue. There wasn't much cover except for a small clump of trees about a half-mile away. He started toward the trees at a fast walk, all the time looking for enemy soldiers. The next time he checked around he spotted two North Koreans soldiers headed toward him, running along the dikes of the rice paddies. He started to run, but loaded down with survival gear he wasn't making very fast progress. He saw that the two soldiers had split up with one headed away from him, while the other was running towards him. The next thing he heard was the whine of a bullet and then the crack of the rifle. That really motivated him to run even faster and to weave from side to side to lessen his chances of being hit. Just about the time he reached the trees, he turned his head to look at his pursuer. The bullet fired by the Korean soldier this time passed through the soft tissue below his jaw. He fell, but realizing he was still able to breathe, got up, and holding one hand against his neck to slow the bleeding, made it into the small clump of trees. Unknown to him, the incoming raid from the task force had been alerted that he was down, and the flight was headed for his last known position. After he caught his breath and realized he was safe at the moment he heard the sweet sound of the approaching aircraft. He pulled out a smoke flare from his survival vest and set it off. The first four airplanes on the scene spotted the bright orange smoke and headed straight for him. They quickly identified him and set up a rescue air patrol over him. The Korean who shot him tried to run away, but tracer bullets fired by Murphy alerted the air patrol and they dove down, killing the soldier before he could find cover. Meanwhile, now that his location was known, the helicopter was dispatched from the LST that was stationed off shore, and he was soon picked up and flown out of the area. Later in the wardroom when he returned to the ship he eagerly told his tale to the large group of pilots. One very close call! All he had from his ordeal was a scar on this upper throat.

On the 30th the division flew a rail strike and afterwards took a trip up the road from Sinchon to Orori looking for targets. There were no sightings of either trucks or ox carts, so the search ended with nothing to attack. The same thing happened on the 31st. These flights were becoming less and less effective because the enemy had developed an effective method of hiding their trucks in the houses of the villages along the way or camouflaging them in the small valleys. The coastal route also had many tunnels where they also easily hid equipment. The picture shows an example of the many tunnels along the coast. Bomb damage as well as ship to shore shelling and subsequent repairs can be seen clearly in this photo.

North Korea Coast

January came to a close and the task force left the combat area to replenish the following day. The weather turned foul during the afternoon and into the next day. The bad weather didn't completely stop air operations the next day, but I sure wished it had. The seas were rough from the storm's high wind making the ship pitch and roll in the heavy sea kicked up by the wind. There was even spray coming over the flight deck when the carrier hit a large wave. While sitting on the catapult waiting for launch I could see these large waves ahead of the ship while the bow was down in the trough. Then when the ship hit the wave and the bow rose up all I could see was sky. The catapult officer timed my launch when the bow was coming to the up to the level position. Off I went into the sky. That was the easy part. We joined up and started our climbed to altitude as the flight leader checked in with the ships CIC. We were vectored out to the northwest and stationed ourselves about 40 miles out at

35,000 feet. Our normal flight pattern was in an easy racetrack form. This one started out in the normal manner, but quickly had to be adjusted. The normal one was to fly four minutes on a westerly direction, make a one minute 180-degree standard rate turn, fly four minutes in the other direction, make another 180-degree standard rate turn and so on. Because of the wind aloft, the Fighter Director Officer (FDO) had to adjust our pattern so we stayed over our spot on the earth. The first adjustment was to fly five minutes headed west and only three minutes east. This didn't work out either, so we were changed to six minutes to the west and only two minutes to the east. We were flying through a powerful jet stream that the controller figured was traveling at about 180 knots. It also was a bumpy ride from the clear air turbulence as we passed through the edges of this jet stream. At least it was different. There were very few sorties flown so we didn't have anything to intercept. After 1.5 hours boring a big hole in the sky, however, it was time to return to the ship.

Released from the CAP duty we made a high-speed let down and approached the task force from the rear. The task force had already turned into the wind to launch our replacement CAP, so passing upwind by the ship on the starboard side I could see that the stern of the ship was still moving up and down a significant amount. The waves were still large, and that was going to make the landing much more difficult. The technique to use when landing on a pitching deck was to make the approach by flying the pattern with the reference point the center of the ship and ignore the ship's stern position. Only in the final stage of the approach, rolling out of the approach turn and into the groove flying straight and level for about 100 yards do you worry about the position of the flight deck. That is the theory; now I was going to try to do it. Making my approach turn I could see the deck was moving at least 20 feet up and down from the horizontal level. I hoped to find the deck coming up when the cut was given to be able to make a good landing. Chasing the deck when it is going down is a sure road to a hard landing and a possible bounce. I lucked out on my first pass with the deck coming up to the horizontal. Coming up the straightaway I got my cut and hit the deck, picking up one of my favorite early wires. It was a damn good feeling to be aboard. Taxiing forward I could see in my rear-view mirror, and then heard Larry taking a wave off because the deck was not in a good position for him to land. It took him another couple of passes to make it safely back aboard. The other two also had to make more than one pass to get aboard. Our many past carrier landings had given us the polished skills to land in most any kind of sea condition. To land this fast moving jet on a pitching carrier deck certainly raised my apprehension level a little higher than normal.

On the third and fourth of February there were strikes and armed-reconnaissance flights. The first one was around the Wonsan area, which was always a dangerous place because of the large number of AAA guns. The second was a bridge at Songjin along the northeast coast. On this latter one we used our division attack technique again. On the first pass we did a good job of messing up the bridge for rail traffic without getting much AAA fire. Because we didn't receive much AAA fire we turned around and did it a second time still without any significant flak, but best of all, no damage to any of us. We were flying well, making our attacks quickly, and hitting our targets and recovering fast. The air group during this period, however, lost two aircraft. One Corsair was lost to AAA fire and ditched near Wonsan Bay. LTJG C. E. Gillette's engine failed while flying a naval gunfire-spotting mission. The helicopter operating in the Wonsan area picked him up. The other ditching due to jet engine flameout was LTJG R. E. Wilson, a VF-837 pilot returning from a CAP mission. He was unable to do an air start and had to take a swim. Both pilots had minor injuries and were back aboard in a short time. After rest, they both returned to flight status.

After replenishment on the 5th, I was squadron duty officer on the 6th and did not fly, maybe because it was my 23rd birthday. The evening of the sixth, the USS *Antietam* left the task force with its escorts and headed to NOB Yokosuka, Japan, for some ship repairs, maintenance, and R&R for everyone. During this trip on the line, the air group expended 816 tons of ordnance, flying 1,017 sorties. The two jet squadrons were busy partners in this effort when we flew 264 sorties dropping 481 tons of bombs and firing 29,526 rounds of 20-mm. Not a bad score card for 14 flying days. There was a price on this effort for the air group. One pilot, Ensign William W. Marwood, was lost from VF-713 when he was shot down, and an enlisted airman with VF-837 disappeared at night from the flight deck. There were two pilots rescued by helicopters after being shot down by enemy AAA. Seven pilots were injured in operational accidents with all of them returning to flight status by the next tour. Besides the loss of seven aircraft, two aircraft were damaged beyond the ability of the ship maintenance crew to repair them. The enemy soldiers firing rifles and the larger AAA gunners were able to hit a total of 41 aircraft, but all of these were quickly repaired aboard the carrier and returned to flight status. The ship and squadron's metalsmiths were a fantastic crew. They could repair almost anything in an amazingly short time. For the pilots, it was a fearful, frustrating, and seemingly an endless war using expensive aircraft against such small targets. The North Koreans rebuilt the bomb damage to the roads, bridges and railroad tracks often overnight. We might be slowing the supplies down, but we could not stop them.

To further the frustration, the jets continued to suffer from 20mm gun stoppages of all kinds. The most pressing problem that created the 152 stoppages (50%) was again related to the hydraulic gun chargers. The jet fueling problem still remained because there was no proportion fuel system operating on the flight deck. Oil was added by hand, six gallons in the after fuel cell, during each gassing. It was the most primitive answer to the lack of jet fuel aboard the carrier. It was like fighting with one hand tied behind your back. To further add to the maintenance difficulties, it was necessary to clean the jet engine ignition system every replenishment day because of the residue left by the oil on the two ignition plugs. Another worry for the jet pilots was the frequent glowing of the low fuel pressure warning lights signaling that the engine had dirty filters. The filters were clogged with rust particles and other junk from the gasoline coming from the ship's storage tanks. This meant that the filters had to be changed twice in 30 hours instead of the usual recommended schedule of once. It was to the credit of the hard-working jet engine maintenance crews that the pilots had the best-maintained jet aircraft possible to fly under such conditions. I had a lot of concern about the aircraft even before reaching the coastline and having to worry about enemy flak.

I had exchanged a few letters with the charming lady I met New Year's Eve and was hoping to meet her again. That was not to happen because her father was transferred from the Tokyo area to southern Japan. So I made other plans.

Chapter 10
Dodging Flak

This trip to Japan allowed Larry and me to take advantage of the R&R hotel in the mountains. The ship was unfortunately anchored this time at berth number eleven about two miles out from the inner harbor, meaning we had to travel by the officers' motor launch when it was available or by a large landing craft for all hands. Not only did we have to use the boats to get to shore, it also meant I had to stand the boat officer's duty one day while we were in port. We both did it early in the stay, and that allowed Larry and me to take a very crowded train from Ueno Station in the evening for the overnight ride. We were unable to get a sleeper, so we ended up sleeping as best we could on the hard seats of third class. After checking in to the hotel early in the morning, we caught some sack time before lunch. With some rest and a great lunch under our belts we headed for the ski shop to make tracks in the snow. Larry had done a lot more skiing than I had, so he was off like a shot down the hill. Larry was fearless and had the nickname of "Boomer" on the slopes. I headed for the "snow bunny" area and began to get back into some kind of shape. It was great fun, and it wasn't long before the muscles starting telling me that I was slightly out of shape for skiing. About that same time Larry came up and said he had enough. Leaving the ski gear with the Japanese crew in the ski shop we headed for our room and peeled off our winter clothing. Dressed in Japanese robes that had been hanging in the room we headed to the lower level. The hotel had a large round pool about 20 feet in diameter in the basement that was fed by a natural hot spring. Gads, did that feel great! We soaked until we both look like boiled lobsters. Larry was first, then me. We let the masseur work us over. I never could figure how old she was, but what a pair of hands she had! She started at my neck and worked all the way down to my feet. Once she finished I felt like a wet dishrag. She knew no English so she did everything by sign language. She had a funny way about her, and if you didn't get off her table quick enough when she had finished, you got a bucket of cold water dumped on you.

A nice nap was always in order before the cocktail hour. The hotel was full of officers because there was lots of snow. The hotel had two entrances on the backside facing the mountain, the one used depended upon the season. The winter entrance was one story higher than the summer entrance. It had already snowed more than eight feet, so the winter entrance was opened. Ten to twelve feet was normal for the area. Our days passed with lots of skiing, good stories around the bar before our meal, and just plain relaxing. But like all vacations, it was over too quickly, and we were off by slow train for Yokosuka via Tokyo.

The R&R was over for the pilots and crew, and it was time to start thinking of the war. During the stay in port the ship had ten days of maintenance and repairs performed on the flight deck and all over the ship. The aft end of the flight deck always needed attention because the jet's tail hook often dug chunks of decking on landing. All fitted out the ship left at 0800 on February 18, 1952 for our fourth tour with the Task Force. There was no refresher flying on the 18th because of inclement weather. The weather cleared enough on the 19th, for 27 sorties to be flown. Our division flew a training flight to give the ship's gunners more practice in tracking high-speed aircraft. I was to make my low pass from astern of the *Antietam* coming up on the port side. In order for me to be below the others in the division who were coming in from different directions, I came up on the port side of the ship about 25 feet off the water, flying at 450 knots. I learned after the low pass that the flight-deck crew was surprised and delighted to be looking down at an airplane. I wanted to give them a good show for all their hard work.

After the ship joined the task force on the 20th, on my first mission I had to abort after receiving my catapult shot for one simple reason. The aircraft's canopy stayed behind on the flight deck. It was a very startling experience to fly around without a canopy, and it sure was cold and windy. In other words, it scared the hell out of me. The canopy had not been properly latched down after maintenance had been performed on the ejection seat. After dropping my bombs on safe outside the task-force destroyer screen, as well as dumping the fuel in my tip tanks, I came back aboard in about 20 minutes. The approach was once again at a higher airspeed to compensate for the extra fuel and an early "cut" for my landing to grab the number 2 or 3 wire. With that landing speed the heavy aircraft pulled out a few extra feet of arresting wire. Air operations were secured early at 11:15, and the ship joined the replenishment group to take on ammo and gasoline.

The following day, it was back to full air operations for everyone. We flew a morning CAP, but after the mission was accomplished we had to head for K-18 when LT Bob Clark could not drop the tail hook all the way down to the landing position. We all landed at K-18 without messing up our own tail hooks or pulling up the metal matting that covered of the runway. After the problem plane was fixed and all the tail hooks checked over and stowed, we headed back to the ship for the next recovery.

While we were at K-18, Bill Jones had the opportunity to escort the author, Mr. James Michener, when he visited the carrier. He was doing research for his book, *The Bridges of Toko-ri.* Bill had a very enjoyable time with him. For his efforts, Bill later received an autographed copy of the book from him.

On the 22nd I flew two missions, one a CAP and the other an armed-reconnaissance mission. The reconnaissance mission was from Hongwon to Hwnzsuch and was as routine a flight as you could imagine—if getting shot at can be called routine! Moving fast along the coast we could stay on the seaward side of the road and railroad. In many areas the mountains came down to the sea with no beach. The last day of this sequence, the 23rd, I was again the squadron duty officer for twenty-four hours. The air group did well and racked up a total of 238 sorties during this three-day period.

Replenishment day was next, and the weather began to cloud up in the afternoon of the 24th. Even with the marginal weather, flight operations started in the morning of the 25th. By noon the cloud cover was solid over all North Korea, and air operations were secured. Before the clouds had completely moved in our division flew with another jet division as part of another coordinated strike. Latter we bombed a group of boxcars discovered earlier by the early morning hecklers, destroying most of them, and made a number of good rail cuts to boot. The flak was not very accurate, and I was able to make good drops. The bad weather closed in, and the ship was quiet. The weather finally cleared on the 27th, and I flew another CAP. An armed-reconnaissance was flown on the 28th and another CAP on the extra day of leap year, the 29th of February. The reconnaissance mission started at Hungnam and ended at Tongmungori. The area around Hungnam bristled with AAA guns, so passing by this area was done above 20,000 feet at high speed and constant changing of direction and altitude. A few minutes into the low-level run, the low man spotted some box cars on a siding. First we made sure that it was not a flak trap and determine it was "reasonably" safe to attack the railroad boxcars. After smashing them into kindling wood, we made more holes in the railbed and destroying the rails. We saw no flak, but there may have been some without tracers. The air group continued pounding the transportation system, flying 291 sorties during this five-day period. On the negative side, there were numerous minor flak hits to the aircraft, but none were lost. Most of these hits were from small-arms fire. I think everyone in North Korea had a gun and fired it at the passing aircraft.

The task force replenished on March 1st with the junior pilots of the jet squadrons again enjoying the privilege of standing four-hour alert duty sitting in the aircraft on the flight deck. Dull work, but because there were not many of us, we did it frequently. None of the lieutenants would stoop that low to stand the duty. It would have been interesting if we had to be launched. A four-plane division made up of all junior officers. That would have been something!

The weather cleared up the following day well enough to allow for 80 sorties to be flown. The AD squadron lost the third air group pilot, LT George Johnson, when his plane was hit making a bombing run on the railroad yards at Hamhung and crashed within the city limits. Our division was in the same general area, and I came back with a small-arms bullet hole in the right wing. I was not aware of being hit, but it does give you a start when you learn that the hit was close. The weather began to close in soon after the night hecklers were launched before dawn on the 3rd. After their recovery all air operations were cancelled. We got out of our flight gear, since for the daytime pilots there was no flying that day. The weather moderated, and the night hecklers were launched on schedule. The Koreans must have figured that the weather would be too bad for flying, so these night fighters had a field day.

The next day, the division went on another armed-reconnaissance mission that was just the opposite from our CAP flight. We were assigned to check out a railroad bridge near Sinpo. The intelligence report based on photos was that it had supposedly been repaired. As we approached the area we could see that not only had the bridge been repaired, but there were a number of rail cars on the tracks leading up to the bridge. The locomotive was probably hidden in a nearby tunnel. We headed down in a loose formation to be able to aim without flying too close together. My attack was along the length of the bridge, and as

I straightened out in my dive, I was able to put the center of the gun sight on the bridge. There was no wind drift, so when I reached 3,500 feet I dropped two bombs figuring one of them might hit the bridge. There was heavy flak coming my way so I made a rapid 6-G pull out that almost blacked me out. At 100% power I climbed quickly and did a high-speed wing over, checking the results of my drop. It looked like I hit the bridge dead on with one of my bombs. Continuing my turn, I was soon nose-down headed for a rail car that was closest to the bridge. The flak was now really getting heavy, but so far it was off my track. I lined up on the rail car and dropped one bomb at a little lower altitude than I should have. I pulled out and then rolled off to spoil the gunner's aim. Reversing my turn I looked back, and sure enough, there was no more railcar. While I was busy doing my thing, the Korean gunners must have had my number again because my airplane was hit in the left wing by small-arms fire. Once again I had no idea that the airplane had been hit until I got back to the ship. The flak was getting too much, so I moved away with the others from the bridge and dropped the rest of the bombs on a group of railcars further up the tracks. I didn't stay around to check out my results because it was time to continue the mission.

Leaving the area with the rest of the division we flew the remainder of the reconnaissance mission without further activity. I had to be careful my next flight because the Korean gunners had hit my airplane on either side of the fuselage; maybe the next one would be dead center. My action on this flight was written up, and I picked up my third Air Medal and the last one for this last period with Task Force 77. Each one was presented by Captain Dufek, USS *Antietam*.

Our missions added to the air group totals, push the number up to 160 sorties during this abbreviated three-day period. After the replenishment on the 5th, the air group flew for four days before replenishing again. I flew five missions during the period, four CAP missions, and an armed-reconnaissance mission. LT Sanders led our division on this flight over enemy territory, and we had a good day bombing railcars and some trucks we found that were poorly camouflaged. We made repeated runs on these targets while using our 20-mm to strafe them and setting them on fire. I am sure the soldiers were firing at us with machine guns, but no one was hit. The saints must have been with us during this one. On the second CAP mission of this period, there wasn't anything going on because North Korea was completely cloud covered. So we bored a big hole in the sky at 30,000 feet the entire time and landed 1.7 hours later. The only exciting event for me took place on this flight was I made my 100th carrier landing. The next day the weather cleared; the last two CAP missions were just as boring. At least we had the opportunity to chase down our friendly flights returning from their bombing raids to exercise our gun sights and our tactical ability, plus buzzing them fast and close.

March 9th was a replenishment day, and so there was not much going on for the pilots. The relaxing day was going to be over shadowed with the events of the 10th. Our division was scheduled in the morning for an armed-reconnaissance mission west of Wonsan. This area is always dangerous because it is on the major east/west rail and road route between Pyongyang (the North Korean capital) and Wonsan. We flew inland at 25,000 feet about half way to make our run eastward toward Wonsan. Billy Sanders went in low at 1,000 feet above the valley floor, Ensign Larry Quiel was number two at 1,500 feet, LT Bob Clarke was in the third position at 2,500 feet, and I was tail-end Charlie at 3,000 feet. The railroad and highway road was in a valley, so there was little chance to surprise the gunners once we started down the valley headed east. The Korean plane spotters signaled ahead to alert all of the gun crews before we arrived.

Things went well for the first ten minutes, then I spotted Larry's airplane nose suddenly come up as a thick stream of gray smoke appeared to be coming from his tail pipe. I radioed to the flight leader, "Larry has been hit."

A moment later, Larry's radio crackled, "I have been hit, and the fire warning lights are on." With all that smoke it appeared that he was on fire even though I couldn't see any flames. His next radio transmission, "I am getting prepared to eject." Just before he was to eject, the smoke suddenly completely stopped.

I immediately radioed, "The smoke has stopped. Try to stay with the airplane."

He radioed back, "All the fire warning lights have gone out; I'm staying with the plane, heading for the coast."

I closed on him from above as he was climbing out of AAA gun range. As I pulled in closer to fly formation with him I could see that there was a big hole on the top behind the cockpit. Dropping down below and looking at the under side of his plane I saw where the AAA shell had gone in the under side of the airplane making a smaller hole.

His next radio communication was, "I'm low on fuel." His fuel gauge indicated that he had lost a lot of fuel, so the question came immediately to mind that he might have to ditch before reaching the front line and safety. The flight leader had made contact with the rescue ships and learned that they were north of Wonsan along the coast. Their position made a dilemma for Larry. If he turned south rather than north, he was flying away from the rescue ship, but closer to friendly territory. By that time we were south of Wonsan crossing the last mountain range. He radioed us that he elected to try for the latter and reaching the coast; we all headed south.

Fortunately for him, there was a small airfield just south of the front lines used by artillery spotting and Forward Air Controller (FAC) aircraft. His fuel supply being just about exhausted, he made a beautiful wheels-up landing on the dirt strip as I followed him in, flying above to his rear and right. I pulled up and made a tight 360-degree turn passing over him. He had climbed out and waved to us that he was okay. I rocked my wings and the three of us joined up in a running rendezvous headed for K-18. By this time, our fuel levels were also getting low. We landed safely and taxied to the operations flight line and shut down. It wasn't long before a Marine helicopter brought Larry to K-18 and a wonderful reunion with much back slapping.

After a late snack at the Marine officers mess and over a beer in the officers club we learned all about his hair-raising flight. Either a 37-mm or larger shell, which fortunately failed to explode, probably had hit him in the rear main fuel tank. It made a hole in the bottom and top big enough to allow all the fuel in the rear tank to flow out the bottom of the aircraft. It moved along inside and out side of the aircraft's skin and was heated up by the hot jet engine exhaust as it passed by the hot tail pipe, causing the gray smoke. Once it was all drained out, the smoking ended. He was doubly lucky. First, the shell did not explode, and second, the gasoline did not catch fire. The F9F's rear tank is connected to the forward tank, and fuel drains from the rear to the forward tank. The connection has a flapper valve, which does not allow the fuel to move in the opposite direction. If it did, he would have lost all his fuel and would have had to eject deep inside the mountainous region of North Korea. He told us the funny side of the landing. As he climbed out of the airplane a very small Korean soldier with the biggest rifle Larry had ever seen greeted him. Larry thought, *Oh my God, I landed on the wrong side of the bomb line.* As he stood looking at this Korean soldier, a small military vehicle raced across the field and stopped in a cloud of dust. A US Marine officer climbed out and walked over to him. Larry said, "I damn near kissed him I was so happy." Knowing macho Larry, that was some statement! We stayed for a few hours, and with a replacement aircraft for Larry from the FASRON, the four of us left for the task force when the *Antietam* had a scheduled recovery. We did not fly for the rest of that day. I thought we had enough excitement to last a while.

Our rest didn't last long. On the following day, March 11th we were back in the air for another armed-reconnaissance mission. We were to fly the road from Yonghung to Pukchon again. We bombed our assigned target and then proceeded with our reconnaissance part of the flight. As we moved along, LT Sanders spotted a North Korean tank moving along the road. We took turns strafing it with our 20-mm, and it appeared we did enough damaged to the tank that it was stopped and could not move.

He called on the radio for anyone with bombs to come and hit it. He was answered by an incoming flight of AD dive-bombers that had just arrived in the area with a full load, and they ended the tank's life with several very close large bomb hits. Anytime you could find a tank and destroy it—that was a good mission.

Quoting from an article published in the *Naval Aviation News*, May 1952:

> When the *Antietam* designated 11 March as New York day, its squadrons joined with those from the Valley Forge to make it a memorable occasion. The two jet squadrons, VF-831 and VF-837, together with ATG-1 planes from the *Happy Valley* made 161 rail cuts in Communist territory, destroyed 3 railroad bridges, 4 railroad bypasses, and 34 railcars, as well as killed an estimated 326 troops to celebrate the day. Returning from the strike, Corsairs and Skyraider of the *Antietam* flew over the ship forming the letters NY in salute to New York and its fighting representatives.

The air group on the whole had a very busy time. The squadrons flew 269 sorties during these three days. It inflicted a lot of damage on the enemy's transportation system as well as other military targets. We paid a small price for being aggressive, with only 14 aircraft being hit with minor damage. The one exception was Larry's aircraft. His was in the major damage category, and that aircraft was headed for the Overhaul and Repair (O&R) facility at

NAS Atsugi. The remaining aircraft were patched up by the squadron's maintenance crews. We called them the miracle workers because they could fix almost anything.

The pilots got a day of rest when the task force replenished on the 14th. The weather held, and we were all back into the air again on the 15th. I flew a photo-escort mission chasing the photo plane from Hamhung to Panchunjang early in the day followed by an armed-reconnaissance mission in the afternoon from Preksongni to Sinup. Even though the rumors were out that we were scheduled to leave the Korean War, the air group continued its aggressive attacks. Our division flew an armed-reconnaissance mission from Sohori to Pungsan on the 16th with lots of speed and much jinxing. On the following days we finished up with a CAP, my last flight for this deployment. At the end of this three-day period, the totals were impressive. The air group had flown 272 sorties, and the damage was excellent. The enemy was busy as well, hitting ten aircraft with various types of anti-aircraft and small-arms fire. There were no aircraft lost, and no pilots were wounded. The ship would replenish on the following day, but the weather was already turning bad and all flight operations were cancelled for the 19th, and the celebration started. For Carrier Air Group 15 and the USS *Antietam*, our tour in the war came to an end. The ship steamed south in route to NOB Yokosuka, Japan and docked there on the 22nd.

The statistics for Air Group 15 were very satisfactory and typical for the Korean War carriers. Ordnance tonnage expended by aircraft type:

F4U-4, VF-713 896.11
AD-4, VA-728 2,675.28
F9F-2, VF-831/VF-837 467.48
F4U-5NL, VC-3 142.99
AD-4NL, VC-35 474.64
Total 4,656.50 tons

Total number of sorties flown was 5,728.

The period from October 15, 1951 to March 18, 1952 the air group lost the services of eleven pilots for the following reasons:

Deaths 4
Psychological 3

Injury 1
Illness 2
Disposition board 1
Total 11

During the entire cruise, the air group lost 23 aircraft and had 14 aircraft damaged beyond the ship's ability to repair them, and they were off loaded and sent back for O&R. The enemy had been busy as well. The antiaircraft gunners had hit 171 aircraft that required the ship's crew to repair.

My personal activity was 72 sorties for all types of missions accumulating 105.2 combat flying hours in the F9F-2. My aircraft was hit three times that I know of with none of the hits being classified as major damage. I completed 87 carrier landings without engaging the barriers. That number, coupled with my 19 landings from the training command pushed my total to 106. None of the eight pilots who came to the squadron from the training command were seriously injured or killed. George Benas and Dick Clinite received some facial cuts from flak hits that fortunately left no visible scars. It allowed us to go back with pride of doing a good job.

From the *Antietam* Cruise Book comes the flowing account:

On March 19th, the *Antietam* left Task Force 77 for the last time to spend a little more than three weeks at port in Yokosuka, Japan. Part of that time was regular Rest and Recuperation Leave. The rest was "standby Carrier." As our date for sailing to the Continental U.S. (CONUS) neared, supplies and bombs were off-loaded for the *Antietam* successors. The ship left port, and all flyable planes were flown to a NAS Atsugi in Japan. The ship returned one last time and on April 17th, she left Japan for good and set her course for Hawaii.

Arriving in Pearl Harbor on Thursday morning at 10:00 A.M. (the 24th) the ship received the personnel of a Marine fighter squadron bound for the U.S., and several civilian guests and newspaper reporters. During the two-day visit, crewmembers enjoyed a final liberty in Hawaii. While at Pearl Harbor, the bunkroom boys met their new squadron command, LCDR Gerald (Jerry) E. Miller. All of the recalled reservists either planned to leave the active military life or if they remained in the service were transferred to shore duty. Most of them chose to leave. The eight of us, however, remained with the squadron to form the nucleus for another sea deployment. LCDR Jerry Miller was finishing up the night-fighter course at NAS Barbara Point and would meet us back in the states. The *Antietam* log showed the following: "At 1000 today, April 26, 1952 the ship left the dock and steamed out of Pearl Harbor, and turning left it passed Waikiki Beach and disappeared around Diamond Head, homeward bound."

On the morning of May 2, 1952 the ship made landfall off of the mouth of San Francisco Bay. After breakfast, all dressed in our Blues, we went topside to get our first look at the U.S. after being gone for almost eight months. The *Antietam*, all polished up, docked at NAS Alameda late that morning. It was a very emotional atmosphere both on the ship and on the dock as the tugs push the ship against the pier and the gangways were both connected. A very proud ship and air group crew returned after many long and dangerous days on the line in the Korean War. Bill Jones and I had no one on the dock to greet us, so we helped the others off-load their personal gear. Later in the afternoon, Bill and I went to the officers club for dinner and some nice refreshments. It was not the best arrival back, but we made the best of it! The following day Bill and I collected our automobiles. He had put his into storage for the period we were over seas. I had the pleasure of picking up my new one. I had written ahead and picked out the one I wanted. It was waiting on the showroom floor when I arrived, all nice and shinny. After all the paper work was done. I drove out in my new, two-tone, blue 1952 DeSoto hardtop. That was my present to myself for all those days at sea. I couldn't spend much money aboard ship so I just salted it way. It was a nice feeling to walk in and pay cash for the car.

Much later a more complete picture emerged of why so little was done by the Navy to support Task Force 77 with more modernized carriers. The WW II carrier had many limitations and handicaps trying to operate jets from their flight decks. Among the problems were the ship could not store jet fuel, catapults were limited to what the jets could carry, and refueling ship's pumps could not move fuel fast enough. The aircraft elevators were load-limited for the aircraft aboard, while the bomb elevators were too small to carry the large number of bombs needed for a strike. These conditions really hit home about the Navy's attitude towards the Korean War and can be found in Admiral Gerald (Jerry) E. Miller's book, *Nuclear Weapons and Aircraft Carriers*:

It is hard to overemphasize the priority that was placed on the atomic bomb delivery mission, particularly the heavy-attack program. Getting that capability was so significant that the Korean War was treated in some ways like a sideshow. As Jig Ramage often commented, the Korean War "was fought by the Reserves." The early days of the war found many reserve squadrons being recalled to active duty, checked out in jets, and deployed in ninety days to combat.

Such was the case with the pilots of the two jet squadrons of Air Group 15. Such was the case of the crew of the USS *Antietam*. All that experience gained in the new type of carrier operations walked off the carrier at Alameda and back to civilian life. The Navy lost a lot of jet combat knowledge and leadership experience that was impossible to replace.

Chapter 11
Training at NAS Moffett Field

On May 6, 1952, the squadron officially left the USS *Antietam* and transferred to the Naval Air Station (NAS) Moffett Field located at the south end of San Francisco Bay. When all the transfer orders had been processed after our arrival there were only the eight pilots and a few enlisted crewmen remaining in the squadron. All the others had been either released from active duty to return to inactive status or those who chose to remain in the Navy were transferred to new assignments. Things were very quiet once we settled into the giant hanger number 2 on the east side of the airfield of our new base. The only activity was the steady rotation of the squadron-duty-officer-job amongst the few who hadn't gone on leave. I was unable to take leave because I had no way to get back to the East Coast, as there were no commercial flights. The oil workers union was on strike, and all the oil refineries had been shut down. I finally lucked out and I was able to get on a Naval Air Transport Command (NATC) flight to the NAS Quonset Point across Narragansett Bay from Newport, Rhode Island. From there I took the shuttle boat to the Navy War College. I had planned to spend almost two weeks at Newport, Rhode Island, with my parents. Unfortunately, they had been preparing a slow cross-country trip ending in southern California, leaving a few days after I arrived.

The biggest reason to return to the east coast was I wanted to see Beverly Greensides with whom I had had a long-time correspondence since leaving Brown University in June of 1949. I wanted to see her after a separation since March of 1951. She was going to graduate from Brown University, and I arrived at the right time to take part in the festivities. We spent many hours together, and it took a serous turn when she opened the package I brought with me. I had brought her a very nice watch for her, and it set off a wonderful feeling in both of us. The night of her graduation dance at Pembroke, the women's side of Brown University, I arrived in my dress blue uniform, and she was in a beautiful, strapless, green gown. Gads, she was gloriously beautiful. It was a wonderful June night under the stars. We were standing by the wall on the roof when a *Providence Journal* photographer approached and wanted to take our picture. To the excitement of all, that picture appeared in the next day's newspaper. What a wonderful way to cap a wondrous week. I rode back to her home in New Jersey with her parents and spent a few day more with her and got to know her parents. It seemed only a few hours, but my leave was going to be up, and I had to get back. That parting was not very easy for both. We were deeply in love.

I took the train from Short Hills, New Jersey to Atlantic City and a bus to the Naval Air Station. I was hoping I could find a Navy flight west. No such luck, but I did find a flight in a Navy TBM World War II bomber that was scheduled to fly to Andrews Air Force base in Maryland outside of Washington. It wasn't much fun on this flight, because I had to sit in the ball turret with my knees almost hitting my chin. I sure was thankful that it wasn't a very long flight. It took me a few minutes to get my legs so they would function again when I climbed out of that airplane. I checked into the base operations, but there was nothing that day. After a layover of a day at Andrews, I was able to get on a flight in a really old R4D (DC-3) headed to San Francisco via Robins, Georgia, Lackland, Texas, and Tucson, Arizona Air Force bases. This "bucket of bolts" could not be flown at night, so it was a slow trip. After four days, dirty and tired, I was finally on a bus to Moffett Field. The aircraft had been on the Berlin airlift and must have been used to haul coal, because every time we hit a bit of turbulence coal dust fell out the overhead. I think I must have looked like a coal miner coming to the surface every time I climbed out of this airplane at each layover. A free flight had to have some downsides.

Back to Moffett the first week in June, things began to get busy with the arrival of the new commanding officer, LCDR Gerald (Jerry) E. Miller. The eight bunkroom guys had met him earlier while passing through Hawaii in early May. In late June 1952 the big job of organizing the new squadron began as well as planning for the arrival of additional pilots. I was assigned to be flight-line officer as my collateral duty. On a temporary basis we were given a few F9F-2 to get our required flying time and to start the check out of the new pilots. As the most junior officer of the eight of us I did not participate in this activity. You certainly couldn't have an ensign telling a lieutenant what he should be doing. That left me very little to do for weeks on end. All of the checkout flights were left to the five more senior lieutenant junior grade officers. The aircraft the squadron used actually belonged to the air base's Fleet Air Support Squadron (FASRON) 10. I was able to fly twice, once each day on the 11th and 12th. The following week I did not get back into the air in the jet, but started my instrument refresher training in the "speedy" twin engine SNB-5 made by Beachcraft Corporation belonging to FASRON 8. It was a far cry from flying a jet. It was more a refresher on Air Traffic Control (ATC) procedures. It had been ten months since I had flown on the U.S. airways. During the week of the 18th I flew five flights in this speedy prop airplane spending 5.9 flight hours under the hood practicing radio-range approaches as well as Ground Control Approach (GCA) procedures. I found the SNB fun to fly, and with its much slower speed there was lots of time to make good approaches. In between flying I started organizing the flight-line crew. I started out with a couple of rated enlisted men and then got assigned a group of sailors who had never been to sea or around a jet airplane. They were just out of airman school after boot camp. It was going to be some challenge to get them into shape. I was able to get some Navy training films about carrier operations that related to flight deck activity to show them that you had to be alert at all times when aircraft were landing or taking off aboard the carrier. Even with the few aircraft, training of the plane captains was ongoing. The three of us had our hands full with this bunch. They had to be taught the most basic steps on everything. We must have done a good job because they all survived the tour and became good plane captains.

In no time it was mid-July 1952, and the pace of squadron activity picked up. The squadron was assigned seven additional pilots with previous operational flying experiences. Coming aboard was LCDR Jim McNeil—Executive officer (XO), Lieutenants Jack Crawford, Robert Chaney, Paul Goodwin, William (Bill) Hitt, Thomas (Tom) Hardy and Theodore (Ted) Wagner. Soon after their arrival, seven new pilots fresh from the training command were assigned. They were: Ensigns Joseph (Joe) Hall, Robert (Bob) Kunz, Irvine A. (Bud) Marler, Francis (Frank) Painter, Belmont Reid, Frank Schindler, and William (Bill) Wilds. The pace of flying increased for the eight of us as we assisted the new pilots with the introduction to the F9F and then their familiarization flights. At least now I could participate in the training of the new Ensigns.

During this month flying was on a regular basis. I flew the F9F one day and the TV-2 another day. The TV-2 was a two-place version of the Lockheed P-

80. The USAF designation was the T-33. The F9F flying was primarily integrating the new divisions into flying together. The eight of us were split up so that there was at least one combat-experienced pilot in each division. Out of the 16 flights, eight of them were instrument related. I was introduced to the jet instrument approach to Moffett Field, first in the TV-2 and then in the F9F. This approach was a typical jet-instrument descent and a final ground-controlled approach (GCA) standardized by the military. It was basically the same whether it was a training flight in clear weather or an Instrument Flight Rule (IFR) approach because of a low ceiling conditions. The approach started out at 20,000 feet headed in a southerly direction until the radio direction compass indicated being over the radio station. It was on top of Black Mountain in the Santa Cruz Mountain range that was south of the airfield. At that point, the speed brakes were lowered, the aircraft airspeed was slowed, and a 4,000-foot-per-minute descent was started. At 12,000 feet, a 90-degree descending right turn was made to the west, followed by a 270-degree turn to the left. These turns effectively returned the aircraft to a northerly heading passing back over the radio station once again no lower than 6,000 feet. After passing over the radio station the descent was continued at 1,000 feet a minute until an altitude of 1,000 feet was reached. At that point the aircraft was leveled out and enough power was added to maintain this altitude and airspeed. At the same time the speed brakes were raised, and the wing flaps lowered. The power setting was adjusted to fly at 150 knots indicated airspeed. About this same time the Moffett Ground Control Approach (GCA) surveillance radar picked up the aircraft on their radarscope. From radioed commands from the GCA controller heading corrections were given to the pilots to make any changes so that the aircraft reached a point in the sky to start the final descent. Upon radio command from the GCA approach controller the final approach started. To start this step was easy. All that was necessary was to drop the speed brakes. The drag created by them was just the right amount to have the proper rate of descent. The rule to follow was that the controller kept up a steady stream of words about your approach, and if you didn't hear his voice for 30 seconds, you were to immediately abort the approach and execute a missed-approach procedure and climb up to 1,000 feet. The controller gave small heading and glide-path corrections until the plane reached the minimum altitude and visibility with the aircraft lined up over the runway. The minimums for Moffett were 100 feet altitude and one-quarter-mile visibility. Either the

TV-2 or the F9F were great aircraft to fly on this approach. Even when it was an actual instrument approach because of fog or low clouds the calm air made this approach especially smooth. Often the approach went off with no corrections, and a perfect pass was made. I made a number of approaches during the training period with good results. During the month I added 16 flights to my logbook while adding 24.7 overall hours and 17.2 hours of it as first pilot time. There were seven formation and tactics flights in the F9F, four instrument flights using FASRON 10 TV-2 aircraft, four instrument flights using VF-831 F9F-2 aircraft and one night-familiarization flight on the 14th in the F9F-2. It was a great beginning for the squadron.

The flying continued in August 1952 with more F9F-2 formation and tactical flights. In the first week I completed the instrument training in the TV-2 of FASRON 8 with two simulated instrument flights for about 3.0 hours under the hood, and making seven GCA approaches on the 6th. I switched over to the F9F-2 and flew five instrument flights adding 3.4 hours with a hood in clear weather and 1.1 hours of actual instrument flying during this period. To complete my night-flying requirements, I made two night flights in the F9F-2 accumulating 3.6 hours, on the 6th and the 28th.

The Navy had obtained operational use of a large tract of land in the Mount Hamilton Mountain range and made it into a limited bombing and rocket range. This gave the squadron the opportunity to fly far more rocket and bombing practice flights than we had in our first training tour. The division could fly a simulated combat flight from beginning to the end. The squadron began to use this nearby range at the end of the month. On the 27th and 28th the division flew two SCAR firing flights using this new bombing range that was southeast of Moffett Field.

I knew that the Air Group Commander, Commander John Parks, had a personal aircraft assigned to him. It was a Douglas Aircraft, AD-2. I asked him if I could get checked out in his aircraft, and he consented. I studied the flight manual and made five flights and numerous touch-and-go landings to feel this big prop aircraft out. I completed my checkout, adding 6.7 hours as well as making nine landings. I flew this only when I wasn't scheduled or on Saturday. On Saturday I had the airfield almost to myself. It was a fun time to try out this aircraft and see what it could do. I flew it first on the 11th and then through the 15th. After my checkout flights in the AD, I ventured further from the field with a local flight to the Sierra Nevada Mountains and the Pacific Coast line south of Monterrey. Flying first to the southeast to Mt. Whitney and then turning north to make my way up the mountain chain, I investigated the many small lakes that dotted these mountains. While flying over one lake, I spotted a hiker's camp and circled around to check it out. As I flew low over the water passing the camp a number of the campers came out and waved vigorously. I made another low pass over them and I could see the faces with big smiles. The following Monday one of the Chief Petty Officers in the squadron came up to me and asked if I was flying the CAG's AD that Saturday. I said I was, and then he told me that he and some of his buddies were in that camp that I had buzzed. They had been up in the mountains that week and were getting ready to walk out that day. It took them a day to walk out; it took me only 30 minutes to fly back to Moffett Field. The mountains were really beautiful to fly over low and at a slow air speed, investigating the terrain. It reminded me of the Korean Mountains in the northeastern area that I had flown over. The only difference was here I wasn't getting shot at. I added a total of 19.7 hours in the F9F-2 with additional time in the AD and TV-2 for a total of 29.9 hours. These hours were completed in the 21 flights flown.

Summer was nearing its end when September 1952 appeared on the calendar. The squadron pilots were busy working to make each division a solid unit with more F9F-2 formation and tactical flights. I also continued to fly the AD-2 adding five more flights. On one Saturday as I was warming up the engine, the tower asked me if I could join in a search for a missing small aircraft. I gladly accepted and was assigned an area to search. Just as I reached the area I was notified by radio that the plane had been spotted, and I was released from my search mission.

I got my courage up and asked the Air Group Commander if I could use his aircraft for an overnight flight. Receiving his permission, I called my uncle in Glendale, California, to see if he would let me stay with him. Uncle Charlie had been a barnstormer in his younger days, so he was all for it. He also arranged that I could land at the small Glendale airport where he worked. All set up Saturday morning, September 13th I filed my flight plan through the Moffett Field Operations with Air Traffic Control (ATC) and took off for the flight to the Los Angeles Basin. When I crossed the mountains north of L.A. I could see the smog that covered the area. The top of the smog was about 4,000 feet. Above that the sky was bright blue and cloudless. Below that, it looked like a brown, dry lakebed. You could look straight down, but couldn't see much when looking ahead. I passed over the Burbank navigation radio station and asked for and received clearance from the airport tower, permission to start my descent from 4,000 feet headed for the small airport south of Burbank. I came over the field at 1,000 feet and made a sharp left-hand-overhead pattern, dropping the AD onto the runway without trouble even though it was narrow and short. I spied Charlie and his young son standing in a parking area by one of the buildings. I headed towards him, and to give his son a thrill, I folded the wings to fit between two small, private aircraft. That AD looked like a giant compared with the small civilian aircraft parked on the field.

After having a pleasant time with my uncle's family, my scheduled time of departure soon arrived Sunday afternoon for the flight back to Moffett Field. I had told Uncle Charlie about how powerful this plane's engine was and to watch the takeoff. It was interesting to taxi out to such a small runway; it was only about as wide as this airplane. After a complete engine check off the duty runway, I radioed Burbank Tower for takeoff clearance, as this field had no control tower. I received my clearance for takeoff as well as my en-route clearance almost immediately because of light traffic. I taxied out onto the runway and ran the engine power up as far as I could before releasing the brakes. The plane rolled only a couple hundred feet before it was airborne. Retracting the landing gear and the holding the airplane close to the ground I built up air speed as quickly as possible. Crossing the end of the runway with a high air speed and still lots of engine power I eased back on the control stick the plane climbed out at a steep angle. I was at 4,000 feet in no time. Rolling into a nearly 90-degree bank I made a tight 180-degree turn to picked up my northerly heading for my first leg of the flight back. It was a good demonstration of the engine power of this airplane. The earlier flights and my cross country to Glendale, California and return netted me another 6.4 hours and five landings in the AD-2.

Finally in September the squadron received its first F9F-5. My first checkout flight came on the 3rd. With a few more familiarization flights it was easier to compare this version of the F9F with the earlier one. They flew almost the same, although the newer one had more thrust, and therefore had a better rate of climb. After these flights, I started to get back in the groove for carrier operations as the squadron started flying FLCP. I had two flights in the F9F-2 and one in the F9F-5. These flights sure brought back memories of days gone by from the first tour when we flew our first set of practice landings. I added twenty-one FCLP landings to the logbook in September.

As more F9F-5s were assigned to the squadron I was able to fly a variety of ordnance flights. The division flew six air-to-air intercept practice flights and five flights carrying either miniature bombs or rockets (SCAR), sorties using the Mount Hamilton bombing range. These flights continued to sharpen our ability to hit the target consistently with these miniature bombs and the SCAR. The range was southeast of the Lick Observatory on top of Mount Hamilton. It also was far from any structures and the civilian population. The divisions could couple these ordnance activities with FCLP at NAF Crows Landing. It accelerated our training considerably.

On the down side, there was still no information given to us about what tactic to use if the North Korean MiGs intercepted any of us. Eventually, we started to try out the shallow "Vee" formation and breaking into an attacking jet. This tactic came from the US Air Force. The few attacks by the North Korean Air Force on Naval Aircraft certainly showed that the best defense was to turn into the attack and take them head on. There was an F-86 US Air Force squadron of jets stationed at an airbase in northern end of the bay, but our division did not have a chance to take part in any mutual training. It sure would have been helpful.

In the beginning of the action reports submitted by the USS *Antietam* during the last tour of the squadron the mission of Task Force 77 was stated as follows:

Conduct air operations from an operating area off the coast of Korea to provide:

Close air support of friendly troop operations,

Interdiction of enemy routes of movement and supply,

Armed reconnaissance of enemy installations and lines of communication,

Provide air cover for replenishment ships and other friendly naval surface forces when necessary,

Protect the force against air, surface, and subsurface attacks,

Provide air spot to bombardment forces when directed,

Conduct photo and visual reconnaissance as required.

Using this as a guideline, one would assume that our training would concentrate on flights to become proficient in those missions that a jet squadron would be responsible for during the forthcoming deployment. As it developed, the training hit only a few of these responsibilities. There were no Ground Control Intercepts (GCI) or shipboard-directed intercepts during the entire training period. Navigational flights were almost always conducted via airways rather than by dead recognition. In short, the training that is described above with a few exceptions did very little to prepare the new pilots for their upcoming combat flights. At least they had the advantage of the experience of the eight of us from the first tour. I stayed away from the older pilots because they sure weren't going to listen to me. After all, I was only an Ensign.

As part of a continual effort to give the new squadron pilots from the training command experience, I flew a number of cross-country flights. The first one was on the 6th I flew an F9F-2 to San Diego and returned on the same day. As a break from this schedule, on the 20th I flew an F9F-5 with Dick Clinite who needed some cross-country flight time from Moffett to Tacoma, Washington, and returned over the weekend of the 20th. I was busy again on the weekend of the 27th when I was with another flight to Denver, Colorado, for a two-day, returning on the 28th. As a bachelor, I was frequently asked to accompany someone to fly on the weekend. That was fine with me because I was always ready to fly. My social life was almost nonexistent with deployment so near on the horizon.

During September it was suggested that the combat-experienced pilots put our heads to together and using the lessons learned from our first tour to come up with the idea of a training flight to capitalize on this. One type of training flight that was put together was to conduct a flight similar to what an armed-reconnaissance mission would be like. The eight of us had flown this type and wanted to prepare the new pilots coming on board for what was done during the first cruise. The concept was to takeoff from the field, fly to an area in the foothills of the Sierra Nevada Mountains, follow a country road to a target, make a simulated attack, and return to base. To make sure that the mission was carried out, they had to identify what was written on the side of the target. In most case, the target was a billboard. I was not sure what the natives around that area thought of these flights, but the area was picked because it was remote and had very few dwellings. This kind of flight gave training in visual navigation, road reconnaissance, target recognition, and fuel management. The Air Intelligence officer briefed the flight and then the pilots had to report back to him their results. It was good training for all hands. It was not an easy flight to complete, and we had a lot of serious fun planning and executing these flights.

On several occasions, the USAF B-36 and B-50 bombers based at either Travis or Castle Air Force bases radioed the NAS Moffett Tower requesting the availability of Navy Jet fighters to participate in air-intercept and practice gunnery runs. The request was for "Little Photos" to allow the bomber's gunners to practice tracking attacking jets. If the Navy flight had just taken off, it took some time to climb to altitude for the intercept. Heavy with fuel, the F9F-5's service ceiling was limited to about 40,000 feet. Intercept of the B-50 was possible without much trouble because it was an all-propeller aircraft. At that altitude, however, it was not possible to make much of a diving attack. It was more of a flat-side attack from the port or starboard rear quarter. Intercepting the B-36 was another matter. In most cases it had already climbed to 40,000 feet before we could start the intercept. On two occasions our division was diverted from the normal schedule to try our hand at an intercept. In the first case, we had already burned off the fuel in our tip tanks, and were at 25,000 feet. The intercepted aircraft was a B-50 flying at 35,000 feet. The division got into an up-sun position at about 39,000 feet and made a mach-needle sectional attack on the lone bomber. The first thing that is remarkable is the size of the aircraft. We were so accustomed to intercepts involving other fighters that this aircraft filled the gun sight even a mile away. Everything at altitude moves slowly because the relative motion is the governing factor, not how fast you were going over the ground. All turns are shallow, because anything steeper caused a rapid lost of air speed. The higher the air speed, the better ability one had to carry out the firing passes.

The coordinated attack was to split the bomber's radar control guns into smaller sectors. The two sections attacked from different angles and later from different sides. We carried film in the gun sight camera to record the attack for analysis later on. The USAF did the same thing. It sure wasn't comfortable watching the gun turrets move around and aim at you as we closed into firing distance of less than 1,500 feet. The multiple attacks lasted about 15 minutes, and then we had to break off because we were getting further away from our base and our fuel levels were getting low.

The second intercept was on a B-36. Now there was a monster aircraft. The flight intercepted it just south of Sacramento. It was already at 40,000 feet, and we were still heavy and could barely get to its altitude. The flight leader made the mistake of letting the air speed to drop while trying to climb to get above the B-36. Not an unusual problem, but one that could be corrected. The flight was in a loose formation below the track on the B-36. Separating from the formation I lowered my nose to pick up more air speed. I lost about 2,000 feet but the trade off altitude for air speed gave me the additional air speed I wanted. I then started slowly to climb, but keeping my nose low enough to maintain my air speed. Climbing above the flight I was able to get above the monster. The bomber commander made light of our failure to reach him. He was a little too assured that no one could reach him. While the bomber crew was busy watching the other three, I began my approach, riding just below the mach needle on the air speed indicator. Just as I was closing in the bomber pilot radioed to the flight leader that he thought there were four aircraft in our flight. The flight leader radioed back that was correct. The next message was telling. The bomber pilot said they only had three aircraft in sight. About that same time I was closing in on them in a shallow dive, and there were no guns pointing in my direction. I pressed my mike button and just said, "Rat-a-ta-ta," as I passed about one hundred feet above the bomber. My gun camera film showed that I had aimed first at the engine nacelles on the starboard side and then the second one. Those 20-mm cannons would have made some big holes in each one of those engine nacelles. It was a nice feeling to have been able to get within firing range. The B-36 was so big there was no way you could have missed it. But that raised the bigger question, why spend time doing this when the job ahead was to perform solely as a fighter-bomber? This time could have been much better spent practicing the low-level rocket and bombing attacks that we would be doing in the near future. Unfortunately, still being only an Ensign I had to keep my opinions to myself. It was frustrating, to say the least. I was not on the best of terms with the CO and XO because I was "too aggressive." I liked to push the airplane hard. I learned that from my combat flying on the first deployment, and I was not about to change because I believed that helped me stay alive during my first tour. I was even told I was an accident just waiting to happen. That comment sure didn't make me feel very good about my place in the squadron. I believed I was a good, aggressive combat pilot and did not take unnecessary chances. From what I had learned from my first trip it was going to be a difficult combat deployment.

September proved to be one extra busy month as we were in the final stages of our pre-deployment training. I found the F9F-5 was just as good as the F9F-2 as an ordnance delivery platform. I flew eleven flights sharpening my bombing and rocket accuracy. I was using the lessons learned on the first trip to Korea to get more good hits by taking into account which side I dropped or fire the ordnance from. During the month I flew a mixture of flights from familiarization with the squadron's new F9F-5 to cross-country flights and in the later part of the month ordnance missions. I flew a total of 57.2 hours during 41 flights in three different aircraft during this month. The break-out numbers of flights by type was F9F-2—13, F9F-5—23, and AD-2—5.

The month of October 1952 started out for me with a cross-country from NAS Moffett to USAF Las Vegas with I A (Bud) Marler on October 3 in the new F9F-5. It was an overnight stay at Nellis USAFB. When we were ready to depart, the operations crew found that their starter jeep's electrical plug did not fit our F9F-5. Unless we could get a start we were stuck. An air force pilot taxied a T-28 propeller aircraft over so that the prop blast entered our air intakes to spin the jet engine turbine. It almost worked, but it just couldn't generate enough rpm to make a safe start. Finally, one of the crew was able to make a jerry-rigged plug that connected the air force's cable to our receptacle. It worked, and we were finally on our way. Just one more inter-service problem solved by good old American know how. After that weekend the squadron started Field Carrier Landing Practice (FCLP) in the F9F-5. It was very much the same, but the newer aircraft had a lot more engine power and took off quicker. It was also a little heavier, so its approach air speed was a little higher. I made 21 FCLPs during four flights. Two of the flights were at NAF Crows Landing and the other two later in the month at NAAS El Centro.

Charlie Clarkson and I were finally scheduled for a long three-day round-robin flight from NAS Moffett and return. As part of the preparations, I got in my required two night flights before going. We left in the middle of Friday afternoon headed for our first stop Albuquerque, NM. On the way at 35,000 feet we picked up part of the jet stream and made excellent time. Our ground speed was an amazing 650 knots, and we had to revise our estimated radio station passage, reporting time twice to shorten the time between the next reporting radio station. The entire trip at altitude was flown on instruments in a deep layer of thin clouds. Halfway along I suddenly saw a large shadow flying in the opposite direction just 1,000 feet above us. I called ATC about this, and before they answered, an USAF pilot came up on the radio and said, "We saw you on radar, so everything was fine." He may have been comfortable, I sure wasn't. After landing and refueling at Albuquerque, we headed east for our next stop, the USAF Sheppard Air Base at Wichita Falls, Texas.

There was a little problem with construction on the beginning of the runway, so we had to fly over the heavy equipment before touchdown, causing us to land long. The wind was good, so there was no real problem. We completed the paperwork for refueling, changed clothes and met Charlie's family. After supper at their home we attended the Friday night local high-school football game. Charlie was the center of attraction, and we both had a good time. The local sheriff told Charlie that the town was having a parade the next morning and it sure would be nice if we made a fly over. Charlie answered him that we would be happy to do so. We stayed the night with Charlie's family outside of the town of Burkburnett.

The next morning we were driven back to the base and got everything in order with operations. We both got good engine starts and taxied out to the duty runway. We had filed to Kansas City as out next stop. We added ten extra minutes to our flying time and with clearance from the tower, we took off in formation. Charlie was leading this time, and holding our altitude down we were soon in the neighborhood of the town. The parade was in progress. I flew stepped up on Charlie as he made a shallow dive to fly down the main street. At 450 knots and one hundred feet we gave them a good show and lots of loud noise. Pulling up slightly we headed for his parents' house. They were standing outside, and Charlie and I lowered our altitude and we flew on either side of the house about 25 feet off of the deck. It was great fun, but one could get grounded real quickly if anyone reported us.

The flight to Kansas City was quick and we were soon within the control area. Charlie was given clearance to change radio channels to check in with the airport tower for landing instructions. The reply was routine with the exception that there was a flood dike close to the downwind end of the runway. That meant we had to be a little higher that normal to clear the dike then put in down on the runway. It wasn't the longest runway we had ever landed on so a modified carrier approach was in order. Passing over the field, Charlie peeled off, and I followed at a short interval. Each of us made a low and slow approach until the plane crossed the dike, then a slight nose drop followed by a little back pressure for flare-out and a smooth touchdown. We taxied to the ramp area of operations and shut down. We stayed in town for the night, and the following morning found us fully loaded with fuel on the way headed west to Denver our next refueling stop. The flight was once again a routine flight, flying over the flat land of the Midwest. Landing at Denver is always different because we were used to sea-level readings on the altimeter. Instead of zero showing on the altimeter, it was more like 5,000 feet. The refueling took some time because it was Sunday, and there were other aircraft ahead of us for refueling, plus a short-handed ground crew. Once we got our fuel and clearance we were ready to roll. We took off together and blew a fair amount of dust at the upwind end of the short runway. As we were climbing away from Denver, the tower called and said that they had found a tire tread on the runway. Charlie, flying lead, radioed back that he had felt a thud just as he was lifting off, and it could have come from one of his wheels. At altitude he throttled back to an indicated 165 knots and dropped his landing gear. Making a visual inspection I spotted that one tire showed nothing but cord; there was no tread. He retracted his landing gear, and we continued the flight to NAS Moffett Field. Reaching the descent point in the flight, approximately 100 miles east of the field, we switched the lead so I could land first in case his tire did blow out and the aircraft fouled the runway. The tower was alerted, and the crash trucks rolled out to greet us. My landing was normal, and looking back in the rear view mirror I saw Charlie touchdown with the crash truck racing after him. The tire held together, and a possible accident didn't materialize.

New models of aircraft sometimes have problems that show up after the plane has been in service for a while. This is what happened to LTJG Bill Jones's aircraft while flying a high-altitude training flight east of NAS Moffett Field. His aircraft suffered complete cockpit decompression when the canopy failed and blew out. The result of this rapid decompression caused both his eardrums to break, and he recalled that he had an oxygen mask full of blood and mucous. The failure of his eardrums meant that he couldn't hear anything. He immediately rolled his aircraft over on its back and made a split S to get to lower altitude. On the way down, he switched his radio to the emergency channel and then broadcast in the blind on Guard Channel to alert the Moffett control tower that he had an emergency and had to land immediately. He also radioed that he couldn't hear anything. He later learned that all the control towers in the Bay Area cleared all traffic, telling them there was an emergency in progress. They closed all traffic into San Francisco International and Oakland Airports, as well as NAS Alameda and NAS Moffett Fields until he was on the ground. He was rushed to the Moffett sick bay where he learned that he had popped both eardrums. He was fortunate that they healed rapidly, and he was able to return to flight status. The damage, however, became slowly progressively worse, and after the passage of many years he had to wear hearing aids, and still does to this day. The result of the canopy failure was quickly addressed both by the aircraft manufacturer, Grumman Aircraft Corporation, and the Naval Air Systems Command. While a fix was being developed, all flights in our new F9F-5 were restricted from flying above 25,000 feet. After several weeks, a fix was ready, and all the canopies were reinforced along the edge where the canopy fit into the frame, and the altitude restriction was lifted. It is always nice to be the tester of this new version of the F9F. The fix was to add a strip of opaque plastic mesh along the bottom of the canopy. It worked, but it took away the additional benefit that the larger canopy added to downward visibility. Oh, well, win some lose some.

The squadron deployed for live-ordnance training at NAAS El Centro later in the month on October 26. On the flight down to El Centro the squadron CO, Jerry Miller had to eject from his aircraft because an electrical fire broke out in the right-hand console of his cockpit. He landed in his parachute in the San Bernardino Mountains but close enough to a road and some cabins to be picked up by Air Force personnel from Norton Air Force Base. A Navy SNB (Twin-engine transport plane) flew up from El Centro to Norton to pick him up. He rejoined the squadron the following day, no worse than lots of scratches from his landing in mountain brush. The squadron was now temporarily based at NAAS El Centro for our scheduled ordnance training. This ordnance training was much the same as before with two flights trying my hand at air-to-air gunnery and other flights doing dive bombing and rocket attacks. The weather was much better than the last time with the temperatures much cooler than before, which were in the eighties. My flying time was again high with 32.3 flight hours during 22 flights. I flew my last two flights in the F9F-2, and from here on out it would all be in the newer F9F-5.

In the beginning of November the squadron was still flying out of NAAS El Centro to continue its ordnance training. I flew five more flights with a rocket, a bombing flight, and three doing air-to-air gunnery. I had one FCLP flight at El Centro on the 7th followed by another one the next day at NAS Miramar on the coast after flying from El Centro in the morning and landing finally at NAS North Island, San Diego. That raised my FCLP landing by another 23. After flying was all done for the day, the aircraft were loaded aboard the USS *Philippine Sea*. Loading the aircraft at San Diego meant that the planes flown to the airfield were taxied over the roadway to the dock, about a half-mile trip. It was no problem for the jets, but the propeller aircraft couldn't see directly in front of them, so the base police force gave them an escort. In one case, a F4U Corsair assigned to VF-713 was being taxied to the dock with two motorcycle policemen doing the escort job. They were well apart so the pilot could see them clearly. He depended upon them for his forward eyes. Unfortunately when they came to a fireplug in the parking area they went to either side of the fire hydrant. Guess what. The aircraft had a sudden engine stoppage and very badly bent propeller blades.

The two jet squadrons began carrier qualifications at sea on the USS *Philippine Seas* on the 25th. It is well known that the Pacific Ocean is noted for large waves that make for great surfboarding. It does not, however, make landing on an aircraft carrier very easy for carrier qualification (CQ). I took my turn and was launched with a good catapult shot. Flying upwind I made my turn to the downwind leg and made my first approach in the F9F-5. A little rusty, but I made my first carrier landing on the Philippine Sea on the 12th. After stopping and then raising my tail hook, I taxied forward to get launched again. The catapult shot was again good, but before I could turn downwind a jet went into the barrier. The sea state was just too much for carrier qualifications. There were too many deck crashes caused by inexperienced pilots and heavy pitching of the ship. Bill Jones was also in the landing pattern and was in the same fix as I was. Cleaning up my plane, I joined up with him so we could fly together from the carrier to NAS San Diego. The two jet squadrons' first carrier qualification attempts were not very good. One of the new members of the squadron, Lieutenant Tom Hardy, had watched the carrier landings from the ship's island, and when the ship docked he announced to the CO that he wanted out of the squadron because carrier landings were not for him. That reduced the number of pilots to 23. My flight time wasn't much during this month, with only 12.8 hours flown during 13 flights.

The ship returned to San Diego and unloaded the aircraft so we could fly them back to Moffett Field. As one of my collateral duties with the squadron was Flight Line Officer it entailed supervising the sixteen plane captains and three rated enlisted men of the squadron. Whenever the aircraft were moved on the ground, my crew kept close tabs on the aircraft. They would either be in the cockpit or standing by when the aircraft were either loaded onto or off of the ship. The F9F-5 had only one place for a large screw eye bolt to be attached at the center of balance of the aircraft. The plane captain removed the faceplate over the hole, but the civilian cable riggers did the actual placement of the large screw eye attachment. Hey, it was union rules. On one of the aircraft, the rigger climbed up and attached the eyebolt. The large overhead crane operator lowered the cable with the hook, and the rigger attached it to the screw eye. The crane picked up the jet and slowly swung it over the side of the ship to lower it to the dock. But as the airplane was only half way in its travel, the eyebolt pulled out and the plane fell to the dock. As it fell the left wing hit the flight deck flipping the plane over, and the plane crashed on the dock upside down. I was standing on the dock about 100 feet from the mangled aircraft. What a mess it was. Now the immediate danger was the fully loaded fuel tanks with 1,000 gallons of aviation gasoline, a full oxygen bottle, and an ejection seat cartridge. The fact that a spark caused by the impact didn't set off the fuel was amazing. I surely would have been caught in the fireball. The squadron plane crew was not involved, but the others were all passing the blame around. Needless to say, the squadron needed a replacement airplane.

We were now getting close to our January deployment, and the flights were concentrated on continued ordnance flights often combined with FCLP. Because I had done well during my brief carrier work I only flew four FCLP flights making an additional 25 touch-and-go landings. The cloudy weather in northern California was becoming more frequent, cutting down our operational days. On the 19th the weather had closed in on the field, and the flight was forced to make an instrument approach after one of the ordnance training flights to the Mount Hamilton bombing range. The base of the clouds was high enough so a GCA final approach was not necessary. The squadron aircraft were under going final modifications before deployment, and I flew two maintenance flights on the 11th and 12th of December.

Never underestimate the influence of the women behind the senior officers. At a party in mid-December I was talking to Mrs. Miller, the CO's wife about my dilemma of getting engaged. My future bride, Beverly Greensides, was an airline Stewardess flying with Pan American Airways in the Eastern Division out of New York. Basically the problem was getting ready for deployment in late January there was no leave allowed 30 days before deployment. I didn't think it would be very romantic to mail the engagement ring to her. Mrs. Miller not only strongly agreed with me, but also she said, "I'll take care of it. Mailing an engagement ring is not the way to do it. It has to be done in person." A few days later, I had been authorized four days leave. My CO wondered how I managed to get this special leave. I explained what I had said to his wife. It turned out that Mrs. Miller was a good friend with the admiral's wife, and the two of them conspired to get the Admiral to make an exception and grant me emergency leave.

There were a number of problems to overcome. Beverly was headed for Europe for a round trip flight and was due back in the states on the 26th. When I called and told her I had four days leave and could she spend Christmas with me in Newport she told me she would try to switch. Crew scheduling was accommodating, and she got a flight change to come back on the 23rd. She did not know about the ring, and I said nothing to her. I had booked a commercial flight to New York and a return, so I was all set. I had also checked with the Navy's Air Transport Service to see what flight they had going back East. I lucked out and was able to catch a flight leaving the afternoon of the 23rd flying to Westover Air Force Base in Massachusetts. Now all I needed was some good weather.

On the 23rd I headed east, and she headed west from Shannon, Ireland. The weather did not cooperate for me. I landed late in the evening at Westover in freezing rain. I was able to get a ride into town at about 2:00 A.M. on the 24th and was dropped off at the bus station. The outlook was not good. The roads were icy, and there wasn't any activity. I headed to an all-night diner for some breakfast and to see what could be done. While eating my food, the owner was curious, so I told him my problem of getting to Providence and then to Newport. A few minutes later he came back after serving another customer. He said the other man was a truck driver headed for Providence and wouldn't mind company on the drive. I finished up my breakfast and took my coffee over to his table to greet him. He finished his meal and off we went. The weather was terrible, but he was an excellent driver, and he navigated that big 18-wheeler down those icy roads with great skill.

Just as dawn was lighting up the eastern sky we drove into Providence, and he let me off at the bus station. He refused my money and wished me good luck. He was one wonderful guy. I got on the first bus out for Newport and in an hour was walking down my street. My mother greeted me as I rolled in, and it wasn't long before I headed to bed to get some sleep. I had been awake for 24 hours. When I awoke later in the afternoon, she told me that Beverly had called and she finally made back to New York and would catch the train from New York, arriving in Providence at about 7:00 P.M.

I was off for Providence to pick her up. The train was on time, and it was a wonderful warm greeting on the cold station platform. On the way back to Newport I mentioned that I had a present for her in my pocket. She reached in and pulled out the small box. That is when I asked her to marry me. It had been a long courtship since we met on a blind date in February 1949.

When we arrived, my mother was in the kitchen and had an all-knowing smile on her face. She had discovered the ring box in my suitcase when unpacking it while I was asleep. She never said anything about it, but once in the house the secret was out, and there was much hugging and joyous crying. Later as we went off to midnight Christmas service we were both a little bit spacey from lack of sleep. It was a fast two days, and then it was time to go back. We departed for New York on the 27th by train, and she saw me off on my commercial flight that evening. It was a most difficult goodbye for both of us. She would soon be off for Europe and I for Korea. If I didn't make it back at least she knew how I felt. I walked to the airplane with a huge lump in my throat.

After returning from my four days in the east I checked in at the squadron and found out that I was scheduled for some more FCLP bounce-drill flights. I was dead tired, but went anyhow. After the first flight, I realized I was in no condition to go flying again, so I begged off the schedule. I managed to stay awake until the squadron was secured, and after a quick dinner, hit the sack for eleven hours of solid sleep. Back in good form, I flew on the 29th and 30th. I added a total of 13.1 hours during twelve flights in December.

The squadron officers set up a New Year's Eve party for our last get together as a group in the states. It was a great time with a surprise twist. After dinner, Jerry Miller, the CO got up and made a short speech. At the end he announced that Larry and I were to be promoted to lieutenant junior grade. But before he did this we had to pass three tests. The first two tests required that we be blindfolded. The first test was to shake hands with each officer and state whether they were a "wheel" (senior officer) or a "peon" (junior officer.) That proved to be a difficult task, as each tried to mask his handshake. We did fairly well with lots of laughs all around. The second one was to kiss each woman and determine if she was married or single. That proved to be a little easier, because the married woman were more comfortable and really gave a big kiss. The single ones, and there were not many, were a little more reserved. We both did better, but the one that got the biggest laugh was that Bob Kunz slipped into the line, and being blind folded, we each tried to kiss him. That just about brought down the house. The laughter from the group could be heard bouncing off the walls. The last test was straightforward and relatively simple. Jerry put the silver bar of a Lieutenant Junior Grade into two empty water glasses and had each filled halfway up with booze. To get the bars Larry and I had to drink the booze down. I was sure going to pass this test, and drank it down in two gulps. That was my last drink of the night! I started out the New Year on a really high note as well as being well oiled.

Chapter 12
Carrier Training, Second Deployment

After recovering from the New Year's Eve and the promotion party to lieutenant junior grade, the squadron pilots were ready to go back to work and into the air. Reporting for duty at 0800 on the 2nd of January 1953, however, we were given notice to report to the base sickbay for a quick deployment physical. I thought that they wanted to make sure we were all breathing. The worst part came at the end when we each got five inoculations shots. These shots had the same effect on me as the last time. I soon ached and started running a slight fever, so I was not very interested in climbing into an airplane and flying around low to the ground doing some more FCLP activity. I voluntarily grounded myself for the rest of the day.

I flew the next day, the 3rd, when I was back in top form. On the 4th the squadron flew to San Diego to be loaded aboard our home carrier, the USS *Princeton*, for the first time. All the emphasis was on getting us more ready for the carrier qualifications that were coming up on the 5th. The *Princeton* was making its fourth tour to Korea and had a very experienced crew. Unfortunately it was a repeat of the last carrier qualification attempt, with continued problems with barrier accidents. Just my luck, these barrier accidents kept me flying back and forth between San Diego and the carrier. Bill Jones and I were again the victims on the 5th when another barrier was knocked down. We both were too low on fuel to wait around so we headed back to San Diego. Before we could get gassed up to fly back to the ship, carrier qualifications were stopped, and the ship also headed back to San Diego. The ship went back out on the 8th; we were to follow later. But when we had just arrived, there was another barricade accident, and back we went to San Diego. We stayed at San Diego until the ship returned and our planes were loaded aboard by a cargo crane. On the 13th and 14th I finally completed my carrier qualification landings in the F9F-5 with three catapult launches and landings each day. It took only a half-hour to make the landings and catapult shots. On the first catapult launch I had to fly around until my main fuel tanks had been partially used up to get my fuel weight down to 2,500 pounds. That meant that I could only get in three landings before I was at the minimum fuel state to be able to make it back to San Diego in the event of a foul deck. The carrier qualification process was simple; the doing was more challenging. After a successful landing I taxied forward and was attached to the catapult for launching. All my landings were done without a wave off, and I picked up early wires on all the landings. After all, I should be able to handle this qualification because I had over 100 carrier landings to my credit.

The ship sailed from San Diego after it had off loaded some of the damaged aircraft, and the following day we were docked at NAS Alameda. Just about a week before deployment I was fitted for my winter exposure suit. The new Mark IV exposure suit was somewhat better than the earlier one, the Mark III, but it still seemed to be too bulky, and I got hot really fast in one.

In one week's time, there was a lot to do at Moffett to get the squadron ready for deployment. Personally, I had only to arrange for storage for my car. The days quickly disappeared, and the day arrived for a repeat of the first deployment. I watched from the flight deck the final sad good-byes. Once again, I didn't have anyone on the dock to see me off, so there was no one to wave to in particular. The big ship was pulled slowly away from the dock by the tugs far enough I could feel the ship's screws begin to turn, and we headed out for my second deployment. Unlike the first deployment, this time I knew exactly what I was getting into. The nagging feeling in the pit of my stomach during the last deployment came back because it was always there. How long will my luck hold? Who would not be there when the ship returned? Lots of questions, but the answers would only come later. To stay focused on the job ahead and to keep the fear inside.

After the excitement of getting ready, shipboard life was much slower. There wasn't very much official business to do, but we kept busy settling into our new quarters. George Benas, Dick Clinite, Bill Jones, and I were lucky enough to get a four-man stateroom on the port side of the hanger deck level. The only reason this large stateroom was not occupied by a more senior officer was there was an ammo hoist for one of the ship's 5-in. gun mount right in the middle of the room. It didn't take the four of us much time to make it as comfortable as possible. We would be on the ship until at least till September, a long time in the future. When the ship arrived well outside Pearl Harbor on the morning of January 30, most of the air group's jet aircraft were catapulted from the *Princeton* to fly to NAS Barbers Point. On the afternoon of the same day the division took off and flew around the western side of the island to the Kaneohe Bay Marine Air station to keep our carrier-landing skills up to date with some carrier approaches to their runway. I ended up making three more FCLP touch-and-go landings before leaving the Marine base for NAS Barbers Point. We took a few minutes to stretch our flying time into a general tour of the island. This tropical island sure was beautiful from the air. It would not be long before we were looking at the snow-capped mountains of North Korea and all the danger that this warfare had to offer. Being at sea for much of the time, January was a slow-flying month for me with a total of only seven flights and 6.1 hours of flight time.

From the cold climate of San Francisco Bay to Hawaii's warm climate at the beginning of February was really great. After a one-day layoff, the squadron left NAS Barbers Point and headed for the carrier. Reaching the carrier, we made a low pass over the ship with all the aircraft in a parade formation. After the ship was into the wind, each division dropped down one at a time, entered the landing pattern and came aboard the carrier. Our division flew air intercepts on the 2nd under the control of the *Princeton*'s Combat Information Center's Fighter Director Officer (CIC's FDO.) This operation was good, and they knew what they were doing. We landed back aboard and the ship headed for Pearl Harbor once again.

When we arrived back at the dock at Ford Island we had our first opportunity to try our exposure suits. The next day after breakfast docked at Ford Island, most of the pilots put on our new exposure suits on and waddled over to the Officers Club's swimming pool like a flock of ducks. What a lark!

Testing Our Exposure Suits

The picture of the pilots swimming and splashing around was quit a funny sight. Some of the pilots found that there were leaks that needed to be fixed as well as some adjustments to be made in the fitting. Mine was okay, and so I tested it completely, rolling around to make sure there was no place for the water to enter. The one thing that had to be done with care was to get as much of the air out of the suit so as to make it fit as close to the body as possible. If you didn't, the air always seemed to go to your feet and legs causing your head to get dunked. The suit was heavy and stiff when walking around and certainly not easy to swim in the water. We also played around with a life raft to figure out the best way to get into it. It was not an easy task. It was going to be doubly difficult with the addition of a survival vest, a Mae West, and the cold water. In the tropical sun, it was fun, and all the pilots had a good time. The dark, cold days ahead seemed far away for many, but for the eight of us, George Benas, Bill Jones, Dick Clinite, Larry Quiel, Charlie Clarkson, Bob King, Joe Perry, and I it was all too real.

The ship went to sea on the 6th, catapulting us once again from the carrier to land at NAS Barbers Point after flying some more air intercepts. The jets stayed at NAS Barbers Point for the next two days. On the 9th we flew out from NAS Barbers Point to land back aboard. Jerry Miller, the squadron's CO, planned to make our takeoff something to be remembered by the base personnel. He had all sixteen aircraft start up and taxi out to the duty runway at the same time. Barbers Point had an unusually wide runway. We lined up in a shallow "Vee" formation on either side of him, and upon his signal we all went to full power. All of us gave him a thumbs-up that we were ready, and off we went. All sixteen airplanes in one big formation took off. What a roar that made for the base personnel. On the second flight of the day I made my 100th jet carrier landing. On the 10th the division flew two flights, the first one was a strike on a bombing range on an uninhabited island and the second one was a series of air intercepts. The air group continued to sharpen its skills with almost the entire air group getting in ordnance flights. Our division flew tactical flights in Hawaiian waters on the 11th and again on the 13th attacking with bombs or rockets on the beat-up targets on the island. During the time in the Hawaiian water I added eight carrier landings, seven catapult launches, but only flew nine flights for a total of 11.8 hours added to the logbook. The ship returned to Pearl Harbor for last minute supplies and then sailed out of Pearl Harbor for NOB Yokosuka, Japan. We were soon to be back to winter flying.

Taken from my logbook it showed that from June 11, 1952 to February 24, 1953 I completed the following:

Total flying time increase 295.6 hrs during 148 flights,
Total FCLP landings 76,
Total carrier landings 16, total catapult launches 19.

After getting all set up in our new home away from home, the four of us discussed how we might be able to quietly set up a nice private bar in our stateroom. We all liked to be able to have a drink before dinner or even after dinner. Either way, we just wanted to be able to relax and unwind from our combat flights. On the way to Japan from Hawaii we put together a plan to reach this goal. Basically we needed a storage container for the equipment, glasses, and the non refrigerated items. I had a large metal foot locker that I used to bring all my clothes aboard that could do the job. We also needed some method of storing the items so they would not bang against each other and break or get damaged from the ships rolling and pitching. Our stateroom was well forward on the ship, so we had a lot of motion. Next, we needed some kind of refrigeration unit. That was a problem for two reasons. First we didn't have much space, and second was the fact that the ship's power supply was not the typical home voltage. We finalized our ambitious plan, and so when we reached Japan, we were ready to start the job of finding all these items.

Chapter 13
Korea, Another Tour over North Korea

After the ship docked at Piedmont Pier, NOB Yokosuka, Japan, a group of the air-group pilots had the delightful experience again to trying our new exposure suits under more trying conditions. We had our fun-filled warm morning swim splashing about in the bright blue warm water of the Ford Island Officers Club swimming pool in Hawaii. Now this time it was going to be very different. After breakfast, the air-group pilots assembled on the hanger deck dressed in our winter exposure suits and cold-weather flight gear. With all this gear on we could just once again waddle down the gangway like a flock of ducks. We climbed aboard a pair of buses and were bussed to the outdoor officers club swimming pool about a half mile away. It was dark gray, overcast day, with the temperature in the low 40s with a cold breeze. The swimming pool was about half full of very dirty, cold water. It did not look like a very tempting place for a morning swim.

We were given a pep talk about cold-water survival while standing around the pool edge. The instructor described the process he would follow for this test. It was to be in three steps. First, after we had all jumped into the pool, he would blow his whistle, and we were to take our right hand out of the survival glove and put it under water. Second, he would wait 60 seconds and then blow the whistle again and we were to pull our hand out of the water and put it back into the glove to warm up. Lastly, when our hands had warmed up enough we were to reach up, unfasten the snap on our Mae West holding our whistle, remove it, and then blow it. The plan seemed reasonable to everyone, so into the pool we went. Gads, was that water cold! I could feel it right through the exposure suit. I had put on my wool trousers and long johns as part of my cold-weather gear under my suit, but I still could feel the effects of the cold water. My suit had no leaks in Hawaii when I tested it, and I was very thankful that it had not been damaged en route because the last thing I needed was that cold water going down my legs.

The instructor's whistle sounded, and the curses uttered by the pilots from the pain were universal after we plunged our hands into that very cold water. The water was a "nice, warm" 42 degrees, and the sensation seemed like sticking your hand into a bucket of ice water. The only thing missing was the ice cubes. Your hand felt like it was becoming a block of ice right away. Everyone wanted to hear that next whistle blast, but it didn't come and didn't come. It was really only 60 seconds, but it seemed like forever. Finally the instructor blew the whistle, and every hand came out immediately and into the glove. Now the problem of being in the cold water became very apparent. My hand was so numb and the fingers so stiff, that neither I nor anyone else could move a finger within the glove or even think about unsnapping the flap to get to the whistle. It must have taken several minutes before a whistle sounded. I finally got my whistle free about two minutes later. It was a valuable lesson on the effects of cold water on the human body. We were certainly no polar bears.

The biggest task we had while in port was to outfit our bar that we had planned during our voyage from Hawaii. Glasses and other equipment pieces were no problem, as we found them all at the Navy Exchange store. We were able to get the old fashioned martini, high ball, and after-dinner-liquor glasses without difficulty. We found various storage separators, and soon the metal foot locker took on the look of a well-equipped bar. The non-refrigerator items came from the base commissary: olives, onions, cherries, etc. From the officer's club package store we were able to buy the other items we needed, like bottles of bitters and other drink mixers besides the booze. The big problem, however, was the refrigerator. Bill Jones was able to locate a small one that very nicely fitted in the space behind the door of our state room. When the door was opened, it was completely hidden. The problem with the electrical supply was taken care of when the electric motor was rewired to operate on ship's power. Bill Jones found a small Japanese shop that could do the job. These owners were great at doing all kinds of things.

With the equipment problem solved getting the booze aboard was not such a big deal. A case of gin, scotch, or bourbon fitted nicely into a parachutes bag. Two of us could easily carry it up the gangway and then to our stateroom. Getting it by the officer of the deck was not a problem because when he asked what we had, the answer was the standard. "Sir, it is crate of china," even if the contents gurgled as we moved it towards our stateroom. Fully outfitted we went on our first trip to the line ready for long days at sea.

My three roommates were all Naval Academy graduates and sure didn't want to be caught with all of this gear. I was a very junior lieutenant JG, USNR, so I volunteered to be the owner of all this stuff. I was also the bartender and made all of the mixed drinks. Our little refrigerator held one six-pack of beer and could make a tray of ice cubes in about half a day. So the drinks usually had one ice cube or they were drunk neat. No sense watering down the High Balls, Martinis, Old Fashioneds, and Manhattans. With the exception of the High Balls we drank all the others straight up, none on the rocks. Why water down a perfectly good Martini?

It wasn't all play time while we were tied up at the pier, because the departure date was quickly approaching. There were a number of briefings by the air group intelligence officers during the period in the officer's wardroom as well as by the staff from the Naval Command bases in Japan. Escape and Evasion (E&E) techniques were high on the list, as well as the location of the rescue ships and helicopter units. The outer part of Wonsan Bay near the friendly islands dominated by Yodo was the most favorable place for ditching. It also helped to have a number of warships that operated in that general area, often willing to enter into the bay to pick up a pilot under the nose of the enemy. There were other warships that operated along the coast but their continuing change of position meant that we were given that information before each mission. They too were willing to move in close to shore to pick up a downed pilot. Maps of the area where we were to operate were distributed and extra material made available for all. I took the opportunity to fill my survival vests with whatever we needed. One of the best things I found to protect small items and matches from the water were to store them inside a condom. It may be a novel use of this item, but very effective way for water proofing. Once again a standard Smith and Weston 38-caliber revolver was issued as well as another cartridge belt. Just as before, I carried only five rounds of tracer ammo in the gun instead of six. The chamber in front of the firing pin was empty. The reason was the same as before. There was no reason to have the gun accidentally fire during an ejection from the aircraft or hard parachute landing. In the cartridge belt I loaded half of it with tracers and the other half with regular rounds. Even though I never fired the pistol on the last trip to the combat zone, it was comforting to have in the event I had to ditch late in the afternoon or on a dawn launch so the rescuers could spot me in the vast ocean by firing tracers into the air.

Our time in port ended when the carrier left on March 8th for some refresher flying for the air group and for the deck crews to sharpen their skills on plane handling, catapulting, and handling arresting-landed aircraft. There were 84 sorties flown that day, and my division was one of the flights to get into the air. The air group did okay considering that no one had flown since February 13th. Almost a month off meant that we were a little rusty. No major problem occurred during these refresher flights other than a couple of barrier engagements. All it takes to get the barrier was to delay by only one second to land long. The pilots were given another Escape and Evasion (E&E) informational briefing on the status of friendly forces and their capability to rescue downed pilots who might land in enemy territory. The second day out the air group conducted joint air defense exercise with the Japanese Air Defense Force, but I was not scheduled to fly and went up to vultures row in the island to watch the action. There were a number of near accidents on deck along with some great saves by the barrier crew, lowering the barrier for a jet making a late wire engagement. The refresher training flights in the morning by the air group added 53 sorties to the record book. Later in the afternoon the ship returned to Tokyo Bay for final preparations to join Task Force 77.

The ship left Tokyo Bay on the morning of the 10th and spent the next three days en route to TF 77 via Van Dieman Straits, arriving in the morning of the 13th. During the voyage refresher flight training and ship's gunnery practice were scheduled, but because of bad weather, there was no flying or ship's gunnery practice. It was now time to reflect on our past experiences and get ready for the actual combat flights. There was a big difference between the start of the second deployment than the start of the first deployment. Arriving in the fall of 1951, I really had no concept of what this air war would be like. I had been brought up on the stories of WW II great fleets with large air assaults. These were the news reports I had consumed about the aerial fighting as a young teenager. The Korean War was completely different. First, the task force was never threatened, and it operated in the same area for months on end. The joke on the ship was it would finally run aground on its own garbage heap. The air war became a daily grind of trying to prevent or destroy the enemy's ability to supply the front-line troops with all the goods needed to wage a ground war. It was also close air support for the friendly troops on the eastern front as well as assisting the naval ships in their role as destroyers of the coastal railroad and highway. It was going to be a lot more dangerous than the first tour because of the many more enemy AAA guns, many under radar control, deployed along the routes, especially around the burned-out cities. Death or injury could come at any second once we reached North Korea while flying towards, over, and out of the assigned target area. The eight of us survived the first tour, but now we were aware of what this war was going to be like. Going back for a second time meant we knew first hand what was in store for us. We were assigned a task, and each of us took it on without any outward signs of stress. It was almost as if we didn't give it a second thought. There were times when the fear factor was very high, and there were times when this folly caused bitterness, particularly when death took one of our friends away.

I had learned from the first tour that there are multiple levels of apprehension or fear during a combat flight over North Korea. It all starts with the catapult launch. That apprehension sat in the stomach and began to decrease when the launch was successful. With the wheels on their way up and the airspeed increasing rapidly the apprehension completely disappeared. As the flight joined and headed off for the coast, climbing on the way in to 15,000 to 20,000 feet, my takeoff apprehension was replaced by the next cause of apprehension; flak.

The second level started as the coast slid under the wing and the target area came into view as we approached our pushover point in the sky. A dive-bombing strike raised the level of apprehension to a major level that often made my mouth feel dry as the nose of my aircraft headed down at a 60-degree dive angle. Once in the dive with the air speed increasing rapidly I would hit the toggle switch to extend the dive brakes to their fully extended position. With speed brakes down, the dive speed could be controlled for good results. The first AAA bursts from the larger guns suddenly began exploding around the flight but with only a visual sensation, no sound. Diving through 8,000 feet the red tracers of the smaller automatic AAA guns begin to flutter upwards, pretty, but deadly. Looking through the gun sight and trying to ignore the flak, I adjusted the nose slightly to make the proper adjustment of mils lead and vertical alignment to put the bombs on the target. Depending upon the target the armament selector switches had been set to drop a single, a pair, or all bombs when the "pickle" button on top of the control stick was depressed. Right after their release a smooth strong 6-"G" pullout was made along with pulling in the drive brakes and adding full power. That is when you felt the fear factor go higher because you were defenseless. The broad plan view of the aircraft made a great target for the gunners. Fortunately my higher airspeed often threw the enemy aim off, and as I reached level flight I dropped a wing, left or right, and continued to pull back hard on the control stick to turn the aircraft enough to spoil any gunner's aim. Unpredictable flight path was always a good defense maneuver. Those tracers flying by you certainly caught your attention really fast. It might have been cool in the cockpit, but the sweat ran down from the stress.

With only a short breather after the attack, the reconnaissance part of the flight added the next level to the danger equation. There were many AAA guns all over North Korea, so I could never really relax. Many of these guns are mobile, and they moved them at night. Constant changing of altitude and direction were the normal technique of combat flying, but the continuous swiveling of the head was a workout. Flights up into the far northeast added the additional apprehension of possible enemy MiG attacks, so the sky had to be scanned as well. Finally relief came when the time and fuel limits were reached, and the flight climbed away from the coast to the safety of the sea. We then carefully checked each other's aircraft for signs of battle damage. If my aircraft was free of visible battle damage, I could just fly along and relax for a few minutes before the task force came into sight.

Reaching the task force at altitude with good fuel levels and a few minutes before the task force was scheduled to turn into the wind we dropped our arresting tail hooks. After visually checking each other's hooks for full deployment we were ready for recovery.

When the flight leader got the radioed message, "Blue 1, your signal is Charlie." The adrenaline level kicked in again and my apprehension of the landing set in. If the sea was smooth at takeoff time, chances were it would be good for an easier landing. But, if there was a pitch to the deck at launch, then the apprehension was stronger. Landing on a pitching deck was never an easy task. Lots of practice helped, but there was always that element of the unknown. Would the hook catch a wire? Would the tail hook bounce? What other possible things could occur during the landing? The division picked up speed in the dive as we swung into a right echelon approaching the ship's starboard side for our entry into the landing pattern. After passing ahead of the carrier, each pilot broke off from the flight at 25-30 second intervals into a 180 degree left turn to the downwind leg. Not until the engine was shut down and I was in the squadron ready room did I let my guard down. Then I felt the let down as the adrenaline stopped flowing and the muscles started to complain about all the physical forces that had been applied to them during the flight. I always stopped at the scuttlebutt (water fountain) to drink a good amount of water to replace what I lost through nervous sweat and breathing very dry oxygen.

Once again on a dark-gray, rainy morning the ship arrived in the war zone and rendezvoused with Task Force 77. The weather in the Sea of Japan was often cloudy and cold during the winter. When it was not cloudy it was usually windy and bitter cold. We had snow and ice on the flight deck the last deployment so I knew what to expect. The weather remained marginal for flying, so the first day of air operations on the 13th was minimal and only 36 sorties were flown. Our division did not fly. The weather was better on the 14th, and the air group got up to speed and flew 117 sorties. Our division got its first taste of live dive bombing when we flew a "Cherokee" strike behind the enemy's front lines. These strikes were named for Vice-Admiral J. J. Clarke's Cherokee family's background. For the other three members, this was their first combat flight. For me, it was just another day like so many in the past. It was just about one year ago that my first deployment ended. We flew into the target area, identified the assigned target that was reported to contain enemy supplies, and then rolled over into a steep 60-degree dive-bombing run. The other rolled straight into their run immediately, but I did my thing and flew a corkscrew pattern down until I lined up my sight on the target. With the necessary mil lead, I pressed the release to drop off my six 250-pound bombs. After release I made my usual six-"G" pull out, hitting the switch on the upper part of the throttle to close my dive brakes and add full power. Climbing away from the target as usual I made fast turns in either direction to change course. I wanted to be the most elusive target I could for those North Korean gunners.

The rhythm of the previous deployment type of task-force "week" had begun. The task force replenished on the 15th and after completing the loading of fuel and ordnance, mainly bombs; the ship conducted AAA gunnery firing. One of the many duties assigned to the junior officers of the air group was to stand as safety officer during the ship's AAA practice. I stood behind the lead gunner and if the tracers were headed for the tow plane I was to hit him on the shoulder to signal to stop firing. I never had to. They knew their business. For some reason, I always was given a quad 40-mm gun mount just aft of the two twin 5-in. 58 turrets. The sound of those 5-in. 58 cannons was just as loud as it was the first tour. I could never get used to that noise even with cotton stuffed in my ears. I watched their effective accurate firing. It was true that the sleeve was being towed in level flight with no change in direction. I wondered how the ship's gunners would do against a twisting, high-speed, jet dive-bomber.

The schedules for the period of March 16-18 gave us three missions to fly. The first mission on the 16th I was forced to abort because my engine appeared to be suffering a potential Turbo Jet Controller (TJC) failure. I climbed rapidly to 5,000 feet and switched to manual control. I figured that with altitude and air speed I would have been able to try a restart or make a good ditching in case the engine flamed out. The switch over went okay, and after I dumped my bomb load on safe into the ocean and purged my tip tanks of fuel, I was ready to land back aboard. Finally the ship had a ready deck, and I was given my "Charlie" clearance by radio. I dropped my speed brakes while dropping my nose and headed down losing altitude until I reached 250 feet to enter the landing pattern coming up the starboard side. I reviewed the landing check-off list, and with everything down, landing gear, wing flaps, tail hook ,and finally my canopy open I started my final approach. I was careful with the throttle movements while on manual TJC control. The landing speed was again faster than normal, being at maximum landing weight of 2,500 pounds of fuel. The touchdown was okay, and I came to the usual sudden stop in 130 feet when my tail hook grabbed the arresting cable. After raising my tail hook upon the plane director's hand signal; right thumb pointed upwards into the open palm of the left hand. The hook clear of the arresting wire I moved forward with a burst of power, clearing the landing area, and was directed to the deck edge elevator to put this dud into the hanger deck. I kept the aircraft's engine running to be able to fold my wings while I was lowered to the hanger deck level. As the elevator reached the hanger deck level, the deck plane director, greeting me with up-raised arms, gave me the come-on signal. I advanced the throttle taxiing into the hanger deck. When I cleared of the elevator with the aircraft rolling, he gave me the cut signal with his hand crossing his throat, and I shut down the engine. I hit the brakes on his clenched fist signal, and when the wheel chocks were in place I turned the aircraft over to the plane captain and headed for the ready room.

I did not fly on the 17th but it didn't turn out very good for one of the other divisions because the squadron had its first death. ENS Joseph S. Hall was killed in action when he apparently was hit and crashed while on an armed-reconnaissance mission north of Tanchon. After the attack by the flight, he did not rendezvous with the flight after recovery and was not seen anywhere. The flight flew a search, but they were unable to locate either the plane wreckage or the pilot. It was assumed he was hit by enemy flak on that dive-bombing run and did not recover, crashing into the mountainside. The mountains were completely snow covered, and his aircraft must have been covered over after impact.

The second mission for us this period was flown on the 18th, and it was a CAP. The third mission flown on the same day was a reconnaissance flight south of Kowon. We were to bomb a suspected rear-supply area and truck shelters. The division was assigned a specific valley to bomb. I could not see anything to aim at, but it supposedly contained enemy supplies. Bomb we did, but there were no secondary fires or explosions. We had yet to see any flak, but without tracers being fired at us there was no way to know when you were being shot at. I suspected that the North Korean gunners were not using tracers in their machine guns. That did not help my apprehension in any way. By the end of the three days the air group pilots had flown a total of 292 sorties. It was not a bad start for this tour. The task force replenished on the following day and after completion of the job in the morning; the ship conducted gunnery firing in the afternoon. The weather turned bad again on the 20th, and all task force air operations were cancelled. So it was another no-flying day. The weather cleared, and for the next three days I flew six sorties, five with the division and one as a photo escort. On the first the division flew a CAP, and then I joined with a photo plane as his armed escort.

After climbing to altitude we joined up with another photo plane and his escort for a short picture-taking session. With the North Korean coast as a backdrop the three planes made an interesting picture. The photo mission was to record the results of a series of major strikes by the air groups from the USS *Princeton*, USS *Oriskany* and USS *Philippine Sea* on the port city of Chongjin and surrounding area. The air group's jets flew flak suppression and Target Combat Air Patrol (TARCAP.) It was a big raid with lots of aircraft pounding the warehouses and mining facilities with high explosives. There was no enemy air opposition, probably because there were so many jets involved. The only jets possible in the general area were Russians. The AAA was light, and as the strike aircraft retired, the smoke from the fires covered the city. When we arrived we found the city still burning, but the photo plane was able to get some good pictures. I was too busy scanning the sky behind us to do much sight seeing.

It was a long mission and was in the air for two hours. As usual for these long missions, I came back with the fuel-warning light burning brightly with less than 600 pounds of fuel. That low fuel level meant I had to get aboard on the first pass. It takes at least 250 to 300 pounds of fuel to take a wave off and then a tight circle for another pass. When the fuel got this low I worried about the accuracy of the fuel gauge reading. The good thing was my fuel weight was so light. I could slow the plane down to about 108 knots to make a smoother landing with this relative slow landing speed.

On the 22nd, we again went after a reported truck-parking area. We headed into the target area with each section attacking from a slightly different direction to force the gunners to choose which section to shoot at. This tactic could reduce the amount of AAA fire that either section received. With the number of AAA guns in this area, we made only one dive-bombing run and dropped all our bombs at the same time. This time there was something there, and we started some good fires. I could see lots of smoke and secondary explosions. This gave me more satisfaction because so often the mission was not very effective, even though I was taking the same amount of risk. We were still doing well, and none of the aircraft had been hit. That afternoon we were launched again for another CAP. As usual, there was nothing to do but orbit and try to stay alert. After a boring 1.5 hours, we got our radio call from the FDO releasing us to come home.

We dropped our speed brakes, turned the cabin heaters to high, deployed tail hooks, and away we went, headed down at 8,000 feet per minute to get aboard as soon as possible. From 35,000 feet it still took almost four minutes to get into the landing pattern. Swallowing frequently to relieve the air pressure in the inner ear I used the time to check out the cockpit to have everything in place for the sudden arresting-wire stop. Passing by the ship on the starboard side, I took an interval on the plane ahead and started my own turn, with speed down to 165 knots, wheels down, speed down to 150 knots, flaps down speed brakes up. Abeam of the island, I opened my canopy and started the final 180-degree turn for landing. All points on the check-off list having been completed now I concentrated on approach turn to arrive 200 feet behind the ship aimed at the center line painted on the deck ready for the final "cut." The control crash, as it is commonly called, put me on the deck. Mission completed.

On the last day of this cycle, the 23rd the division flew as flak suppressors for the props on a strike on barracks in the Hungnam area. These missions were rewarding because it gave the props good protection from flak while they made their dive and recovery. The eight jets entered in to their dive from about 20,000 feet, planning to pass the props that were flying at 12,000 feet. As we passed the props, they also started their dive. About 8,000 feet I commenced firing short bursts from the 20-mm cannons concentrating on my assigned flak gun positions. I stopped firing my guns as my altitude decreased, and I adjusted the nose slightly to position the gun sight with a mil lead on my target. I hit the button, pickling off at 3,000 feet my 260-pound fragmentation bombs. Speed brakes retracted as a hard 6-"G" pull-up was effected. As the nose came through the horizon, I pushed the throttle up to 100% as my jet angled up in a steep 45-degree climb. I was trying to keep all of the other planes in sight all the time. At the top of our climb all together we made a tight hard 90-degree banking turn to pull the divisions around in tight 180-degree turn so we could dive again. We were in our dive as the props came off the target after their bombing was completed. Once clear, the 20-mm guns spoke again in short bursts to keep the gunners off their guns giving the props time to clear the area.

The division returned later in the day to add another ordnance load in the same general area. So far we had all escaped being hit by flak. I added 9.9 flight hours in this three-day period. The Corsair squadron, VF-152 had its first injury due to AAA fire when LT C. B. Purcell received wounds on the left forearm from enemy automatic weapons fire while on a Close Air Support (CAS) mission.

The air group pilots flew a total of 314 sorties in the three-day period that just about drained the ship's supply of aviation fuel and bombs forcing the task force to replenish on the 24th, first from the tanker and then from the ammo ship. There was no ship gunnery firing because the weather closed in again from a slow-moving frontal system. For the next two days, there were very limited air operations because of the bad weather. Not only the task force but also most of Korea was cloud covered. There were only 14 sorties flown during the period, most of which were weather reconnaissance and anti-submarine patrol sorties. I did not even suit up in flight gear.

The following two days, the 27th and 28th, full air operation was the order of the day when the weather improved around the task force and over North Korea. The air group flew 216 sorties during these two days. The description of the type of action the air group flew comes directly from the USS *Princeton* action report.

Air operations were devoted to concentrated attacks on a major supply complex located approximately ten miles north of the eastern main line of resistance. Aircraft from the three carriers, USS *Oriskany*, USS *Philippine Sea* joined USS *Princeton* planes in saturating the one-and-one-half mile square area.

The division flew in these efforts each day. It was amazing that none of the air group's aircraft were hit. I saw plenty of tracers and flak air burst, but the North Korean gunners seemed to be always behind us or well off of our flight path. On the 27th we also were scheduled and flew a CAP as well. As with most of these defensive missions, there was no activity. Being the last planes to land because we had more fuel than the returning strike aircraft, the pressure was always there to make it aboard on the first pass. On the second flight of the day, we went back to the same general area 10 miles north of the eastern end of the bomb line to hit a suspected troop billeting area. I never knew if we hit anything, but we did our job. We went in and dropped our bombs and because this was a troop area, we carried 260-pound fragmentation bombs. The bomb drop results were hard to determine because the exploding bombs kicked up so much smoke and dust that the area was obscured. With the colder air of late winter and good wind over the deck we could carry six of these bombs. This fuse, when armed, was capable of sensing the ground and could be pre-set to go off at a low altitude. Unfortunately, if the bomb armed while on the aircraft it could sense the plane itself or another and explode. I made sure the arming wires were doubled clipped, and I frequently visual checked them as the flight traveled to the target area. The division had no problems, so we came back with no bombs or flak holes to make our landings. Another mission completed, and another daily grind finished. The days seemed to be much the same. One or two missions flown slowly push you down the fatigue slope. The body starts to complain from the constant stress of forceful 6-"G" pullouts incurred during the dive-bombing runs. With limited hot water for a shower, I could not get my shoulder muscles to relax. But a good stiff shot of a gin martini sure did help.

After flight quarters were secured for all carriers, the task force moved south to meet the replenishment ships and replenish our fuel, ordnance and general stores on the 29th. The ships were all low on everything so there was no shipboard gunnery practice, as it took a longer time to replenish the large amount of fuel and ordnance that the air group had expended. The carrier had to go alongside three different ships to accomplish the job of filling up with fuel, ordnance, and finally general stores. The tanker was the one that everyone liked to see, that meant there might be some U.S. mail from home.

During the next two days of air operations, the 30th and 31st, the division flew a mission each day. This time, we concentrated on armed-reconnaissance missions. The first on the 30th was from Wonsan to Hungnam where we were under heavy anti-aircraft fire all along the route. In spite of the heavy flak, the flight got through without any battle damage. There were moments when I thought I was going to be hit, but the tracers missed by a comfortable margin. I also tried to make sure that I was some place else. A constant change in direction threw their aim off enough to get me through. Of course, they could be sloppy in their aim and hit me anyhow. This area between Wonsan and Hamhung was relatively flat and has many small rivers coming out of the mountains. This means there were many railroad and highway bridges, large and small that could be hit. This flat coastal plain made it a major shipping route for war goods traveling from the northeast to the eastern side of the battle line. Even though there was a lot of nighttime traffic, targets were hard to find in the daylight. Careful observation by experienced pilots of the suspected hiding places along the road often turned up some hidden trucks. The Koreans also hid supplies in the many villages and in the small valleys leading from the coastal plain. This way we were able to detect the occasional truck or ox cart that could be attacked. These attacks were typically strafing ones. The North Koreans were good at fixing the small bridges and building bypasses around the larger ones. In the winter that was not difficult because the ground was so cold and the rivers were covered with a thick layer of ice.

The mission on the 31st was from Ichon to Wonsan. Once again there was no damage to anyone in the flight. If the flights appear to be routine, they were not. Once over enemy ground, each pilot was constantly changing direction, speed, and altitude to minimize the aircraft as a steady target for the enemy AAA gunners. This meant that you needed to keep the other three in sight, look for targets, and watch out for flak, while all the time zigzagging or jinking. Twisting high-"G" turns and rapid pullouts were normal. I really tossed the aircraft around often riding on the edge of a high-speed stall. Then added to the flying job there was the need to be aware of the time over the enemy terrain and your current fuel state. These were nerve-racking flights every time. For every 1.5 hours in the air, we had to get dressed, get a half-hour briefing, a half hour to man the aircraft and finally get launched. Back after the flight there was some more time for a de-briefing. It was not unusual to have one mission take almost three hours. Two in one day could really drain your energy. If the ship was early carrier, breakfast was at 4-4:30, and lunch wasn't until 11:30. If I had two flights without a break, my stomach growled most of the time on the last one complaining that it was empty. No matter how tired I was, being alert during the approach and landing was essential. So I had to call up that extra shot of adrenaline to get me through those last minutes in the landing circle and on to the deck. This was no time to be relaxed!

Late in the afternoon after flight quarters were secured the ship with its destroyer escorts left Task Force 77 for Yokosuka via the Van Dieman Straight. In 10.5 operational days I flew 16 flights for a total of 24.1 flight hours. All my landings were good touchdowns, and I grabbed early arresting wires. The pilots of the two jet squadrons flew a total of 628 sorties. Of these sorties 127 or 27% were defensive CAP and 39 or 6% photo escorts. The majority of the total sorties, 393, were direct attacks against the enemy in the form of direct bombing strikes (287), or armed-reconnaissance missions (106). The bombing flights were often followed by an armed-reconnaissance of a road or railroad. The air-group pilots flew a total of 1,154 sorties for an average of 109.9 sorties per operating day. On the negative side, one VF-153 pilot was lost to enemy AAA fire. Although the two jet squadrons also showed improvement around the carrier there were still problems during landing. There were five barrier engagements and two barricade engagements; the numbers were certainly too high. The long layoff from air operations was a contributing factor along with the stress of combat for the new pilots. The first barricade engagement was caused when the plane came in too low at the ramp with a rising deck, and the tail hook hit the edge of the ramp, knocking it up into the locked position. The second one was caused by a hard landing breaking the tail-hook point. It took ten minutes and nine minutes respectively to re-rig the barriers and the barricade. On the bad side, these engagements still represented 1% accident rate. On the plus side, the jets had no problems during catapult operations with 719 launches. The average wind of 35 knots helped measurably with the launches. This strong wind kicked up larger waves , however, making it more difficult for landing with a pitching deck.

During many of the CAP flights there were frequent problems with the jet engines over speeding for both jet squadrons when the aircraft was above 25,000 feet. This over speeding was due to a condition called auto-acceleration. The problem was caused when the Turbo Jet Controller (TJC) unit sensitivity to altitude "froze" and the engine started to accelerate because too much fuel was being sent to the engine. Thus the engine could go over the 100 %-power level. The only thing the pilot could do to stop this condition was to pull the throttle to the idle position and switch the TJC control switch to manual. The procedure could possibly generate another problem causing the engine to flame out. I had one experience with this auto-acceleration problem. It was during a CAP flight at 35,000 feet. We were flying in an open, spread-out formation with a power setting of about 86% when I felt the aircraft suddenly start to accelerate. A quick check of the engine power-setting instrument revealed the engine gaining rpm. I snapped the throttle to idle with my left hand just as it passed through the 105-% mark, and then dropped the same hand to the TJC-selector switch, snapping it to the manual position. I lucked out when the switch over went okay. There wasn't even a rumble when it was made. I started to breathe a little easier after that experience. The rest of the flight went off with out any difficulties. I moved to tail-end Charlie position so I could move the throttle slowly or as little as possible. In the landing pattern, I made very smooth throttle movements to insure there would be no flameouts at low altitude. The landing was normal, and I went down the deck edge elevator to have the fuel control replaced. Even though this was a short period with TF 77, the air group dropped 4,497 bombs in those 10.5 operating days. There were 99,866 rounds of 20-mm fired. It was not that bad beginning.

One of the unusual events that took place during this deployment is the story of the "Blue Tail Fly." It all started at Moffett Field when the squadron was due to receive new Grumman F9F-5. The Navy made the new commanding officer, LCDR Gerald (Jerry) E. Miller an unusual offer. Although the squadron was to receive new F9F-5s during the summer from the Grumman factory painted in the standard Navy blue, he was offered two experimental aircraft that were not painted to meet the 16 aircraft assigned. He gladly accepted the offer and VF-153 became the proud owner of two non-painted, silver-colored aircraft. One of these aircraft (Bureau # 126652) was destined to standout in Naval Aviation History. Based upon the history card in the National Air and Space Museum microfilm files this particular aircraft was manufactured at the Grumman Bethpage factory and rolled off the assembly line on February 28, 1952. After production flight test at Bethpage, it was ferried to the Overhaul and Repair O&R at NAS San Diego via O&R NAS Quonset Point arriving on August 27, 1952. Two days later it landed at NAS Moffett Field and was checked it to FASRON 10. On September 15, 1952 it was assigned to VF-153 and became part of squadron's flight line. The metal smiths painted with the side number 312 in black rather than the usual white.

There were minimal differences between the standard blue F9F-5 airplanes and the non-painted ones. The most noticeable one was the link up between the cockpit and the trim tab on the horizontal stabilizer. The squadron pilots flew the planes during the period of training at NAS Moffett Field, NAAS El Centro, and during carrier qualification off of San Diego. We thought that the non-painted ones were slightly faster, but no one could prove it. There was no question that flying this plane in formation was different. We were so used to flying blue-painted aircraft that it just seemed out of place.

The aircraft was with the squadron as part of CVG-15 when it deployed from NAS Alameda on January 24, 1953 aboard the USS *Princeton* (CV-37). The picture of this specific aircraft was taken at NAS Barbers Point in Hawaii in early February 1953 during the ship's stop in the islands.

VF-153 combat flights began on March 13, 1953 when the ship went on station with Task Force 77 operating in the Sea of Japan. Our offensive and defensive combat flights were filled with flying the different missions typically assigned to the jet-fighter squadron. On March 18, 1953, Panther 312, piloted by LTJG Richard (Dick) Clinite on a routine armed-reconnaissance mission, was hit in the forward part of the vertical fin by an explosive anti-aircraft (AAA) shell. The damage to the tail portion of the airplane was too great to be patched or repaired aboard ship, and the aircraft was declared, "Aircraft on Ground" (AOG). The only thing to do was to replace the entire tail assembly, but no tail assemblies were available.

Soon after this occurrence, an enemy shell from an anti-aircraft gun hit the aircraft Ensign William (Bill) Wilds was flying in the nose section. He was able to return safely to the ship. This aircraft turned out to be damaged beyond repair aboard the ship. Now there were two aircraft grounded. The creative squadron and ship maintenance crews, however, came up with a unique answer. They put the good blue tail section from the damaged aircraft Bill had flown onto the Panther 312. The Blue Tail Fly was hatched. It only took a very short time before the crew painted that name "Blue Tail Fly" on the nose of the aircraft. It was the talk of the ship; a light-hearted event in the time of war!

The Blue Tail Fly taxiing forward after recovery March 1953, official Navy photo

This was our squadron's new secret weapon. When this plane was flying in formation with other aircraft, the eyes could have a trick played on them, because looking at the Blue Tail Fly against a bright white cloud; it appeared as if there was nothing but a flying tail. Then, the reverse was true when the plane was seen against the dark blue ocean; then it was a flying wing. We hoped that this strange plane would startle and confuse the Korean gunners so their aim would be off. We can all dream. On March 31, 1953, the author flew the Blue Tail Fly for the last time on an armed-reconnaissance mission that ended at the enemy's city of Wonsan, Korea, and then back to the ship. The *Princeton* left the task force the following day for Yokosuka, Japan, for maintenance, repairs, and R&R for the air group and ship's crews. But the Blue Tail Fly was not to fly again in this configuration. When this hybrid plane came to the attention to the powers that be, the plane was ordered removed from the squadron. The picture shows the Blue Tail Fly being offloaded on April 6, 1953 and sent to FASRON 11 for repair. It later saw service again as an all-silver aircraft with VF-63 in the fall of 1953. It was sent finally to Litchfield Park and removed from active service in 1978. Although the Blue Tail Fly disappeared, it lived on in the memory of those of us who flew it in all its glory.

Blue Tail Fly Being Offloaded

Chapter 14
Our Luck Runs Out

The ship was en route to Yokosuka for two days, arriving on the morning of April 3, 1953. One of the things that struck us was nobody had a light robe to wear going and coming from the shower. The head (toilet and shower) was about 50 feet from our stateroom. The air handling blowers within officer's country generated more of a gale coming down the passageway than a breeze. It was especially true when the hatch to the hanger deck was opened. So after docking, we went ashore to find a Japanese shop to see what we could get. Walking up one of the streets in Yokosuka we spied a shop that made summer Kimonos.

Now we had the task of making our needs known to the owner of the shop through sign language. He quickly got the picture and motioned to Bill Jones to stand on a small stool. Taking out a tape measure he measured Bill from his neck line to just below the knee. Then he measured him from the center of his back out to his wrist. Then he did the same around his waist. When all this was done he motioned to George Benas to undergo the same procedure. By this time, a group of people were gathering outside the shop watching this goings on. Bill and George were not that much taller than the shop owner, so it wasn't a problem. When it came my time the owner had a little more difficulty because of my height. He could barely reach from the center of my back to my wrist. When he measured me from my neck to the calf, the crowd began to giggle. It was going to take a lot more material to make mine.

Then it was Dick's turn. This proved to be a big job. The owner could not reach from Dick's neckline to below his knees. It took two of them to do this operation. By then the crowd had gotten larger and the giggles had turned to laughter. The crowning touch came when he tried to measure Dick's reach. Even with two, it was a job. The crowd went into great peals of laughter and much finger pointing to Dick's height and arm reach. We certainly got into the spirit of the event and laughed along with them. We put a down payment on the robes and got a promise he would have them finished in two days.

We returned as promised, and there they were. Not only were they beautifully made, but the pattern of the material; blue on a white background, was excellent. The shop owner had put Dick's finished robe in the window on a support that showed off the height and the sleeve length. Just after we walked in another crowd quickly formed, and Dick proudly put his on and modeled it for them. They were enthralled by the size of the garment. I'm sure Dick's robe could have covered two Japanese with ease. With big smiles all around, we paid our bill and left the shop with our robes carefully wrapped up in paper and a few thousand yen less. They were perfect for each of us, and we used then throughout the cruise. (I lost mine to my wife after our marriage.)

Once things settled down, Larry and I obtained a few days of R&R leave for the rest camp in the mountains, and we were off to try our hand at spring skiing and relaxing. It was a repeat of our last trip with one exception. On this trip a group of officers staying at the hotel were taken down to the village inn for a Japanese-style banquet. The building did not have central heat, but the room was heated by burning charcoal in containers imbedded in the floor under the table. It was a grand feast with wonderful food and a generous amount of hot sake to drink. Afterwards, one of the waitresses arranged a game of "Knock you off the pillow." Two people stood with their heel on the edge of a pillow back to back. The object was to hit the other one to knock them off with your butt or duck their attempt and have them lose their balance and fall of the pillow. One of the waitresses got Larry to join in, and he put his heel on the pillow and she on the other side. Larry had been enjoying the sake; she was cold sober. They halfway tried to dislodge each a couple of times, but then she hit Larry with a fast quick blow with her butt, knocking him not only off of the pillow, but propelling him a few feet forward. He tried to stop his fall by putting his hands out. The only problem was the "wall" was a rice-paper-covered screen in front of the glass windows. He put both hands through the paper. We could only roll around because we were laughing so hard at this picture of Larry struggling to pull free of the paper screen. We made sure that the owner was compensated for our high jinks. It reminded me even today of a great time we had in the mountains. As usual, the R&R ended too quickly, and the two of us caught the train back to Tokyo and then the local train to Yokosuka.

Our little bar operation was fully in business by the time we went out on our second trip to the task force. All was going well, and then it happened! The air group commander somehow found out about our little operation and came into our stateroom unannounced to verify that we indeed had an operating bar. I figured I was sunk. Not so, it seems his favorite drink was an Old Fashioned, and I made a good one. So properly bribed, we continued in operation with a slight twist. As Commander Parks was finishing dressing for the second seating in the wardroom his strong Texas voice would come down the passage way. "Lieutenant Schnitzer, five minutes!" I would get all the stuff out and mix his drink with great care. I carefully stirred the mixture so as to keep ice particles out of his drink. I did not believe in shaking my drinks. It bruised the booze. When he pulled the curtain of our stateroom open and walked in, I handed him his perfect Old Fashioned. He enjoyed his one drink before dinner and always left with a smile.

One time he asked me how I made my drink. My answer was simple. "Sir, that is a military secret." We all enjoyed his company. He was very approachable and enjoyed a good laugh. In my view, CDR Parks was one fine naval officer and air-group commander.

One of the other visitors we had on occasion was the Catholic chaplain, Father McGovern. He was a devoted martini drinker and I fettered him with my famous one. In fact, one night before replenishment, we plied him with a number of these tasty drinks. When he left I am sure he was feeling no pain. It was a great stress reliever and made life aboard ship a little easier, but we never abused alcohol.

On April 13, 1953 at 1600, the ship left Yokosuka for the task force. We were en route for the next three full days to rendezvous with Task Force 77 on the 17th. The first two days out the weather was so bad there was no chance for refresher flying or to allow the ship to conduct gunnery practice. On the 16th the weather improved, and the air group was able to fly 91 refresher sorties. Our division was picked to fly in a parade formation for official pictures by the photo plane. It was fun flying, but it was not easy when it came to land on a pitching deck after a layoff of almost two weeks.

The *Princeton* arrived in the darkness of early morning to rendezvous with Task Force 77 and started conducting the first air operations of our second period in the combat zone. We were up at dawn about 07:00 with a full schedule of 107 sorties to be flown. Our division joined with two others to hit troop-and-supply build-up areas in close proximity to the front lines. These strikes were officially named "Cherokee strikes." We were the late carrier this day, meaning the air operations started about two hours after dawn and ended when the night hecklers were recovered about 10 in the evening. After only one operational day, the task force had to replenish on the 18th. This was followed by shipboard gunnery practice. I stood ready-deck-alert duty with three other pilots in the morning during replenishment. It was dull, cold, and boring. We could walk around the aircraft to stretch our legs, but we could not leave the immediate area. Most of the time was spent in the cockpit either listening to the Japanese radio station or reading.

The *Princeton* was scheduled to be the morning carrier for this next three-day period. On the 19th, the air group flew 109 sorties including morning hecklers around Hamhung and northeast along the coast towards Songjin. The daylight flights began just before dawn flying close-air-support mission along with Cherokee strikes against personnel and supply areas. I was squadron duty officer on the 19th and did not fly. Being SDO meant it was a long day from early morning, when flight quarters started, until the end of air operations around 5:00 P.M. After dinner I was ready for the sack. I was usually beat!

On the 20th, bad weather moved in over the front lines, and the flights were sent north and northeast to the area above Hamhung. When the ship was morning carrier, we were up at 3:30 A.M. for breakfast, then off to the ready room to dress in flight gear, then be briefed for the first mission. Briefing finished, we waited for the command to blast out of the squawk box, "Pilots, man you planes." The pilots headed out of the ready room to climb the short flight of steps up to the flight deck in the pitch dark to find our aircraft. On a blacked-out carrier deck that was no small task, especially when there was no moon. The worst hazard was the tie-down lines attached to the nose wheels. I stumbled into my share of these lines trying to locate my aircraft. The first jet launch began just as the eastern sky showed a thin line of light. Our division joined with two others to participate in this strike. With 12 jets all diving and bombing at the same time I needed to be alert for flak but mostly the other airplanes. With our higher speed, most of the flak was behind us. Those red tracers coming up, however, sure made me wonder if one had my name on it. I had learned that if the tracers began to drift away there was no problem. If it didn't drift away it meant that it would be close. Some were so close I could smell the burned cordite from the burning tracer shell as I passed through the smoke trail left in the air. Those were the ones that sure caused me to have a high level of apprehension. Fortunately, no one was hit in spite of the heavy flak.

Later in the day the division flew a CAP, for the second flight. These CAP flights were as boring as ever. What a difference it was! Go from physically hard, dangerous work on one mission to boredom on the next, sitting in the cramped cockpit strapped in so tightly you could not even wiggle your butt to ease the pressure. All you wanted was for the flight to end and to get back aboard the ship for some water. Breathing the dry oxygen for an hour and a half dried the up the fluids, and it wasn't unusual to drink for a bit from the water fountain outside the ready room. The sorties by the air group totaled 118 for the day.

On the 21st the air group flew all-day and racked up another 114 sorties. Also on this day the flights could choose where they wanted to go and what target they liked to hit. We didn't join in because we were sent on a defensive CAP flight to bore holes once again in the sky. While we were doing this, the squadron had another casualty when an AAA shell hit the aircraft being flown by LTJG Charlie J. Clarkson, one of the original eight. He had to ditch his crippled aircraft in Wonsan Bay. Fortunately he received only minor facial lacerations from the shrapnel entering the cockpit. It does not matter what the cause may be; it is always difficult to make a successful ditching. He did a great job and did not suffer any further injuries from his ditching. In his own words, he recounted the events of that day.

On April 21, 1953, our flight (of four) was assigned an armed-reconnaissance flight on one of the known and more infamous transportation routes in North Korea; roadways and/or railways through the mountains on which troops and materials were moved sporadically. Our normal formation and search technique was to have the lead plane fly low (around 500 ft if the terrain allowed) in a weaving pattern from side to side across the route. The second plane was a little higher and weaving out of phase so he could observe the lead plane at all times. Third and fourth planes were still higher (about 2,000 feet above terrain) and trailing about 1/4 mile. All four planes constantly weave across the route while keeping an eye out for those in front, looking for ground-to-air fire directed toward any of them, and for any possible enemy aircraft. We were armed with six 100-pound fragmentation bombs with nose and tail fuses each, plus our standard 20-mm cannon ammo. The first part of the search was quiet, but circumstances changed as we came around a sharp bend in the route where the terrain was a little less precipitous. From my position as number three I could see flashes of enemy fire from under cover of a small group of trees, off to one side. I immediately announced my intent and turned into the threat, diving in a strafing run. I could see my 20-mm shells detonating around the area, and just as I was starting to pull out of the run my plane was hit twice with some type of heavy-weapon shells. The windscreen shattered. I felt the rapid pressure change in the cockpit, and the plane responded sluggishly to the flight controls to pull up. I knew I had been hit! As my nose pointed above the horizon I took a rapid inventory of the damage. I was bleeding from some facial wounds caused by windshield shards, my flight instruments were all screwy, and the nose section in front of the windscreen was gone. Everything up front was smashed or blown away, including the battery from one hit, and about three feet of my right wing tip, including the tip tank, was gone from the other hit. About that time I noticed Bob Chaney moving into position on my right wing. Through hand signals he informed me I was losing fuel and signaled me to punch out. I let him know I wanted to get to the water if possible, and noticed the safety wires on my six bombs were gone. I could see the bombs but had no way of knowing if the arming vanes had spun any or enough so that the bombs were, in fact, armed. The other two pilots in the division were ordered to head for the ship while Bob and I headed for the Wonsan Bay. A few miles offshore from Wonsan, North Korea, a small LST converted into a hospital ship with a helicopter aboard was anchored for just such emergencies. As soon as we reached the bay I attempted to punch out (eject), but the pre-ejection mechanism was broken and did not respond.

It finally occurred to me that I had a serious problem and that I might not make it back alive. Even faced with that likelihood, the human's will to live was so strong there was no way I could not fight on. There was one possibility to bail out, except for the fact the airplane would not trim for anything close to level flight. With so much of the wingtip gone, and with no hydraulic aileron boost, I couldn't hold the plane level with just one hand. It took both hands to hold the aircraft in level flight. I feared the aerodynamics of the situation would cause the plane to roll rapidly around the longitudinal axis, and if I bailed out the tail section could hit me as it rolled over. Bottom line, even though I was uncertain if the bombs were or were not armed, I decided they most likely were not and elected to land wheels up in the water. I signaled my intentions to Bob, and he relayed them to the two search-and-rescue helicopters already airborne. Having made my decision I unfastened my safety harnesses and slipped out of my parachute, reattached the safety harness, and started a right-hand spiral designed to set up a landing into a light breeze, fairly near the ship. As I descended I reduced the airspeed to test for signs of a stall, and found it started to fall off at about 200 knots, primarily because of the loss of so much of the wing.

I had no battery power nor hydraulic power, so I could not lower the landing flaps to further reduce landing airspeed. I decided to lower the arresting hook to let it drag in the water to work in opposition to the air-cushion effect of the wings and the water surface to reduce airspeed as much as possible before touchdown. With the power still at about 85% I felt the tail hook make contact with the water. I held the aircraft off the water until it touched down at about 185 mph. This action threw up a rooster tail spray for about a mile (I was told later) while I held the plane out of the water as the hook tried to drag it in. When the plane hit and finally stopped it tilted up on its nose to almost vertical and immediately sank. As it reached vertical I released my safety harness, and since the parachute was already off stepped from the seat to the windscreen frame and right into the water. It was very cold, but I had earlier decided not to wear the cumbersome exposure suit.

I was in the water only about two minutes when a helicopter was over me and dropped its rescue harness for me to put over my shoulders. Within seconds I was in the helicopter, and a few minutes later I was aboard the hospital ship enjoying a brandy and receiving first aid treatment for minor cuts and scratches on the face and right leg. As was customary under these circumstances I gave my .38 revolver to the helicopter pilot and he gave me his .45 caliber automatic. The *Princeton* was rather far away to the north involved in flight operations so I stayed on the hospital ship overnight and was transferred to a cruiser the next day. I was on the cruiser for two days while she pursued her mission of shoreline bombardment. During my stay on the hospital ship the helicopter crew took me over to Yodo Island, at the mouth of Wonsan

Bay, and introduced me to the CO of the South Korean Marines that manned the island and regularly shelled the North Korean coastline. A fascinating island honeycombed with caves and tunnels, and a few howitzers. They also had a short, dirt runway with an arresting cable across it for emergency use by prop planes such as the F4Us or ADs, when needed. The ship returned to the task force, and the helicopter flew me back to the *Princeton* where I was welcomed back aboard by CDR Harmer, the ships XO. On April 27, I was back in the air for a CAP flight.

After all aircraft were aboard and air operations were secured the ships headed south to rendezvous with the supply convoy. The task force replenished on the 22nd, which ended up being a long time for the *Princeton*. The air group had flown 341 sorties and depleted the store of ammo by dropping a lot of bombs from the magazine and burning up a lot of fuel in the process. Because of this delay all shipboard gunnery practice was cancelled.

The ship was now the afternoon carrier and the air group pilots flew 112 sorties on the 23rd, including the launching in the evening of the night hecklers. Earlier during the day, the flights included Close Air Support missions along with Cherokee strikes against personnel and supply areas along the central front line areas. Our division flew flak suppression for the props during the strikes. For CAS we remained in orbit south of the bomb line until called down to attack either a specific area or the Forward Air Controller had a definite gun emplacement to hit. These guns were most difficult because they were already manned and were willing to trade shots with the attacking aircraft. Once again our speed and agility gave us the advantage. It still was a nerve-racking type of attack. I did not like to trade shots with an AAA gun. It is a damn good way to get shot up.

The night fighters flew along the northeast coast from Hungnam without much success. In spite of the heavy AAA ground fire, all aircraft returned safely to the task force. The daylight hours at this time of the year had begun to grow longer, and the air group increased the number of sorties to 119 on the 24th. Concentrated close-air-support sorties were flown against the enemy's position in the eastern and central sectors of the front lines. There were excellent results from these sorties. Our division flew flak suppression again for some of these close-air-support attacks near Kumson. Flak suppression was a nice name for trading cannon fire with the enemy. It took guts to bore in on the many guns that were trying to knock you out of the sky. The rules of war were simple: find the enemy guns, and kill them before they could hit or kill you. It sounded good except for one thing. These gun emplacements were difficult to attack. The reason was that the direction of attack was limited. The attack run was made to avoid hitting friendly forces. The North Korean gunners knew this, and it sure made it easier for them to know our course into the target. Later in the day the division flew a CAP mission. Soon after reaching our orbital station we were vectored out by the CIC controller to intercept an USAF RB-45 photo-recon bomber. Needless to say we saw it, but to make an intercept was impossible. It was too high and had a speed advantage we could not duplicate because we were still heavy with fuel. It was a good thing that it was a friendly.

While we were playing games in the sky, the other jet squadron, VF-154, lost their first pilot when LTJG Anderson M. Clemmons' aircraft was hit south of Tanchon and he crashed without ejecting from the crippled jet. It was more than likely that AAA fire had hit him as well as the aircraft that brought him down. On the 25th the air group flew sorties against the coastal defense guns that had been shelling the friendly islands and the US warships in the Wonsan area. We flew, however, from Songjin to Kilchu on a reconnaissance flight. We were briefed that both of these towns were well protected with many AAA guns. We flew in at 20,000 feet and passing to the side of the town rolled into a high-speed pass over the Kilchu. The enemy's response was light while we kept going along our assigned route. Just before Songjin we broke off our mission and climbed south to return to the task force. Not much to see, so we just blew more holes in the railroad roadbed. The flight leader picked a spot that was free of known AAA. I also made sure to pull out of my dive high enough to avoid the ever-present small-arms fire.

My long-time flying buddy, Larry Quiel, was killed that morning when he stalled and crashed immediately after takeoff. His aircraft hit the water in a left-wing-down attitude, and the plane cartwheeled and disintegrated upon impact. Only a small amount of floatable aircraft parts and a few pieces of Larry's personal equipment were found during the search by the helicopter and one of the destroyers. I was assigned the very emotional difficult task of doing an inventory of Larry's effects. It was one of the most difficult tasks I have ever done. I had known Larry since July of 1949, almost four years. He was a great guy and a good pilot. I personally missed him, and I still remember him to this day with a lump in my throat. His loss made me even more bitter about the endless missions that seemed to go on and on with no end in sight. How many more of us would not come back? The odds were certainly not in our favor.

The task force replenished on the 26th, and in the afternoon the ship conducted gunnery practice. Just try to nap with those guns firing. The air group flew 99 sorties on the 27th, including night hecklers northeast of Hamhung along the coast. Prior to the night hecklers, the daylight flights continued close-air-support missions aided by our division performing the flak-suppression duties once again. We were getting good at destroying these North Korean gun emplacements or driving them off of the guns, allowing the props a flak-free attack. Once they started to fire on the attacking props, they gave way their position, and the controller would have us strike them with our 260-pound fragmentation bombs. With those bombs you did not need to make a direct hit because the shrapnel from the bomb going off 50 feet above the ground spread out over a large area. That either kept them in their holes or they were either killed or wounded. Other jet divisions made strikes against personnel and supply areas in the same sector of the front lines. In addition to the close-air-support mission, we flew another CAP that was as boring as could be. After all the attacks, everyone returned safely to the ship.

Air operations on the 28th were limited because of the inclement weather conditions that moved in and covered North Korea. Only 64 sorties were flown, but we got stuck with another CAP. We burned up almost 3,500 gallons of aviation gasoline boring holes in the sky. The other jet squadron, VF-154, had a second death when LTJG Russell J. Lear was killed when his aircraft exploded after being hit by flak. He crashed without ejecting while on a mission in the Wonsan area. The enemy gunners were getting better and better with all the practice we gave them. On the 29th, the weather moved in, and all but a few weather reconnaissance sorties were flown. The weather improved some, but TF 77 had to replenish on the 30th. With better weather, the target-towing airplane arrived, and in the afternoon the ship conducted AAA gunnery practice. There would be little daytime sleeping during this activity. If I didn't have to stand gunnery safety officer I usually went to the officer's wardroom to play cards, backgammon, or shoot the breeze with other members of the squadron over the usual cup of good Navy coffee.

Beginning in the month of May, flight operations became more frequent as the weather was very good for flying almost all week until May 7th. On May 1st the *Princeton* was the late carrier, so air operations began for us after the arrival of dawn. The air group concentrated its attacks on the enemy's coastal defense guns on the Hodo Pando Peninsula. The naval forces had come under increasingly intense shore gunfire. During the month of April an all-time high of 2,091 rounds were fired against ships of TF 95. Our division was not scheduled for this type of mission, but flew one of those exciting CAP missions instead. We burned up another 3,500 gallons of fuel making contrails in the sky. Our only relief from the boredom was to intercept the returning flights. After landing I had reached a milestone in my flying career, my 100th combat mission. Like so many things about the Korean War, it meant nothing to the Navy. It was just another day.

A total of 113 sorties were flown for the entire day. This included the night hecklers who were launched just at dusk to attack vehicle traffic around Wonsan. When they returned about 10:00 P.M. one of the ADs was involved in a night deck crash on recovery when the aircraft piloted by LT Vince Mahoney flipped upside down after floating up the deck and hitting the barriers while still airborne. He received only minor injuries as a result of the crash. A little black humor took place when the crash crew raced out to get the pilot out of the airplane. It was pitch dark and only red flashlights were being used. The Catholic chaplain knew who was flying, so he raced out with the crew on to the flight deck. He found the pilot's arm and realized it was covered with a warm fluid what he was sure to be blood. He began to recite the last rites of the church when a weak voice was heard from inside the cockpit. "Damn it, Father, I'm not dead yet." It wasn't blood, but hydraulic fluid. May 2nd found me again as duty officer, and I did not fly. The air group did fly some Cherokee strikes with excellent results. The weather deteriorated in the afternoon, cutting down on the number of sorties. All told, 91 sorties were flown.

On May 3rd I made up for not flying the day before, and I was launched twice. The first mission was more difficult than most. We were assigned the task of trying to hit the enemy's coastal defense guns on the Hodo Pando Peninsula. These enemy's guns were well hidden and difficult to destroy unless it was with a direct hit. We used our 250-lb. bombs trying to do the job. That meant making multiple runs dropping only one at a time. It gave the enemy AAA gunners a lot of practice. Some of the shore gun emplacements could only be attacked in one direction. Not the best or easiest thing to do when being shot at. We all made it back safely without any known flak holes. How lucky could we be? I guess the duty gunners were either tired or had bad eyesight. The second mission was a routine CAP. Ugh, it was so boring. The only excitement was when we passed the starboard side and began the process for our landing. Then all boredom ended and the nerves were taut to make a good, safe landing. The LSO graded us on every landing, but the main reason was I wanted to stay out of the barrier no matter what.

On that same day, LTJG Joe Perry flying with his division made a direct hit on one of those gun emplacements, causing a large secondary explosion. He must have set off the stored ammo in the cave. The crew on the island and ships in the area were delighted with the results. The night hecklers had a field day once it got dark hitting truck traffic around Wonsan. They would almost always find vehicle traffic after dark. They stayed hidden all day and came out like rats at night. There were 105 sorties flown by the air group this day. Right on schedule the task force replenished on May 4th, but in the afternoon the ship did not conduct gunnery practice due the inclement weather that moved in bringing rain, wind and low clouds.

The frontal condition passed that night, and the weather cleared on the 5th. The air group went back to the attack. Our division was again assigned the coastal defense guns around Wonsan and the Hodo Pando area. These were the same gun emplacements we tried to hit before, and again they were difficult to destroy because of their well-constructed layout. We attacked with shallow dives and even tried to do masthead bombing. With these guns it was difficult to know if we made a direct hit. After our bombing attack on these guns with our external ordnance we checked up on the airfields north of Wonsan. The division was in a spread-out formation, flying low and fast to evade the AAA. There was no apparent activity at the fields as far as we could tell. We made no attacks because there wasn't anything worthwhile. As part of the control of the air, the USAF listed 30 major North Korean airfields to be kept unserviceable. The Navy was assigned six of these airfields all of them in the area between Wonsan and Hamhung.

Meanwhile the Corsair squadron, VF-152, lost another pilot, ENS William M. Quinley, when his aircraft was hit during a naval gunfire-spotting mission in the same Wonsan area we had bombed. The flight he was with encountered heavy flak, and his aircraft was spotted burning on the ground after crashing.

There weren't any signs that the pilot survived. On the plus side, the results of the day showed that the air group had flown 111 sorties for the day.

On the 6th the division was assigned another CAP, while the air group made raids on the Komdok mining area destroying a processing plant. Other attacks were made against supply and troop concentrations as well as a number of close-air-support missions by the props. A total of 101 sorties were flown for the day. It was another black day for the air group, however. First, LT Leland R. Rickey, VF-152, was shot down during a strike south of Wonsan. Later in the day my squadron lost another pilot when ENS Francis (Frank) Painter was killed while trying to ditch in the sea after his aircraft had been severely damaged by AAA gunfire north of Tanchon. He had flown his badly damaged aircraft towards the coast, all the time leaking fuel. He wanted to eject over land, but the division leader, LT William (Bill) Hitt encouraged him to stay with the plane as long as possible. He reached the coast but was too low to eject and set himself up for a ditching. His attempt to make a successful ditching ended in disaster when he touched down, hitting the water too fast and hard, causing the airplane to explode and disintegrate upon impact. The F9F was not the best aircraft for ditching because often the nose section broke off and injured the pilot, or the engine exploded when the water entered the hot engine area. He sank with the aircraft with no chance of survival. These deaths hit all of us very hard. The flak was heavy and well aimed, so it was always in my mind when I crossed the coast line. Will this be my turn?

The good weather did not hold, and it became overcast once again on the 7th. There was little flying except weather reconnaissance, ASW and CAP missions. There were only a total of 19 sorties flown. I did not participate. The task force replenished on May 8th but with poor weather in the afternoon the ship did not conduct gunnery practice. It was a welcome respite from the endless missions we were flying. There were plenty of signs of fatigue showing among the pilots.

The weather cleared some the following day, the 9th and the air group tried to go back to the attack, but was forced into a reduced schedule by the marginal weather. For our first mission our division was assigned flak suppression for a Cherokee strike on supply areas in the east and central front. The division was also assigned a CAP for its second flight of the day. Being the first to be launched the flight joined up in a running climb. The flight leader checks in with the CIC air controller and is given a vector to fly to our orbital station. As we climbed to our assigned altitude, the current CAP was released and it dove for the task force to make it in time for recovery. We reached our assigned altitude of 30,000 feet and started our endless orbit. We flew four minutes in one direction, made our 180-degree turn using up another two minutes, and flew another four minutes in the other direction and continued this endless routine for the most of the mission. The flight spread out to make it easier for the four sets of eyes to keep scanning the sky. One really never knew if the enemy jets could approach undetected. It was a known fact that the task force's radar was often very limited when it came to picking up jets at higher altitudes.

About 15 minutes into the flight, the CIC Flight Director Controller called the flight leader, Paul Goodwin. "Blue One, this is Eskimo, vector three five zero, Buster, over. Paul, answer, Eskimo, Blue One, Wilco." (The command "Buster" meant for the flight to go to a maximum-engine-power setting.) That was surprising because we had never had that command given before. The controller's radio call was followed by another call, "Blue One, this is Eskimo, unknown bogies twenty miles, angels unknown."

I thought, *Gads, something has shown up on the radar that has upset CIC.* It was too early for any returning flights, so it seemed very unusual.

The flight leader returned his call, "Eskimo, this is Blue One, request altitude of bogie."

For whatever reason, the FDO controller's return call was, "Blue One, this is Eskimo, no altitude information available."

I suspected the radar was not performing up to par. We closed rapidly on the target but without any altitude information the target could be at any altitude. The CIC's radar return showed that our "blips" had merged, and the radio call from the controller said, "Blue One, this is Eskimo; your blips have merged; reverse course to one seven zero."

We still could not see anything. The flight leader immediately gave us a hand signal that he was going to drop his dive brakes and head down in a steep, diving turn. His radio call was, "Eskimo, this is Blue One, reversing course, diving to lower altitude, over."

This brought a "Roger" from the controller. His voice gave me the feeling that it was getting tense and exciting aboard the ships of the task force.

Riding the mach needle we made a high-speed descent closing from the rear of the bogies. At about 18,000 feet the flight spotted the aircraft ahead flying at about 15,000 feet. The flight leader sang out, "Tally-ho, Eskimo, this is Blue One. Have the bogey in sight."

217

The FDO radio back, "Blue One, this is Eskimo; requested immediate recognition, over."

"Eskimo, this is Blue One, Wilco."

Closing rapidly they could see that they were twin-engine propeller aircraft. Could they possibly be the Russian made PE-2? We were too far away at that moment.

He radioed his first impressions. "Eskimo, this is Blue One. The pair of aircraft are twin-engine flying at angels 15, over."

"Blue One, this is Eskimo; need immediate recognition, stress immediate."

The flight leader's call must have set off the alarm bells with the task force. All ships were ready to go to general quarters. Things were really getting tense. The next hand signal from the flight leader was to change the selector switch from the charge position on our 20-mm cannons to the firing position. The four aircraft were flying lose, and so he pushed the second section out even more so each pair had an aircraft to aim at. My heartbeat was up, and the tension was rising fast.

We were closing fast, and I thought to myself, *Was this going to be my first attack on an enemy aircraft?*

Now we had closed to about 2,500 feet, and he could see the aircraft clearly. They were Grumman F7F twin-engine fighters. "Eskimo, this is Blue One; bogeys are friendly, Fox Seven Fox."

We were told earlier in the tour that only the Marines had them and they used them for night fighter and photo planes. They must have been on a familiarization flight of Northeast Korea and took a shorter course across the ocean from the far northeast of North Korea headed for the bomb line and home. After the flight leader radioed his sightings everyone relaxed. By this time we were on top of them. We buzzed those two aircraft really close, and the pilots were really startled. Paul, the flight leader finally got them on the "guard" or the emergency radio channel and requested that they should check in with the task forces CIC. I do not know how much trouble they got into, but both the task force and we were ready to blow them out of the sky if they came much closer. We all relaxed and headed back to our station, turning our gun switches to safe. The adrenaline had been flowing for each of us. That was the closest I ever came to firing on an aircraft. I realized that my flight suit was damp and my heart rate was up there. At the end of air operation the air group did manage to fly a total of 82 sorties. All strike aircraft returned safely to the ship.

The good weather did not hold, and it became overcast on the 10th, limiting the action except for weather reconnaissance, ASW and CAP sorties to 26. I did not even get dressed in flight gear. The same thing happened on the following day, when only 11 sorties were flown. To relive the boredom Bill Jones had worked out an arrangement with the ship's officer of the deck (OD) to fire our pistols. Several of us went aft to the fantail for some firing practice. The ship was pitching, and the wind was strong, but we had a great time burning up our 38-caliber ammunition trying to hit those tin cans we tossed overboard. Almost all the cans were safe from our gunfire. That night the task force moved south for replenishment on May 12th.

The weather finally cleared on the 13th and the air group flew 113 sorties. Our division flew a CAP and then on the second flight of the day late in the afternoon the division was scheduled for an armed-reconnaissance flight beginning west of Wonsan and then eastward to end close to Wonsan. There was a railroad and vehicle road through the mountains from Wonsan that leads to Yangdok and then all the way to Pyongyang, the North Korean Capital. It was a heavily defended route with many AAA guns of all sizes. We carefully checked the latest overhead photos to spot as many gun positions along the route as possible. I noted them down on my covered map in grease pencil. Being late in the afternoon, the shadows in the valleys were going to make it even more difficult to see very much. Spring had come to the country and the trees had completely leafed out adding to the difficulty of finding targets. By late afternoon any trucks would have long been covered over. It would be after dark before they came back to the highway. We could be lucky, however, but there was not much excitement about finding any meaningful targets. Once the briefing was completed, we got ready for flying. The excitement of the upcoming launch began to take over my thoughts. No matter how many times I did it every launch created an adrenal rush. We manned our aircraft when ordered, and I walked around the aircraft for a quick visual check, got strapped in, and I went through my cockpit pre-flight checklist.

We each carried six 250-pound bombs. That was about the maximum loading for this aircraft. Whether we got airborne with them depended upon the relative wind over the deck. We were parked aft of the deck edge elevator with our wings folded. Earlier the plane captain had spread the wing for the loading of the ordnance. The bomb-loaded wings were folded, and the aircraft positioned with the plane's tailpipe directed outboard at a 45-degree angle. It is not always possible to load this size bomb with the wings folded. There is too much weight to lift that high up on the folded wing.

The task force, now with three carriers began its turn into the wind for launch. It was always an impressive sight to me as the task force of over twenty ships swung into the wind. Admiring the view was quickly ended as the air boss gave the orders to start the engines of the Combat Air Patrol (CAP) jets already spotted on the catapults. After the command, the three-wheeled starter jeeps made their way down the fight deck, starting each jet in turn. After I had an engine light off, I went through my take-off checklist and when finished kept an eye out for my plane director. The flight-deck crew had already put on a tiller bar on the nose wheel of my airplane while I was getting ready for my mission. The sound of more jets turning up began to get louder as the ship approached the wind line. Just as the ship reached the wind line, the two jets on the catapults were at full power and were shot off, one after the other.

The plane director's upraised arms with his fists closed for me to lock my brakes caught my eye, and he then signaled the deck crew to pull the wheel chocks. I taxied forward upon his upraised arms giving me a come-on signal. Next, he signaled me to spread my wings by closing his arms across his chest and then spreading his arms outwards. With my wings down and locked, I gave him a thumbs-up, and he motioned me to start forward. Starting to roll forward, his right arm came down pointing to the deck signaling me to hit my left wheel brake turning the aircraft towards the catapults. Moving forward one plane length at a time as each plane was catapulted, I was soon next in line behind the blast shield. As the jet ahead left the deck, the blast deflector was lowered, and I was signaled to move forward again. With a good wind over the deck, a higher rpm was needed just to get the airplane moving again. The catapult crew picked up the tiller bar, and I rolled into position over the catapult track. Properly positioned, the plane director commanded me to lock my brakes with two closed fists. The catapult crew rolled under the plane and the hold back mechanism was attached to the rear underside of the airplane. At the same time, the bridle was hooked to the aircraft and around the catapult shuttle. The plane director then signaled me to release my brakes with a rapid opening and closing of both his fist. I felt the catapult shuttle moving to tighten the slack in the bridle, locking my airplane to the catapult. The catapult crew had already rolled out from under the plane, and I was now almost ready to get shot off.

I dropped my feet from the brakes and lowered my flaps to the take-off position when given the command by the catapult plane director. He put both hands together parallel with the deck, and holding his wrist together opened and closed his hands.

The catapult officer turned towards me and took charge. With a thumbs-up from the catapult crewman in the catwalk that there was a green light meaning there was a good head of hydraulic pressure, he gave me the two-finger turn up. I moved the throttle smoothly forward until it reached 100% power. One glance at the entire set of engine instruments told me everything was okay for launch. I looked directly at the catapult officer and saluted him with my right hand that I was ready to go. I immediately grabbed the control stick, putting my head back against the head rest while putting my right elbow in my gut. In the next two seconds I went from about 33 knots of air speed to 125 knots, and I was airborne. Free of the catapult acceleration, my head jerked forward slightly, and I was off. All this took less than thirty seconds to accomplish after the aircraft ahead of me. Leaving the deck at close to stall speed with the load I was carrying, it was just a reflective motion to move my left hand that I had wrapped around the throttle and the catapult post moving the landing gear lever to the up position. There was a momentary noise as the landing gear door opened, the gear folded into the wheel well, and the landing gear doors closed. As soon as this happened I felt the plane start accelerating. Closing the canopy and raising the flaps was next as I picked up air speed to reach climbing speed. I passed close by one of the destroyers that were part of the task-force screen. I gave them a wing waggle plus a hand wave as I passed 100 feet off to the side at 50 feet and I was off to join the others.

The flight to the coast was routine as we climbed slowly to 20,000 feet. It was a beautiful day with dark blue water and bright blue sky. In a short time the green North Korean coast came into view, and soon the flight passed over the coast. It was so peaceful, yet it was fraught with danger every minute while we were in enemy territory. The flight leader changed course slightly to head for our pushover point to start our mission. All was quiet without any indication of what was to come. We maintained radio silence to reduce the chance of detection.

We reached our pushover point and dove down with speed brakes out. Reaching the proper altitude over the ground we took up our positions and soon started the actual reconnaissance part of the flight. In short order, the flight leader spotted a road bridge that had been repaired. We circled around and made a shallow dive-bombing attack to hit the bridge. Dust and smoke obscured the results of our strike, but it appeared that we had hit the bridge. The photo plane could determine what our damage was later. That is if they got there soon enough. Otherwise the Koreans quickly repaired it again. Further along we attacked a small valley off the main one because truck tracks in the dirt from the main road up into the valley indicated that there may be trucks stored in the area. The remaining bombs that were not dropped on the bridge found something because there were additional fires burning when we left. By this time, we were getting close to the Wonsan and needed to avoid the AAA guns that ringed the city. The flight leader started his climb to altitude with everyone following. Just as we passed over the harbor area it happened.

There was no radio communication but out of my right eye's peripheral vision I saw an F9F moving fast about 200 yards away. Just as I turned my head to look the canopy flew off and the ejection seat came out of the plane. It was Dick Clinite! I pushed my microphone button; "Mayday, Mayday, Mayday, Blue 3 has ejected." To this day, I do not know what happened to cause him to eject. The aircraft was flying in a wing-level attitude, slightly nose up. There was no fire, smoke, or fluid trailing back from the plane, nor could I see any indication of flak damage. His parachute opened, and I saw his plane roll slowly over to the right and dive straight into the harbor. He had ejected at about 8,000 feet, and as soon as he was clear of the ejection seat he opened his parachute. I flew slowly by him and as I did he waved to me, holding his D ring with the ripcord attached. He appeared to be okay. The weather was clear, but there was a strong wind blowing from west to east that was moving him out to sea. That was good and bad. Good because he was clear of landing in enemy territory, but it did mean he would land out to sea in the wind-whipped water. As I followed him down, flying big figure eights, the flight leader and wingman staying at altitude had alerted the rescue ships. The helicopter was launched from the LST up the coast from the Wonsan area and was headed towards us where he would be expected to hit the water.

Then disaster struck. The wind was blowing very strong off of the mountains, and when he hit the water he was unable to free himself from his parachute harness. He struck the water hard because of the wind drifting him fast over the surface. I watched in horror as his parachute continued to drag him through the water. I was helpless to do anything. Flying low and slow above him I made large figure eights to keep him in sight and to give the helicopter a target area to head for. It seemed like forever, but finally the helicopter was over him, the helicopter pilot used the down wash from his rotator blades to collapse the parachute. I saw the crewman descend to the water close by him and I figured my job was done. There was nothing more that I could do. Unknown to me, just as I left the area the helicopter had to bring the crewman back aboard and head for its base because it could not lift Clinite and his billowed parachute into the helicopter. The helicopter had alerted the closest surface ship in the area which moved in for the pickup.

Now it was my turn to start to worry. I had to quickly leave the area and gain some altitude because I was getting dangerously low on fuel. The other two had been at altitude, and they headed off for the task force with considerable more fuel than I had. I noted that I had only 1,200 pounds of fuel to fly out to the task force and land aboard. It was going to be very close. I climbed slowly to 10,000 feet, carefully monitoring my fuel-flow instrument, trying to maintain the highest air speed for the least amount of fuel used. Adding to my growing concern was the growing darkness. I had never made a night carrier landing, but I figured that might happen. The two others were about 30 miles ahead of me and with more airspeed were able to make a normal landing. They were safely aboard, but I was still many miles out. My first radio contact with the *Princeton* began the final process. I squawked my IFF on radio command, and they picked me up on their radar. The CIC's FDO gave me a slight course correction to the task force. They asked for my fuel state, and I stated I had 800 pounds of fuel. I still had too many miles to go. Their next message was that I was cleared to land on the first carrier I could find. The task force was steaming into the wind with all the carriers having a ready deck. Then it hit me, there wasn't another aircraft airborne and this entire fleet was waiting for just me. Talk about a lot of pressure. I watched the fuel gauge slowly move towards zero passing through 600 pounds. With this low fuel state I was in no condition to do anything but make a straight in approach. I had just enough fuel for one pass. I had never made a straight in approach, but there was no time to be concerned about that. That red fuel light had been burning all too long, and I knew that landing had to be right on. A wave off was an invitation for a swim. I picked out a carrier that appeared to be the closest and headed right towards it. It turned out that it was the *Princeton*, and heading directly towards the stern I pulled the throttle to idle to save as much fuel as possible. It was going to be a really tight squeeze to make it before the engine stopped from fuel starvation. I found some mental strength to overcome my fatigue to carefully go through the landing checkoff list. I could never figure out how I found that extra measure to see me through this landing. This was going to be the most important carrier landing I had ever done.

The LSO visually picked me up about 600 yards astern of the ship in the growing darkness as I started to close in on the flight deck. All the color had gone out of the sea, and now everything was dark gray, except the wake of the ship that glowed white head of me as I continued my let down. I kept my eyes moving so I wouldn't stare at one place for too long. I kept tell myself, *Concentrate, concentrate.* I leveled out a little too high and a little too fast, mainly because I was so light. I was now down below 300 pounds, almost a thousand pounds lighter than normal. I eased up on the throttle, losing altitude, while at the same time raising the nose slightly to bleed off the excess airspeed. I was given a high signal, and then I got my cut from the LSO. I eased the nose down and then flared out just as my tail hook grabbed the number-two or -three arresting wire. All I cared about was that I was aboard, and I wanted to find out what had happened to my roommate. I rolled back to let the arresting wire fall way from the tail hook and expected to get a come-on signal to move forward. The plane director instead gave me the two-closed-fists signal to hold my brakes while two deck crewmen ran out and tossed chocks around my wheels. I got the engine-cut signal as I felt the ship heel over as the task force turned out of the wind. I just sat there in my parked aircraft. I had made it with only a few gallons of fuel left! The entire task force was just waiting for me to land. A plane captain climbed up to the cockpit and with the plane all tied down, he offered and I accepted his help unbuckling my shoulder straps and lap belt, then the parachute harness. I was so tired that it was all I could do just to get out of the aircraft and with the help of a crewman stagger with weak knees up the deck against the wind to the catwalk, and down to the ready room.

Walking into the ready room, the Teletype machine in the right front area of the ready room was pounding out the message that came from the USS *Samuel N. Moore* that had been sent to the area. "Pilot was picked up, pilot dead, drown." I was totally exhausted mentally, physically and emotionally. I just sat there completely numb. No one asked because they could see that I was drained. I slowly pulled off my flight gear and put on my uniform. I was functioning like a zombie. I finally made it back to the stateroom somehow and sat down. That is when it hit me, and I lost it. I pounded the desk in complete frustration as the tears rolled down my cheeks. I could not have done anything to help him. I was so close but so far away. I just had to watch him drown. The picture of the parachute billowing in the wind on the dark blue sea dragging him through the water will be in my mind's eye forever. It was a hell of way for a great guy, a good friend, and fine pilot to die.

His body was recovered without injury other than those sustained by his hard water landing. The destroyer that picked him up from the water, transferred his remains to the battleship USS *New Jersey* the following day by whale boat, and his body was later shipped back to the states for burial. The next step for me would be another emotional roller coaster ride. I had to inventory his effects, tossing what was not useable; selecting what was to be sent back to his wife, Pam, and what could be recycled and used by his roommates. That would happen, however after the ship left the task force. Tomorrow was another workday. Dick's death didn't give me a holiday. It left me only with even more bitterness towards this stupid war. I kept flying, and slowly I became mentally and emotional exhausted from the endless cycle of combat flying. The mind and body can just take so much. I woke up tired and numb. It took a major effort to get the energy flowing when I climbed up the flight deck to man my aircraft so as to be safe to fly. I certainly did not want to become a statistic as well.

The weather remained clear on the 14th, and the air group flew an increasing load of 117 sorties. Our division flew two attack missions. The first was against supply areas around the city of Wonsan and the second was flak suppression for a combined strike against Pachunjang in the afternoon. We were very alert for AAA gunfire. We didn't want a repeat of the previous day. It was on this day that I flew my 100th offensive combat mission in the Korean War. That didn't count the CAP flights or other non combat sorties. Once again it meant nothing to the Navy. No recognition, no pat on the back, just keep going! It was also the last day on the line for the air group and ship for this period.

I added to my logbook another 23 flights and 33 hours during this period on the line. Out of the twenty-nine days with Task Force 77 there were 18 days of flight operation. The other eleven were either replenishment days or the weather was too poor for combat flying. It was a tough period for the squadrons. The air group lost four pilots during this period. The toughest part was for the four of us who roomed together. We had made great plans for an R&R in Hong Kong, but with death of first Larry Quiel and then Dick Clinite, our roommate, the three of us remaining were really not up to having an exciting time. It seemed that the law of averages had finally caught up with the eight of us. We were now down to six. How many more deaths would there be before either the war was over or the tour would end? Time was not on our side! The carrier replenished at sea on the 15th and then proceeded to Sasebo, Kyushu, Japan, for additional stores on the morning of the 16th. The carrier left Sasebo that evening for Hong Kong. The first day out I began the difficult task of inventorying Dick's effects. Once again, I had a very difficult and emotional job to do. One minute he was among us, and then the next minute he was gone. I could not stop crying as I looked at his effects. Damn this stupid war!

During this longer tour in the task force, the F9F-5 suffered from several ordnance problems that reduced the effectiveness of the missions we flew as well as endangered the deck crews. The first major problem was with the bomb racks. Quoting from the USS *Princeton* action report:

> Difficulty has been encountered with the Aero 14A bomb racks in use on the F9F. [The F9F-5 was equipped with a different bomb rack than the F9F-2.] The Aero 14A bomb rack suffered from design defects that affected loading, maintenance and releasing bombs. In accordance with Task Force 77 directives, the racks are now disassembled after each malfunction and a report was made on the failure. It has been found that bent and broken sears and defective arming solenoids are causing the most trouble.

The most troubling problem from the pilot's standpoint was to carry a dud bomb or worse, bring the bomb back that could not be released. Quoting further from the same action report:

> Aero 14A racks, while an improvement over the previous racks, are generally not sturdy enough to stand up under the rigorous conditions that must be imposed upon them. Bombs up to, and including five hundred pounds must be supported on taxiing aircraft with the wings in folded position, on catapult launches and on arrested landings.

The second ordnance problem was with the 5-in. rockets carried on the jets. The rockets were of WW II design and were failing to fire because of broken electrical connections. This was attributed to the jets' much higher air speed. Directly from the action report: "The pigtail electrical connection for rockets is the weakest link in the rocket system. The high speeds of the F9F whip the wires into pieces or sawed the wires at the rocket base."

The result of these types of failures was that the rockets' motors did not ignite, and the rockets came back aboard with the airplane. There were 30 cases of hung rockets, representing 5% of the rockets carried. It was not a very satisfying record. Fortunately for the flight-deck crew, most of the rockets stayed on the rack during arrested landing.

The last problem area was with the 20-mm guns. The guns failed on an average of one stoppage per 1,800 rounds. The F9F-5 carried four 20-mm cannons with each carrying 600 rounds of ammo. That meant that someone had a jammed gun on almost every mission. It sure was not a comforting fact. Compared to the 50-caliber gun, it was a very high failure rate. The 50-caliber gun performance was one stoppage per 8,500 rounds. It appeared that the demands of wartime flying were ahead of technology for these new jet aircraft. The Navy seemed to be running on a peacetime schedule even though we were fighting a war.

Now let me tell you one of the funnier events that happened during this period. I had just made a normal carrier landing in my trusty jet, and after the plane director had given me the hook-up signal he waved me forward. He held up one finger, the first one on his right hand telling me I was to taxi all the way forward to park up near the bow. I gave it almost full throttle to get the airplane rolling against the strong headwind coming down the deck. I picked up a lot of speed to be able to clear the barriers and the barricade so that the deck was ready for the next aircraft that was nearing its final approach. Just as I crossed the barriers, the flight deck officer moved away from the island and held up two fingers indicating he wanted me to go to the deck edge elevator. I held up my right hand and raised two fingers and then shook my head telling him I could not do it. I dropped one finger and to this day do not know which one it was. I was traveling too fast to make a safe turn with my wings almost folded and was afraid of turning the plane over, blocking the flight deck. I parked my aircraft and headed down to the pilot's ready room. I was there only a few minutes when my CO burst into the room yelling at me that I had given the "finger" to the flight deck officer. After he stopped shouting at me, I simply told him that I did not. He insisted that I did. I explained to him what had happened, and he started to calm down. In any case, I found the flight deck officer after recovery and told him why I refused his direction. He was not bothered by it, and realized that his plane director had already given me the signal to go forward, and that there was no way I could have made the turn safely. I said that my CO said that I had given him the "finger," and he laughed. He said he never saw it that way. Such is life!

The ship was en route to Hong Kong for two days arriving on the following day May 19th. After the cool weather in the Sea of Japan, the hot humid weather Hong Kong was a shock. We took in the sights and drank a number of toasts to our departed buddies. I treated myself to getting some civilian clothes made and purchased additional items of civilian clothes. Up until now, I had very little reason to wear civilian clothes. Life moves on!

The USS *Princeton* anchored in the Hong Kong harbor for seven days. The minute it was docked, small boats surrounded the ship. It was so bad that the crew broke out the fire hoses and drove them away. Finally there was no choice, but to use the "bumboat" to ferry the officers and crew to and from the dock. What a time it was.

We rented a suite of rooms in a small hotel, the Miramar, on the mainland and enjoyed the sightseeing, shopping, and the night life. Except to stand the duty as SDO one day, we soaked up the food, booze, and we slept late. We hired a houseboy to take care of our clothes and make breakfast for us. Every morning when we woke up he had pressed our clothes, washed our underwear, shined our shoes, and had a great-big pot of freshly made coffee just waiting. What a life! He did not speak any English, but sign language was all that was necessary. The second day he arranged for a tailor to come to the room, and we all got measured for clothing. Two days later, our new clothes were delivered, and every things fit like a glove. It was a great rest, but much of the fun just wasn't there. Our hearts were not into much celebration after what had happened.

The ship departed Hong Kong for Yokosuka after about a week's stay and arrived in Japan on the 30th. Prior to arrival, still well at sea, the ship launched a large part of the air group's aircraft to NAS Atsugi, Japan south east of Tokyo. Depending upon our assignments, we either stayed there or went back to the ship for other duties. A little over a week later, on June 9th, the ship left NOB Yokosuka. Clear of the mouth of the bay and out of the sea-lanes it was ready to recover aircraft. We took off from NAS Atsugi and flew back all the aircraft to rendezvous with the ship. Arriving overhead each division entered the landing pattern, and the 36 aircraft were recovered. As the ship plowed through the Pacific Ocean we did not have an awareness of what was ahead of us. For the pilots it seemed to be back to the same daily routine, but it would turn out not be.

Chapter 15
Korea, the Longest Tour

While the ship was in port for maintenance, the communist army launched a major ground offensive against the II ROK and X U.S. Corps along the east central and eastern fronts. Despite poor weather, the Navy's effort was to help turn back this attack with an all-out aerial support. When the USS *Princeton* and its escorts joined the task force on the morning of June the 11th to participate in this "Herculean" effort we were briefed for a full flight schedule. With the arrival of the USS *Princeton* the task force was now made up of four carriers. This was the first time during the conflict that four large carriers were active against the enemy at the same time since WW II. The *Princeton*'s air group went back on the attack and with the longer days of late spring, were able to fly a high of 135 sorties. After a 29-day lay off, we got back into shape on the first day. Our division flew three separate missions, all of the same kind, that first day back. These were bombing missions like we were high-level bombers. The USAF had been using the MPQ-1 radar system to control bombing for some time. In late May the task force launched its first flight to familiarize the Navy pilots with this system. The technique was to fly in below the main line of resistance for identification and not to be taken for an enemy flight. Crossing the coastline the flight leader made radio contact with the radar controller as we spread out in a loose formation flying at 18,000 feet. Coming in from the coast the controller would give us specific vectors (headings) to fly to be sure he had the right flight on his radar screen. Then when all was set, we made a right turn on orders from the radar controller and took up the heading and Indicated Air Speed (IAS) to maintain. All spread out we waited for the command from the radar controllers to drop all our bombs through the overcast. Just before drop, the controller would alert us and give us a count down to the command to drop. "Three, two, one, drop," and 24 bombs left our aircraft to hit somewhere close to the front lines. At the same moment of release we felt the weight loss as each plane dropped 1,500 pounds. It was weird, to say the least.

Late in the afternoon on the third flight, one of my 250-pound bombs did not release from the bomb rack. I had no choice but to bring it back to the ship. This is one of those things that could happen, but nevertheless, I was very apprehensive about bringing this damn bomb back aboard the ship. The bomb rack had apparently failed, or the bomb was jammed such that the bomb would not release. On the way back to the ship I had my wingman carefully inspect the bomb to check on the status of the arming wires. If one of those wires had pulled loose then the bomb was armed, and I would have to eject. No one in his right mind would attempt to land either on the carrier or at K-18 with an armed bomb that could drop off and instantly explode. An earlier attempt to land at K-18 with a hung bomb by an AD pilot ended up with him being killed by the explosion when the 500 pound bomb dropped off upon touchdown at K-18 and exploded under his aircraft. The report back from my buddy was that both wires were in place.

Before arriving back at the task force, I pulled out of formation and tried every trick I knew to shake that damn 250-pound bomb off. I tried negative "Gs" as well as "skidding" the aircraft with rudder deflection first right and then left. Nothing worked! The flight leader reported to the carrier CIC that he had one aircraft with hung ordnance. Their instructions to him were that I would be the last plane aboard and for me to call in when I started my final 180-degree turn for landing. As the task force turned into the wind our flight was given clearance to descend to enter the landing pattern. The dive brake extension signal was given and with full brakes out we started to make our descent. I broke off from the formation at 2,000 feet as directed by the ship's air controller. I pulled up my dive brakes and set the throttle to maintain only 180 knots. I set myself up to orbit outboard from the approach pattern while all the other returning aircraft went into the landing pattern. This gave me even more time to worry about coming aboard with this bomb.

When the last jet division entered the landing pattern, I moved in behind them to start my own approach, taking a longer interval than usual behind the plane ahead, so the pilot before me could get parked, shut down and get off the flight deck. The air boss warned the flight-deck crew that the last aircraft had a hung bomb. Everyone knew that the flight deck was not a place to be when an aircraft with a hung bomb was coming aboard. I made my radio call as I rolled easily into my shallow turn abeam of the ship's island to start my normal approach.

Landing Signal Officer

Reaching the "groove" with a "Roger" from the LSO, he snapped me a cut. I tried to "grease" the plane onto the deck. It was a good landing, but the damn bomb fell off anyhow. I could not duck because I was all strapped in. The bomb bounced first on its nose then flew up in the air a few feet, and tumbling, it landed on its tail. It then flipped over on its side and slid, nose first, up the deck. It stopped close to the ship's island without going off. Whew! It was a tense few seconds while this played out.

The ordnance-disposal crew waited only a brief moment before they came out of the island. The first ordnance man was looking for the bomb out on the flight deck. It wasn't there. That's because it was only a few feet from where he was standing. He was surprised, but with great care he and his crew picked the bomb up and gently placed it on a bomb cart. It is not an easy job to pick up a 250-pound dead weight. Wheeling it slowly to the port edge of the flight deck, they tossed it over the side and everyone started to breathe again. Especially me! The flight-deck crew reappeared, and the plane director signaled for me to taxi forward. Rolling up the deck I pulled the oxygen mask free as I passed the island with a broad smile. I sure did not consider this a typical flight. Meanwhile, the air group had a busy and successful day without major flak hits on any of the aircraft. It had flown a respectable total of 135 sorties.

The 12th was a marginal flying day with solid cloud cover to 15,000 feet. We flew a CAP mission without incident. I sure needed sun glasses or dark lens in my goggles while flying over this solid overcast. The white clouds reflected back the sunlight with such intensity that it could be painful without those dark-lens goggles on. All I could see was blue sky and white clouds. There was no other color. In the afternoon we again flew another radar-drop mission. The weather continued to get worse, and on the way back it was an instrument let down all the way. We were in the "soup" for half an hour before breaking out below the clouds at 800 feet. We flew in a tight formation because the clouds were so thick that visibility was down to about feet. I was tense all the way, and I was working up a sweat with the cabin heat on full high. It was difficult flying because I had a bad case of vertigo. I had lost all visual reference so I flew with my eyes glued to the wing of the aircraft ahead of me. I had his tip tank only a few feet from my nose with a slight step down to stay out of his wing wash. Just to make it even more exciting in the descent we picked up some ice on the wings but it soon burned off at the lower altitude. We broke out below the clouds, and I could relax a little bit. The air group was limited by the weather and only flew 68 sorties.

The ship refueled that night after flight quarters had been secured. This was a foreshadowing of things to come. The weather improved on the 13th, and we were back to the attack. Our division made a reconnaissance flight over the airfields around Hamhung to verify that there still had been no work done to improve them. Flying low spread out by a hundred feet we could all get a good look at the airfields from different angles. The cloud cover was still present over the front lines, so the second flight of the day was another radar drop. With marginal weather, the division mission was to do high-level bombing once again from 18,000 feet. This time as we approached the drop point, a large caliber

AAA shell exploded right between us, rocking my wingman, Bill Wilds, and me. He was flying in a loose-formation position on me, and the enemy radar controlled gun must have seen us as a single radar return and placed the shot right on target. Fortunately for us, we were far enough apart that neither picked up any flak holes. It sure did startle the hell out of both of us. That was a little too close for comfort. The gun that fired that shell was a big one, and that air bust was big, black, and very ugly. Other than getting a damn good scare the division arrived in time for recovery. After recovery, Bill and I went top side to look at our aircraft to see for ourselves there were no flak holes in either airplane. By the time flight quarters were secured, the air group had flown 138 sorties. That was not bad for the first 3 days back. The ship re-armed from the ammo ship that night after flight quarters.

The 14th was even a busier day than the previous one for all hands. The air group flew a record breaking 152 sorties with our division flying two Cherokee strikes. The first was around Hyon-ni, the second Hoieng. This type of attack is designed to fly in at about 20,000 feet, make a steep dive, get lined up on the target, drop the bombs, and get the hell out of the area as quickly as possible. The AAA had been getting steadily heavier and heavier, as well as becoming very accurate under radar control. Every time I was ready to start the dive, I took a deep breath, rolled into the dive, and hoped for the best. Diving into the muzzle of a lot of AAA guns was not my favorite pastime. I know how a duck feels when he crosses over a number of hunters. After the strike, the division made a reconnaissance trip over the road system looking for targets of opportunity. Finding nothing we returned to the ship with all our 20-mm ammo. The ship once again replenished the fuel burned up from the tanker after flight quarters were ended that night.

The 15th was another repeat of the previous day but even more so. It was a day that Air Group 15 set the record for the highest number of sorties flown by any air group in the Korean War, flying an amazing 184 sorties. Our division on the first mission attacked areas around Changjon and on the second flight hit Song-do. We had racked up 11 flights in five days, and the fatigue level was getting very high for everyone in spite of having almost a month off. With that kind of intensive operation over 20 hours per day it doesn't take long to become tired. There was no question that the ship and air-group crews as well as the pilots were beginning to show the effects of this continuous operation. No matter how we felt, the ship, however, had to rearm during the night as the air group was very quickly emptying the fuel tanks and arsenal with this high level of combat flying. Our stateroom was close to the hangar deck, which meant the rearming and refueling generated one heck of lot of noise. It did not keep me awake very long because I was dead tired.

There was no rest for anyone on the 16th as we all went into another full day of flying. The first mission was to attack a truck storage area west of Anchor Hill along the front lines, and the second one was to attack a truck-parking area at Hoidong-ni. The flight carried six 250-pound bombs and delivered them to a specific target area reported to be a truck shelter area just north of the bomb-line. After the strike was completed we proceeded to fly over our assigned route. It was during this flight that we got caught in a flak trap. Jet strike and reconnaissance flights over the North Korean area are never the same. All the preparation may look the same, but the possibilities of heavy enemy flak, target conditions affecting the approach, weather, and getting hit by AAA are different each time. One of the most important things is to remain alert, keep your plane's track in constant change, and know where everyone else in the flight is located all the time. Navigation over North Korea was not difficult for me after flying so many strike and reconnaissance missions. I probably knew the road and railroad system better in the eastern half of North Korea than I did in northern California. The tactical approach was whenever the lower two planes came under AAA fire; the second section was used as aggressive flak suppressors. In most cases the AAA guns stopped firing whenever the second section's two aircraft open fire with their 20-mm cannons. There were, however, times when they didn't, and a full press attack by the second section was necessary to extract the lower two planes from being shot at without being capable of returning fire. These attacks sure did raise the adrenaline level to a high state for everyone, especially me.

After the first part of our mission was done, the flight took up its secondary mission of flying a road route looking for vehicle activity. It was poor pickings and as the time and fuel were running out the flight was just about ready to climb to altitude and head back to the task force when the flight leader spotted a truck partially hidden on the side of the road. As he headed down for a strafing run on the truck, the second pilot started his dive for a strafing run as well. With both in their run, the flak trap was sprung, and the four well-hidden AAA guns opened up on the flight leader. The tracers from the guns were flying all around him as he started his pull out from the dive. The second pilot shifted his fire from the truck to the AAA guns, trying to give the flight leader covering fire. In the past that had been enough to shut them down, but this group didn't know the rules and kept firing. The flight leader plane cleared the area and climbed rapidly up and away. These gunners, however, were now all firing at the second airplane as I jammed my throttle to full power, rolled over into a near vertical turn, and dropping the nose of my airplane into a dive heading towards the guns to give him firing cover. The gunners were concentrating on the number two so much they did not discover I was coming until I opened fire. I was in a good strafing attack position with lots of air speed for an excellent firing run. As I lined up on the first AAA gun emplacement, which was aimed away from me, I fired a short burst that caught them flat-footed, knocking them out of action.

With a slight back pressure my airplane's nose rising slightly put my gun sight on the second gun emplacement. They had also not spotted me, and I was able to hit them before they could return fire. Two down, two to go! The gunners in the third and fourth emplacements must have either seen me or heard my shells hit the other gun sites and had spotted me. They started to rapidly swing their guns around towards my flight path. As they completed their re-direction of the guns they started to fire as I continued in my firing run. It was too late for them. Their shots were wild, not well aimed, but mine were right on. The frontal profile of a jet is small, but their gun emplacement was much larger. I could see my 20-mm shells exploding right in the third gun emplacement as they did with the other two gun sites. This set of AAA guns stopped firing and it appeared that it was knocked out, as the other two had been. It was hard to tell whether they took cover or if I killed them where they stood.

By this time the fourth gun had moved around and was firing at me with better aim. Raising the nose slightly to line up on the fourth gun emplacement I was running out of altitude and was too damn close. I fired a quick burst and pulled out. I was in a shallow dive so there was not much of a pullout to do. By this time I had used up all my altitude but increased my air speed as I pulled out to a level attitude and crossed over the gun about 25 feet. Not wanting to give them an easy going-away shot, I rolled into a 90-degree left bank, and making a high-G turn flew up a short valley, putting ground between my airplane and their guns before pulling up and climbing to rejoin the flight. This firefight lasted about half the time it took to read this description. At about 470 knots indicated airspeed, the airplane was moving at almost 800 feet per second. A small target moving fast was my primary defense against these gun emplacements. Another defense was my aggressive attack with my four 20-mm cannons. After getting some saliva back into my mouth I was able to find my voice. I radioed the flight leader that I was okay, and in a running rendezvous soon joined up with them for the return trip to the task force.

Back in the ready room, the four of us talked about this hair-raising flight as we were being debriefed. Suddenly the back hatch (door) of the ready room opened and the maintenance Chief Petty Officer walked in to the ready room and asked who was flying 303. I said I was, and without a word handed me a green sprig from a pine tree. Then he said it was found between the wing and tip tank of my airplane. I must have dragged the plane's wing tip through the top of a pine tree in my low-level, very tight 90-degree bank. This kind of low-level flying is not permissible in the states, but in North Korea, there are no such rules. It took a while for me to calm down, and when I did I suddenly felt like a wet towel. The strangest part of this event was it was done in complete radio silence. There were no radio calls or yelling for help. It was a measure of the professionalism of the members of the division. Because of the number of sorties the air group had flown the ship had to once again re-fuel again during the night. I slept well after calming down with a good stiff snort of good old Navy booze supplied by the air group flight surgeon along with one of my own from the house supply.

The weather began to close in on the 17th, and the air group flew only 36 sorties before the task force called it quits. The division tried to attack Tongchon on the East Coast, having to fly under the bad weather. We didn't locate anything because of the low clouds and the general darkness, making visibility very poor. Unloading our bombs on the railroad tracks we headed back to the task force with plenty of fuel. Since starting on the 11th, I had flown one CAP and 13 combat flights over North Korea in the last seven-day period. By that afternoon, all flight operations were cancelled, as the weather closed it. The air group had almost emptied the ships stock of ordnance, so it had to replenish during the night. After supper we watched a classic B-grade movie and then came back to our stateroom. A couple of drinks finished me off, and I fell asleep the minute my head hit the pillow.

The 18th was a welcome relief with bad weather stopping all air operations. It was one very quiet ship. I think I slept for 12 straight hours. The 19th was a marginal flying day, but the division was sent on a close-air-support mission at Suogu. Reaching our target area the flight leader reported in by radio and was assign to a Forward Air Controller (FAC). We were vectored to our general target area, and the flight leader raised the onsite FAC on the radio. This one was airborne, and once contact was made he described what we were to attack. We were to bomb the north side of the ridge close to the top. When questioned by radio about the position of the friendly forces by the flight leader, he said they were on the south side of the ridge near the top. Great, we had 200 yards between the two forces. The FAC made a quick, diving turn and fired a smoke rocket at our assigned target area. Peeling over one section after the other in a tight diving turn, we dove for the area the FAC had marked with his rocket. It was just after dawn, so the air was still without a breeze or air turbulence making it a lot easier for a steady stable dive. We dropped half our load on the first pass and got a "Job well done" for the accuracy of our bombing. The FAC assigned us another target, and we did the same thing. We didn't hear it, but the FAC told us by radio that we were getting a fair amount of small-arms fire and to make any additional dives steeper and faster. We strafed the last target area, and we pulled up, flying south before turning east and home. These dives were difficult because of the small margin between the North Korean or Chinese forces and our own friendly troops. There was no way I knew when we came under AAA fire because in this area the enemy did not use tracers to give their gun position away. CAS was a crapshoot for the pilots. We had to hold a steady dive in order to place our bombs on the specific target but it also made me a good target for the enemy gunners. At least I might have the opportunity to use my excess air speed to let me get over friendly forces if the plane was hit and had to eject. Even with all the small-arms fire that was fired in our direction, we came back without anyone being hit. Lady luck was with me once again.

For the next four days we were all grounded because of very poor flying weather. The ship re-armed on the 20th. Other than that, it was a restful period that we all needed. The weather finally broke up a little on the 24th and the division was back into the air. We attacked targets on the waterfront of the village of Chako in northeast Korea. The weather wasn't good for dive-bombing, but it turned out that the targets were just too good to prevent us from attacking them in any way possible. The bad weather had aided the North Koreans to be able to move supplies down the coast either by rail, small ship, or barge. Between the bombing raids and the constant shore bombardment by the ships of TF 95 the movement was slowed, but not stopped. We were lucky in that there was a backup of supplies in this area along with the watercraft used to move the supplies. I was able to make a number of shallow-glide bomb drops as well as strafing runs. The first run was successful in knocking down a 40-foot pier with two well-placed bombs, and on the second run I strafed and sank a 30-foot barge alongside the pier. Those 20-mm shells made some big holes in the barge. The remaining two bombs were used against four buildings on the waterfront. The bomb hits were right on target, and when I pulled up, the buildings were already burning out of control.

Climbing out of the run with full power I did a climbing 180-degree turn to get oriented to make another run. The last target was a railroad coal-loading station, and I lined up my gun sight on the center of the structure and squeezed the trigger. I held the trigger down to fire a good, long burst. I could see the line of tracers headed right into the target. The HEI shells sparkled as they hit all over the side of the structure. Strafing with the 20-mm cannons created a lot of damage to the mechanism of this coal station. The 20-mm ammo was belted with three types of warheads; one was a high explosive incendiary (HEI), the next was an armor-piecing (AP) head, and the last was a tracer. The AP could do a lot of damage to any metal structure. It was one of my better days. I felt I had done something to slow the supplies to the front lines. The marginal weather, however, restricted the rest of the air group's activities, and so only 90 sorties were flown by the time flight quarters were secured that night.

The weather cleared completely on the 25th and the air group set another record of 172 sorties in one day. We had only one flight, an attack on targets in the Kojo area. With good weather we could come in close to the target. I rolled the airplane over until I was almost inverted while pulling the nose towards me, then rolling upright into a steep dive. I aimed carefully and released high enough to avoid any small-arms fire. The target was clobbered, and we headed along our route, but found nothing. Once again we made it back safely to the ship. The next three days were all washed out due to the bad weather. On the 29th, the weather cleared, and the division was sent to attack the airfield at Kilchu. Air intelligence indicated that there had been enemy activity noticed at this airfield, and we were to check it out. We attacked the damaged building on the airfield and added our own bomb holes to the others already there. We also added a few more craters to the already-damaged runways. I couldn't see any activity or indications that repairs were being made. Sometimes I thought it was just a big waste of time, energy and pilots' lives to make more holes in an already-damaged air field. There was only a small AAA defense around the airfield that was ineffective, because we made only one pass over the airfield. No matter, tracers being fired in my direction kept me constantly changing direction while checking the area.

The ship had to be re-provisioned, re-armed and re-fueled during the early morning hours of the 30th, and air operations started later than usual. The division first flew a CAP and then later headed for Chongjin to check out the railroad and highway south to Kilchu. We started just south of Chongjin and bombed some of the small bridges that had been repaired. We did not find anything on the road or alongside the road under the trees as we moved south. Reaching Kilchu we broke off and then headed back to the task force to await our landing assignment. June ended for me with 21 missions flown and 33.0 flight hours added to the logbook during the 13 days of air operation. The air group had been with Task Force 77 for 20 days, seven of which were washed out because of bad weather. It had been a rough month, with almost every flight facing moderate to heavy AAA fire. The air group's aircraft often returned with small-arm bullet or flak holes. The maintenance crews worked long hours repairing the planes and getting them ready for another flight. I found that flying multiple times in a given day was exhausting. There were times when all I wanted to do was sleep instead of eating. I lost weight, and finally the flight surgeon warned me to cut out the cigarettes and cut down on the coffee. I finally had to go "cold turkey" and stop smoking. It was probably the best thing that came out of this event. I never smoked again.

The month of July started out with two flights on the 1st for our division. The first mission was a strike at Hari-Dong, and the second was against targets at Hwagye-ri. We ran into moderate AAA fire while in the dive, but higher altitude pullouts kept us out of range of the small-arms fire. Our bombing accuracy suffered with the higher drops, but we were more interested in living through another day. After the second mission, the division headed for K-18 because one of the other aircraft had a tail hook problem. After landing and refueling the tail hook was quickly fixed by the FASRON mechanics, and we were soon on our way to return for the next scheduled recovery. The Corsair squadron lost an airplane and the service of one of its pilots when LT W. A. Jensen was forced to ditch after being hit by enemy AAA. He was picked up by a rescue boat from a ship in the area and later transferred to the Naval Hospital in Yokosuka because of his injuries. The air group flew a total of 108 sorties. The weather became a problem on the 2nd limiting the number of sorties to 41. My roommate, LTJG George Benas, flying a reconnaissance mission, received lacerations about the face and neck when an enemy AAA shell hit his jet in the nose section. The aircraft remained flyable, and he was able to return to the ship and effect a normal landing.

Taken from the USS *Princeton* action report covering the period, 9 June 1953 through 3 August 1953 has a short statement on page 13 that reads as follows:

On 2 July LTJG G. Benas, 521247/1310, USN of VF-153, received lacerations about the face and neck when his aircraft was hit by an enemy AAA Fire. LTJG Benas flew his damaged plane back to the *Princeton* and received treatment aboard.

What really took place is an interesting story of a great guy and courageous pilot. George was one of the original eight pilots who had flown the earlier tour with the squadron and was now on the second tour. During his first tour, George had been hit by flak several times. On his second tour he was hit several more times, with three of them resulting in the loss of all hydraulic pressure. Both the landing gear and flaps on the F9F used hydraulic pressure for operation. The landing gear has a back up system using air pressure stored in a bottle in the nose section, but once the gear is down using this system it cannot be raised. So George was a pro, having made three no-flap landings already. On this particular mission he was leading the "Jokers" division on a bombing raid north of the front lines on a suspected North Korean Army Corp headquarters. As the flight was retiring from the raid his aircraft was hit by 37-mm anti-aircraft shell. It entered in the nose wheel well on the starboard side, continuing at an angle up into the cockpit, under his right leg, narrowing missing him, and then exploded in the right-side console, destroying everything. Some of the shrapnel from the exploding shell smashed the windscreen as well. He immediately lost all electrical power, flight and engine instruments, and hydraulics aileron boost. The exploding shell made a complete mess of that side of the cockpit. The aircraft at that moment seemed barely flyable, but he headed for the ocean in case he had to eject or ditch. As things calmed down he found that the aircraft remained flyable, so he took the risk and the flight headed for the task force. At this time George did not know whether the nose wheel would deploy, as he knew he had been hit in that area of the aircraft. To add to his problem, he could not verbally communicate with the flight because his radio was all smashed by the flak damage, and he had to rely on hand signals to the others flying formation with him.

The flight returned to the carrier, and George got himself ready for another no-flap landing. The ship had been told of his plight so the arresting crew was ready. Once on the downwind leg he pulled the handle that is forward of the throttle, and the air-bottle air pressure activated the main gear, but the nose wheel was too damaged to deploy. So this time it would not only be a no-flap landing but also a trickier landing to snag an arresting wire before the nose dropped to the deck. If the nose dropped to the deck, the tail hook would be too high off the deck to grab a wire, and he would go skidding up the deck into the barricade. His approach was good, and he settled the crippled aircraft down, slightly nose high, to be sure to snag a wire. It went as planned, and after the arresting wire stopped his aircraft it slowly nosed over. The definition of a successful carrier landing is one you can walk away from. He was taken to sickbay and had the wounds on his face attended to. Fortunately he suffered no permanent scars from his wounds. After a few days of rest and allowing these wounds to heal before putting on an oxygen mask, he was back on flight status. Bill Jones and I later kidded him that he really cut himself shaving.

With bad weather moving in, the task force used the time to re-fuel and re-arm when flight operations were cancelled. The bad weather was still a factor on the 3rd and there were not many sorties flown by the air group. The total was only 80—well below our capability. Our division, however, did fly a CAP and then a strike on a supply area in the Wonsan area. Wonsan is a place where you came in at a high altitude, made a steep dive, dropped your bombs, and got the hell out of there. The AAA was always heavy, but with the jets, the enemy was usually late getting started and the North Koreans didn't have a lot of time to get us in their gun sights. In my dive I saw a lot of tracers coming up and air burst above us in the rear-view mirror. Most of the flak was wide of our flight path so it looked like it was well off the mark, and the guns were not well aimed. Consequently, we came back without any known battle damage. The metalsmiths in the squadron would give our planes a careful going over no matter what we said.

We had the fourth of July off because of bad weather. I think it would have been nice to celebrate the 4ᵗʰ with some more fireworks. The weather was still poor on the 5th, but even so, the division made a Cherokee strike North of Finger Ridge hitting possible troop concentrations. The rest of the air group however flew only 39 sorties. That evening, the ship first went alongside the tanker to refuel and then alongside the ammo ship to rearm. While the weather was a problem for the task force, LT Guy Bordleon of VC-3 shot down his third and fourth "Bed Check Charlie" over Seoul. These aircraft were small training biplanes that the North Koreans used to attack targets around Seoul at night. The US Air Force had requested a prop night fighter from the Navy, and Guy did a great job. The weather got really bad on the sixth and only four weather reconnaissance got airborn. There was no other activity during the night. The weather improved some and the division was scheduled for an armed-reconnaissance mission around Pachunjang. During the flight over the route, the flight leader spied part of a train on a stretch of tracks. There was no apparent defensive AAA fire; we were able to make repeated runs on the boxcars with the destruction of at least three and damage to the remainder. Whenever a target like this turned up, we made a major effort to do as much damage as possible. That was a good mission. The rest of the air group was hindered by marginal weather, and including ours only flew 55 sorties.

On the 8ᵗʰ of July, the weather cleared, and the air group went back to the attack, flying a full schedule of 162 sorties for the day. I started out the day with a photo-escort mission that was memorable for being boring and then the division flew a Cherokee strike in the Tonggumyou Area carrying 250-pound bombs to hit our assigned target. A full ordnance loading can only be carried in the summer when there is good wind over the deck. Usually in the warm weather the loading is reduced from six to four bombs. Right after a frontal passage, however, there is a good chance of 10 to 15 knots of wind over the water to help the jets into the air with a full load. Whereas the CAP flight was boring, this mission was not. The area we were assigned was heavily defended, and the North Korean gunners were very accurate with their firing. From 20,000 feet the target area looked just like the photos and map. In a spread-out, shallow Vee formation we all dove at the same time. I lined up on a thickly tree-covered area, figuring that this might be a good storage area. The flak greeted us as we passed through 10,000 feet. It seemed like a long time to be under fire, but diving down in a steep dive with full dive brakes extended, the altimeter spun rapidly and dropped going through 3,500 feet. I pulled back hard on the control stick and darn near blacked out from the high G load on my body. The flak followed me, but fortunately the gunners did not give me enough lead, and the shells fired from the enemy gun once again ended up behind me. Leaving the target area at full power and high speed, I looked back and saw many secondary explosions in the area where I had dropped my load. The photos later showed I had set off a good size ammo dump. It was a good feeling, and I was awarded for my efforts with my 8th Air Medal. With that many sorties flown, the ship, as usual, had to refuel that evening after flight quarters were secured to replenish the fuel we used as well as going alongside the ammo ship to replace the bombs we had dropped.

The weather was marginal on the 9th, and only 34 sorties were flown, but I did not fly. No matter how skilled a pilot is, there are factors beyond his control that can lead to disaster. Such was the case of my roommate LTJG Bill Jones. He was launched for a mission on a marginal weather day. Soon after launch the task force sailed into a thick, foggy condition. The fog was so thick that from the bridge they could not see the LSO platform area. The aircraft that were airborne were directed to fly to K-18 to land. The K-18 tower was reporting the weather within acceptable limits. When the flights arrived and attempted to land, one by one they found that the weather had dropped well below limits. The actual state of the weather was 50 to 75-foot ceiling and visibility down to one-eighth of a mile or a little over 600 feet. A landing jet can cover this distance in about 5 seconds. (For comparison, the minimums at NAS Moffett Field were 100 foot ceiling with one-quarter mile (1,320 feet) visibility using Ground Control Approach (GCA) radar guidance.) After waiting for other aircraft ahead of him he started on his first pass. As Bill made his final approach he broke out of the fog but could not see the runway because of the 35-foot-high sand dune. As he closed on the sand dune he found he was not lined up with the runway, but was off course. He had to do an emergency missed approach. Adding full power he started his climb to try another approach. Just to make it even more exciting, mountains surround the airfield on three sides.

Breaking out above the fog after climbing out, he headed out to sea for another pass. By this time his fuel was dangerously low, and before he could get very far his engine flamed out, even though his fuel gage showed he had 200 pounds of fuel. He immediately made a 90-degree turn in order not to run into the waves but to parallel the swells coming in to the shore. He dumped the nose down to maintain his air speed as the altimeter move rapidly towards zero. As he closed with the water he dropped his speed brakes and flaps, using the auxiliary hydraulic pump powered by his battery to make the best ditching. Still in the fog and on instruments he started his flare-out based only on his altimeter. When he felt his speed brakes make contact with the top of the waves, he immediately raised his flaps using the auxiliary hydraulic pump. He picked up his flaps so that they would not give him a nose-down pitch when hitting the water. He didn't want the nose to dig in because in other ditching, the nose of the F9F broke off. Without ever seeing the water because of the thick fog, he hit. After the aircraft came to a stop, he unbuckled his seat belt and shoulder harness and climbed out of the cockpit and on to the wing. He inflated his life raft and climbed in before the airplane sank.

The sea was calm with heavy swells, but it was very foggy, and he was getting cold. He pulled the emergency radio out of the life raft pocket and found that the battery was dead. Meanwhile the control tower at K-18 had alerted the rescue crew and a Marine helicopter was sent out to try to find him and to pick him up. There was only one problem. They did not know were he was. He could hear the helicopter flying back and forth searching for him under the fog at a very low altitude, but he was further out to sea from where they were searching. Then the sound died away. Bill was hoping that they went back for fuel. By this time he was really suffering from the effects of the cold water. Before long, the helicopter was back searching once again. The helicopter was still closer to shore than Bill was. He could hear them going back and forth several times. The helicopter on this second flight continued the search, but within an hour the sound disappeared again. Finally on the helicopter's third search flight Bill was able to see the helicopter's wheels and he quickly fired off a flare. There was no reaction to this flare. A short time later he saw the helicopter again; he fired off a second flare, and that did it! The helicopter came directly at him, and in no time he was hoisted aboard and he was on his way to K-18. He had been in the water for almost seven hours. Besides being very cold he was very thirsty as well. Immediately after arriving at K-18 he was treated for hypothermia and given lots of fluids. A few days later, traveling in the back of an AD he was flown back to the carrier. George Benas and I were sure delighted to have him safely back aboard.

Air operations were secured early, and the ship went alongside three different supply ships. The first was the tanker for fuel, followed by the ammo ship for another load of ordnance, and finally from the last for aviation supplies and general stores. After the fuel lines were in place the next thing was to carefully bring the U.S. mail aboard. Mail call took place soon after the mailbags were all received.

I remembered July 10th very well for two reasons. The first reason was that it was the day of my first jet-aircraft accident. The day started out with a routine CAP mission. The flight was without incident, and when released by the FDO we headed back to the task force. Everything was normal during the descent and approach to the ship. I was flying the number-three position. When it was my turn to break, I passed the lead to the fourth man and started my 180-degree turn to the left. As the speed dropped below the 165 knots I dropped the landing gear. Immediately the aileron boost appeared to fail. *What the hell is wrong?* Scanning the instruments I noticed the hydraulic pressure gauge dropped to almost to zero, then to my surprised came back to normal. Next the nose-wheel indicator showed that it was down and locked, but the main landing gear showed unsafe. *Oh, hell, I have a problem!* Raising the landing gear I continued my downwind leg. Slowed to 150 knots and flying straight and level, I lowered the gear again. The same thing happened. The aileron control became stiff; the gauge went to zero and then back to normal. The main gear was down, but still showed unsafe. Using the polished spot on the left tip tank that acts like a mirror I could see the left landing gear was down. *Now I know I have a major problem.* I radioed the ship, "I have a landing gear problem, and will take a wave off, so have a visual check of my landing gear flying."

The LSO radioed, "The landing gear appears down."

That did not make me feel any better, yet I thought, *It could be a microswitch failure.* I flew upwind far enough to start another 180-degree turn to the downwind leg. Starting my approach I pulled the red emergency handle to activate the emergency landing gear air bottle to lock the gear down. *Damn, nothing changed on the gear indicators.* I radioed the ship that I still had an unsafe landing gear condition and was given clearance for landing. There wasn't another aircraft to be recovered, so if I fouled the deck it would not have screwed up another landing aircraft. Continuing my second approach I was going to be as close to the center of the deck as possible in case the main landing gear failed.

Unknown to me at this time, the air boss had told the deck crew that a possible deck crash could occur with the jet approaching for landing and to be ready. The last turn of the approach was made and in the straightaway, I got a "Roger" on my altitude and air speed and then I received my "cut" from the LSO. Just before touchdown my tail hook engaged the number-two wire, and when the aircraft hit the deck, the main landing gear began to slowly fold against the air pressure. By the time the airplane stopped, the rear of the fuselage was resting on the deck. The nose wheel had remained down and locked, but the two main landing gears collapsed.

Deck Crash

The cause of the gear failure was the rupture of a hydraulic fuse in the lock cycle of the main landing gear. The official determination was material failure.

In spite of the deck crash the aircraft had surprising minimal damage. The left inboard flap had to be replaced, and the dent in the left tip tank was determined to be minimal, and it was not changed. The aircraft was quickly fixed and was flown in the next launch one and half hours later. It was just a small part of the aircraft, but it sure gave me one hell of a scary landing. What is the old saying? "A good landing is one that you walk away from. A great landing is one that they can use the aircraft again."

The second reason was personal. I was approaching my two-hundredth carrier landing, and the LSO and I had a bet that I couldn't make that number without a landing accident. The bet was a bottle of booze. This deck crash happened on my 191st landing. I was really ticked off. I went on to make 216 carrier landings before the tour was over. Of that number, 197 were jet landings. After I recovered from the landing and getting my breathing back to normal I climbed out of the aircraft on the deck, when the LSO came running forward against the wind from the LSO platform. What was the first thing he said? Not, "How are you?" but, "I won." Because the emergency was known in advance, there are numerous pictures of this accident by two official Navy photographers as well as many pilots in the air group. Potential accidents bring out the "vultures" for the excitement and pictures of a potential deck crash. Fortunately, I disappointed them, much to my delight.

This date was the beginning of almost continuous flying for all the air groups in the task force. With the exception of the 15th and bad weather on the 20th and 21st the pace began steady and then culminated in an all-out effort right up to the day the war stopped. The following day, July 11th, found the division flying on top of the overcast north of Seoul on the North Korean side of the front line on a bomber mission. Flying under the control of the radar controller, we flew at 18,000 feet and dropped our bomb load upon radio command. What damage we did was unknown. After completion we headed back towards the ship. This was a long flight all done at altitude unlike a usual combat flight. The target area north of Seoul was some distance from the east coast, plus the task force was operating about 100 miles off the east coast. With the marginal weather the air group managed only 96 sorties. That night the ship took on fuel and then ammo after flight quarters had ended. Flying during the day and replenishing at night had become the norm rather than the exception. Rumors were flying around that there might be an end to this nightmare.

The division flew one mission on the following day, while I added an additional flight with another photo-escort sortie to my total. The photo plane was to take pictures around Kapson. So trailing along above and behind the photo plane I did not see any flak or air opposition. It turned out to be a routine mission. The next mission was to attack the bridge at Sachangin. The strike was effective in spite of moderate flak fired at us, and the bridge was destroyed. With all the practice we were getting, the division was consistently hitting the target even with higher pullouts. The North Korean repair crews, however, would rebuild the bridge in a few days. They started on it as soon as we left the area. The air group flew a total of 133 sorties for the day. Fortunately the ship did not replenish that evening, so it was quiet, and we could all sleep soundly.

The 13th was a no-fly day for me because flight operations were curtailed early due to poor weather. Only 60 sorties were flown. The ship took advantage of the weather and spent additional time replenishing both fuel and ordnance. The weather continued to be poor for flying on the 14th, but the division did get launched and once again got to play big bomber. We joined up below the clouds, tucking into a tight formation for our climb to altitude. It was dark inside the clouds as we slowly climbed to 20,000 feet, finally breaking out into the bright sunshine. The formation loosened up so we could relax for a few minutes. As we were crossing the coastline the flight leader contacted the radar controller. I was identified by the controller by making a couple of turns. We got a northerly vector to await his command to drop. All set up with the bomb arm switches on salvo, we dropped on the end of his countdown. Free of our bomb load the division made a roll to the right and headed for the coast. It was a dull mission, very much like a CAP. The air group only managed to launch 30 sorties before the task force called it quits and secured air operations, but not before a pilot, LTJG Jacob L. Pawer on the staff of Commander Carrier Division 3 (ComCarDiv 3) crashed into the sea during a practice-rocket run. He was on an anti-submarine patrol (ASP) escort flight. A search of the area by the ASP plane and later by a destroyer was done without any indication of the pilot's survival. When the sea is calm it can be difficult to judge one's altitude when making firing runs at low altitude. He either misjudged his altitude or he got target fixation, but he dove right into the water.

The spell of bad weather continued through the 15th. Our division did not fly at all, even though there were 34 sorties flown. Mostly the sorties were defensive with anti-submarine warfare (ASW), anti-submarine patrol (ASP) or CAP being the predominate flights. I could do without a boring CAP mission. The weather cleared on the 16th, and the air group flew a full schedule culminating in 119 sorties being flown. Our division went out on a strike around Ichon. The big news of the day was that LT Bordelon had shot down his 5th aircraft to become the Navy's first propeller Ace of the Korean War.(To the best of my knowledge this has not appeared in print.) The interesting aspect of this was how the ordnance crew of the ship and VC-3 bore sighted his guns before his departures to South Korea. They jacked the F4U up on the flight deck to a level flight condition that would occur with the Corsair's flaps down. The reason was that he was going after slow-flying aircraft. He would be intercepting them at slow speeds with his flaps down to be able to stay behind them. A number of us were on the flight deck watching this activity. It paid off very well when he was able to shoot down these pests. The USAF was unable to do it because their jet interceptors were traveling too fast, and the targets were flying too low to be easily spotted by radar. He returned to the *Princeton* with a great deal of excitement for all hands.

The weather again became marginal on the 17th, but the division did manage to fly a strike around the village of Hwachon-ni. The strike specific target was a bridge in that immediate area. After the bombing attack we then flew reconnaissance on the road system around the same village checking for targets of opportunity. Like so many I had flown and would fly in the future there was nothing in sight. The remaining pilots of the air group were restricted from much flying so the record shows only 26 sorties completed. The weather was still marginal the following day, but the division got in another flight to perform an armed-reconnaissance mission in the coastal area north of Wonsan. We lucked out, and the flight leader spotted a lone truck that was poorly hidden and was immediately dispatched to the graveyard with direct hits. During all these flights I saw very little flak. The other members of the air group managed to mount only a total of 29 sorties for an overall total of 33.

The 19th was another milestone passage for me when I made my 200th carrier landing after flying a routine CAP. There was considerable cloud cover around the task force and we were in the soup for over 15 minutes going to station and returning to the task force. The second flight of the day was another strike, this time aiming at a bridge in the area of Chando-ri. Bridge strikes were always dangerous because of the usual defensive AAA emplacements. The best tactic we had was to attack by sections with each diving in from different directions. For best results we had to dive in the same direction as the length of the bridge. Some were very short so there was not much leeway on your mil lead. The best way was to make a steep dive and make it count on the first pass. More than one pass was an invitation for getting hit by flak.

The Corsair Squadron, VF-152 lost an aircraft and the use of a pilot when ENS R. W. Turner crashed into the sea on takeoff. He suffered major injuries to his left leg and had to be rescued by the USS *Fletcher* (DDE-445) because he was unable to be hoisted by the helicopter. He was latter transferred to the Naval Hospital in Yokosuka. Also on July 19th, we found out what could happen to our water supply. Like all Navy ships, the aircraft carrier produces all its own fresh water. There were three sets of evaporators and condensers on board the ship. Under normal operations only one is needed to produce enough water for the ship's boilers, galleys, and the crew's washing and drinking needs. When the summer arrived, the water use went up because the ship needed to use all eight boilers to provide the extra relative wind speed for flight operations. The crew was now working longer hours and needed to wash more often. This meant that the two sets of evaporators and condensers were needed to meet these additional needs. On this day, one of the evaporators failed and had to be shut down. No problem, because the other two could meet all the ship's needs. A day later a second evaporator failed, and the available water was drastically reduced. To meet the three requirements of the boilers, galley, and sick bay, there was nothing left for the other uses. There was water for drinking, but that was it. You could not shower, wash your hands, or brush your teeth. It wasn't long before this problem became very evident, as we all started to stink. You could imagine what it was like in the officer's wardroom with that many smelly officers. You could scrape the oily sweat off of your hands. A lot of deodorant was used, but to limited effect. It was all we could do to sit and eat a meal. There was no reason to put on a clean uniform, because we stank just as badly in a few minutes.

Fortunately this condition did not last for more than two days. The necessary parts were flown out to the ship by the carrier on-board delivery (COD) aircraft, and a second evaporator/condenser system was put back into commission. Water was restored to all outlets, but that did not mean long showers. It meant you turned the water on for 30 seconds to get wet, turned it off and soaped down, then turned the water on for another 30 seconds to wash the soap off. The good old Navy shower! At least I was clean and had a sweet smell, even though the shower was brief. Long showers would have to wait until the ship was in port, hooked up to the base's water supply. Then you could have the luxury of a longer shower.

The weather became worse on the 20th, and there were only 29 sorties flown. As part of the 29 sorties one of squadron's divisions was launched for an armed-reconnaissance mission north of Hamhung. LCDR Charles M. Jones of the air group staff was killed when his F9F was hit by AAA fire while in an attack run, and he never pulled out of the dive. His plane crashed into a hillside. George Benas had the sad experience of witnessing the crash.

After flight operations were secured the ship replenished provisions. The weather closed in completely on the 21st, and only three weather reconnaissance sorties were flown. During the evening the task forced took the opportunity to replenish the fuel supply. I realized that it was becoming hours and hours of flying never knowing when an AAA shell would hit. The stress was showing on everyone. Tempers flared and then died down just as quickly. We kept an eye on our buddies to make sure that each one was fit to fly. There were a few pilots who were reaching the breaking point, but the ever-present air-group fight surgeon ordered them grounded for a day or two. We each had to deal with our own stress level as best we could. The challenge had left, and it was replaced with a just-staying-alive attitude.

To make matters worse, beginning on the 22nd the naval air war went into over drive. It would be almost a round-the-clock effort. I found that each day was a repeat of the last one. The weather slowly improved, and the division flew two missions into North Korea. The first one was a bombing strike on a suspected truck storage or staging area, and the second was an armed-reconnaissance around the Hongwon area. The air group flew only 63 sorties for the day because of weather restrictions during the morning hours. The 23rd found me chasing a photo plane around on an escort mission. No problems occurred during the mission and no indication of AAA fire. All I had to worry about was my fuel supply. As usual, I was back aboard with the low-fuel light burning brightly. This fuel condition always added to my stress level. A foul deck could have serious implications. The air group was back into a higher number of sorties for the day. A total of 136 were flown. The ship replenished that night, taking on fuel from the tanker and ordnance from the ammo ship.

The 24th was a very full day for both the air group and our division. The air group with our division's sorties as part of this total flew a total of 160 sorties. Our first mission was a high-level bombing strike north of the front lines under the guidance of the radar controller in South Korea. Our next mission was an armed-reconnaissance flight along the coast to check up on bridge status and search for whatever targets we could find. When targets were nowhere to be found, we tried our bombing skills to try to knock down high-tension electrical power towers. Once in a while it worked, but it was a tough target to hit. We rounded out the day with a defensive CAP. I was in the air for 6.1 hours that day. Add to this airborne time about four more hours for briefing and debriefing, and I was really tired at the end of the day. Sleep was at a premium. As the ship refueled during the night, the noise of the refuel activity could be clearly heard in the forward part of the ship, however, I was tired enough that once I fell asleep I slept soundly.

This was the time of year when dawn came early, so I was up at 3:00 on the 25th for breakfast and briefing. I got all ready for launch and went through the standard routine. Everything was okay during the launch and not until I was with the division did I discover that my tip tanks did not transfer any fuel. Nothing I could think of helped, and I had to abort my participation in the mission. I returned to the task force and set up an orbit, awaiting landing instructions. Once the ship had completed re-spotting the deck and was ready for recover, I dumped the fuel in my tip tanks and entered the landing pattern. It was at a higher landing speed than usual because I was right at maximum landing weight of 2,500 pounds of fuel.

The second mission went off okay, and we headed out to do the high-level bombing once again. We flew a loose formation, and upon the radar controller's call, made holes in the Korean countryside. The air group was dropping so many bombs that it was necessary to re-supply every other night. We got a light schedule for the 26th, and I flew only one mission. Our mission was to bust the re-built bridge at Kaenmal. It was in and out as fast as possible, and we did it in royal fashion. Heck, we were practicing every day. We should be good at hitting small targets. The Corsair squadron unfortunately lost the last pilot of the war when LT William C. Blackford Jr. was shot down while on a reconnaissance mission with no chance for survival. The air group flew a total of 167 sorties. Once again we were using so much gasoline that it was necessary to re-supply every other night.

Our squadron was normally assigned to fly twelve aircraft per launch. The interesting fact was we only had twelve operational aircraft. During this maximum effort the ground crew worked long hours to keep all of them flying. Several of our aircraft went over 30 hours of flying without being grounded for small maintenance repairs. There were a few of our aircraft that gave off a whistling sound in the approach for landing. The bullet holes that did not affect their flying ability were not patched. That could never happen in the states. This meant that every night something was happening on the hanger deck. The squadron maintenance crew worked many long hours to perform this daily miracle.

The 27th was a maximum effort day for the division as well as the air group. We flew three missions beginning at dawn and going on all day. The first was an easy one. It was a CAP just boring holes in the sky. The second mission was a strike south of Wonsan in areas suspected to contain trucks and supplies headed for the front. The last mission for us in the war was an airfield strike and reconnaissance of the airfield at Hoemun. It was another day. 6.1 flying hours. On the last recovery, the pilots in the last jet division to be recovered were all trying to be the last aircraft aboard. The first two took a voluntary wave off and the air boss got the picture and ordered them to get aboard, "NOW!" The air group did its job in great style, flying 124 sorties for that day. I was launched 12 times in six days, and when it was all over I slept for 12 hours straight. A few extra drinks after supper sure did help me go to sleep. I felt I had earned them.

On the morning of the 28th there was an unusual stillness throughout the entire ship. The crew had worked 18 to 20 hours each day for about a week while the pilots each had flown an unusually high number of missions. Everyone was physically, mentally, and emotionally exhausted. I flew 30 sorties during 21 flying days in the month of July. The missions consisted of five defensive Combat Air Patrols, two photo escorts, one aborted flight, and 22 missions over enemy territory. The ship had been at sea since June 9th. The record book showed that the USS *Princeton* and Air Group 15 had set a number of records for a carrier operating in the Korean War. I also had completed a respectable number of combat flights during the four-month period we were operating in the Sea of Japan. Adding to my combat flight from the first tour, I was engaged in offensive and defensive flights in the war zone 161 times.

The *Princeton's* action report for the period summed it up with these words: "It is believed to be one of the longest periods of sustained combat operation conducted at sea by any aircraft carrier during the Korean Conflict."

We were at sea 56 days. Other records were set when:

On two separate occasions, the combat sortie record for aircraft carriers is believed to have been broken when one hundred seventy-two and one hundred eighty-four sorties were launched during two single days' operations.

When the peace talks at Panmunjom took a turn for the better, and in order to maintain the pressure on the enemy the task force engaged in a maximum effort. This effort increased the average number of sorties from 110 to 165. Whenever weather permitted it, we flew every day and replenished at night. VF-154, our sister jet squadron set a record by flying 54 sorties in one day. The air group flew 3,421 sorties and expended over 2,700 tons of ordnance during this same period.

My little bar operation needed replenishment as well. I had figured that a case of each kind of booze would last us the thirty days we were normally at sea. I didn't figure on a 56-day trip, so by the end of the war we were down to almost nothing. It was necessary to ration the drinks near the end. The guest list was pared down as best we could. I had only a small amount of booze left when we finally headed into port.

Chapter 16
After the Armistice

Even though the conflict was over for us, the task force continued operating in the Sea of Japan until the end of July. There was nothing to do to replace the hectic pace we followed during the last days of the war. Finally, on August 1st the carrier with its escorts left the task force and headed for Yokosuka arriving on the 3rd. The ship was docked at Yokosuka for ten days. On the 14th the ship left Tokyo Bay, and after recovering five aircraft flown from NAS Atsugi, headed back to Task Force 77. We were en route until the 16th when the *Princeton* joined with the task force. The weather was poor for a number of days, so there was little to do. I did not get into the cockpit until the 21st. I flew again on the 26th and 27th. In all these flights we either just bored holes in the sky or we made some low, fast pass at the task force to let the AAA crews on the ships of the task force track high-speed aircraft. There was an air group fly by of the ship with the jets flying in a formation that was a big letter "P." It was a fun day and a way to show our appreciation to the *Princeton*'s crew for all their hard work keeping the aircraft well maintained and us in the air. I flew my last flight with the task force on the 29th with no objective in mind except keeping up my skills and staying alive.

On the 1st of September the air group launched all the flyable aircraft from the carrier for the last time, and this fleet of aircraft headed for NAS Atsugi. The jets, being faster than the props, arrived in the Tokyo Bay area first. The weather did not cooperate, and our flight of eight jets ended up landing at the USAF Base, Kisarazu. The flight of eight VF-153 jets led by Executive Officer Jim McNeil, stayed on top of the overcast until we reached the Tokyo area. Instead of changing the flight plan to IFR and making an instrument descent to the naval air base, he hunted for a hole in the overcast. All of a sudden he spotted one, and without any warning to us he dropped his wing into a vertical bank and dove for the hole in the overcast. It took all of us by surprise, and the seven of us also did a steep wing over to try to stay with him diving down as well. There was nothing like a vertical dive in a crowded air space to make me feel comfortable. I sure was not impressed with his leadership on that flight. The other squadrons did even worse. It was one very wild ride for most of the other pilots in the air group because everyone was trying to fly under visual flight rules. One AD from VF-155 ended up crash landing in a rice paddy near the Naval airbase, while a Corsair from VF-152 had engine trouble and was forced to landed wheels up on an off shore island, O-Shima. What a mess! Those of us that landed at the USAF base stayed overnight. After breakfast in the morning the weather began to improve enough that we could complete our ferry mission landing at NAS Atsugi later that morning. That was the end of my flying in the Far East. It was not a very glorious ending. I finally finished up my second Far Eastern deployment on the 2nd of September. From then I would leave the excitement of carrier aviation, the fear of being shot down, and head back to the United States. In spite of our poor performance on our last flight, the air group did its job with pride and a sense of accomplishment.

What we did as part of the war was soon forgotten by the nation in general and the war earned the title: "The Forgotten War." To those of us who went through the hail of enemy AAA fire, it never was forgotten. Eight of us started out on this adventure; six of us came home alive after flying an average of 150 missions. Of the remaining six, two suffered injuries from enemy fire that hit their airplanes. Those two, George Benas and Charlie Clarkson, had their aircraft severely damaged by enemy flak. George suffered facial injuries from one of his flak hits and had to make several difficult landings aboard ship. Charlie had to make a dangerous high-speed ditching under the nose of the enemy in Wonsan Bay. He, too, had been hit in the face from his flak strike. Bill Jones had to ditch his aircraft under very bad weather conditions when he exhausted his fuel supply trying to land in the fog at K-18. He was rescued after spending many painful hours in the water. Almost everyone in the air group had his aircraft hit by enemy anti-aircraft fire many times, but each was successful in either returning to the ship, landing at K-18, ditching, or bailing out. I was very fortunate to have received only a few small-caliber bullet hits, all in the wing area. I did have the pleasure of a crash landing aboard ship because of a material failure.

My own record taken from my pilot logbook covering both of my tours was as follows:

161 missions completed of all types.

I went into the operating squadron with 19 carrier landings and left with 216 carrier landings.

Best of all, I had no barrier engagements.

My flight hours started at 362.6 and ended at 952.6.

The Navy honored me for my action against the enemy with eleven Air Medals and one Personal Commendation.

Air Group 15 on its second tour in the Korean War from March to July of 1953, a period of 4 ½ months, generated some very impressive records. A brief summary is as follows:

Flew 7,865 sorties.

Twelve pilots had to ditch, crash land, or bail out of their aircraft and were rescued.

Expended approximately 4,833 tons of heavy ordnance.

Made 6,974 carrier landings with the two jet squadrons making almost 55 percent of these landings.

There were 4,258 catapult launches with 3,956 being jet launches.

To accomplish all of this the aircraft burned 4,279,229 gallons of aviation gasoline.

The carrier steamed 58,897 miles and burned 10,713,286 gallons of fuel.

Unfortunately the air group lost 11 pilots and three enlisted crewmen.

It is interesting to note that during the naval air operation in supporting the UN forces approximately 2,900 fixed-wing pilots were involved in the Naval Air Arm action during the entire Korean War. This number includes some duplicates because some pilots flew during more than one deployment. Air Group 15 had eight pilots in VF-153 who flew in a second deployment. Further, there were less than 900 of these pilots who flew the jets off of the carrier. (My research found from the action reports that of the estimated 2, 900 pilots, at least 179 died from enemy action or operational accidents.) These three years were no walk in the park for any of us but were especially painful for those who were injured. The emotional scars of the loss of our squadron buddies will stay with me forever.

Chapter 17
Last View from the Cockpit

The USS *Princeton* arrived off of the entrance to the San Francisco Bay in the early morning hours of September 22, 1953. After breakfast at 0800, I climbed the ladder to the flight deck for my first view of the USA after eight long months. This arrival was not going to be a repeat of my return after the first deployment. Today I was going to have someone very important to me standing on the dock. Unlike so many mornings in this area, it was a wonderfully clear day with no fog nor clouds to clutter the air and sky. As the ship slowly approached the entrance there was a pause in our progress to take the civilian harbor pilot aboard to guide this large ship through the twists and turns required to reach the dock at NAS Alameda. The harbor pilot climbed the ladder to the hanger deck and he went immediately to the bridge to get underway. Now the excitement began to build with the steady progress the ship was making. We soon passed the mouth of the bay and majestically sailed under the Golden Gate Bridge. One had to be on a ship to feel the full effect of this magnificent bridge. It had a symbolic meaning that stated, "Welcome Home." There were people waving from the bridge railing as the ship passed under the bridge and entered the San Francisco Bay. As the ship cleared the bridge the distant drone of aircraft engines became louder, and within moments the roar of several formations of naval aircraft was heard as the squadrons of another air group flew in parade formation over the ship to salute our return.

The ship's pilot was supervising the OD as the *Princeton* slowly moved the ship under the Oakland Bay Bridge, and finally the dock at NAS Alameda came into view. My last view of this pier as it faded away was still in my mind's eye. Then I wondered, *Will I ever see it again?* Now it hit me as I could make out that the large pier was overflowing with people. For me it was very special because my future wife, Beverly, was among this crowd, having flown out from the East Coast for this very exciting and emotional occasion. As soon as

259

the ship approached the pier at NAS Alameda, I scanned the crowd looking for her. We finally spotted each other and our smiles were as big as the ocean I had just crossed. The ship was finally nudged by four big tugs against the dock. At that moment the ship's whistle blew a long loud blast signaling the exact time of arrival. The "anchor pool" was divided among the crewmembers that had guessed the closest time to the second of official arrival. It was a beautiful moment that washed away all the fears that had built up inside of me leaving only the sadness of the loss of my flying buddies who did not come back.

The two gangways were put in place and locked in solid by the dockworkers. Joining the stampede down the gangway and on to the dock, I headed over to where Beverly was standing and with one sweep I picked her off her feet and we met in a long, wonderful embrace. It had been almost nine months since our last time together on Christmas of last year when I proposed marriage. There are not enough words to describe the picture of the air group and ship's crew during their reunion with family and friends. The dock was covered with people smiling, crying, and cheering. One has to be there to comprehend the huge level of emotions that poured out from the thousands of people on the dock.

After a short time, many of us went back aboard, and I carried my personal clothes and effects off of the ship. Loading our gear into Clarkson's car, we drove down the eastside of the bay with them to Mountain View. There was much to do and a million words to be spoken. With all that was going on I was finally able to get my own car out of storage the following day. We stayed two days and left Charlie and Zelda "Zee" Clarkson and drove down the central California valley to Los Angles to stay with my older brother for another few days. From there we drove across the country following route US-66 to St. Louis and then to Beverly's home in Short Hills, New Jersey. It was a long five-day trip, but we welcomed the time to talk up a storm about our future life together. After a few days with her family, I continued the journey by myself to Newport, Rhode Island, to be with my family for a few days before the wedding. I returned to Short Hills, and on October 10, 1953, we were married. To my delight and surprise, two of the previous squadron officers made the wedding with their wives. They were LT Billy Jo Sanders, my division leader from my first tour, and the LT Von Southern, the squadron Air Intelligence Officer. Ensign Bob Kunz of VF-153 was my best man and LTJG George Benas was another of the ushers. It was a wonderful, warm fall day. The following morning Beverly and I had breakfast with both our families at her parents' home. During breakfast my new father-in-law was in the kitchen, and his wife called to him to bring some spoons to the table. He didn't hear her, so I said, "Dad, would you bring some more spoons?" He spun around with a startled look on his face. This was the first time he had a male voice call him dad. We all got a good laugh over his reaction. After a long breakfast, we finished packing the car, and after our good-byes we headed back to the West Coast to return to Moffett Field area to set up our household as a newly married couple.

After reporting back to the squadron at its new home on the eastside of the field, I found that all the officers with the exception of the ensigns received orders for new duty assignments. The six of us were being split up. Bill Jones was off to southern California, George Benas was headed to NAS Alameda to be on the admiral's staff, and Bob King was headed to test pilot school in Maryland. Joe Perry was leaving the Navy. Charlie Clarkson and I received orders to FASRON 8 at Moffett in the third week of October. That was great, because it was only a move across the Moffett airfield to the main base side, which was the opposite side from the squadron area. We reported to our new assignment and then in typical Navy fashion, we waited. Not to be sitting around doing nothing, I was able to get checked out in the twin-engine SNB-5 that was used primarily by this squadron for instrument instruction for naval aviators flying propeller aircraft. I made three flights in the SNB during the latter part of October with the first one being a checkout flight, and the last two as first pilot. I flew one more time in early November just before we expected our Temporary Additional Duty (TAD) orders. Charlie and I were scheduled to attend the All Weather Training School in the jet instrument course flying the TV-2. (The USAF designation for this aircraft was T-33) LCDR McDowell, formerly XO of VA-155, was also scheduled for All Weather Training on the propeller side using the SNB-5.

In mid-November we finally received our TAD orders to attend the Fleet All Weather School at NAS Corpus Christi, Texas. Before thanksgiving, the three of us headed southeast from Moffett to drive the 1,600 miles to Corpus Christi. We drove in shifts and slept when we could. It was a nineteen-hour drive through the wide-open spaces of the American southwest. It turned out that over half the trip was through Texas alone. Arriving on Sunday, we checked in with the Naval Base Officer of the Day and then with the school when it opened on Monday. We started the training immediately with ground school and time in the flight simulator. Charlie Clarkson and I were to be trained in the TV-2 two-seat jet trainer. One of the pleasant surprises was when we were to be assigned a flight instructor. LT John J. Barteluce's name came up on the board, and sure enough he became my instructor. We had flown in the same squadron, VF-831, on the first Korean Tour. I started flying the training syllabus on December 1, 1953, in the TV-2 with John flying the front seat while I was under the cloth hood in the back seat.

The first flight was an orientation on flight operations around the area and over the air base. The next six flights were all under the hood. We covered the first stage of the syllabus, which was mostly air work using just the flight instruments, but we did not do any radio-range work. It wasn't until the last flight in December that started me into radio-range flying as well as jet penetration descents from altitude to make an approach to the air base. The training command, as usual, closed down for the Christmas holiday so I booked a commercial flight from Corpus Christi to Los Angles. I went on leave on the 19th for Christmas with my wife at my brother's place in Whittier, California. The flight I was on was one of the few that were able to land at Burbank Airport because of a dense fog that had rolled in over LA. My wife started driving our car out from my brother's house, but the fog was too thick to see much so she returned to the house. By mid-morning the fog thinned out, and she was able to get to the airport. After Christmas we then drove north to Mountain View for the remainder of my leave.

Before New Year's Day came, the three of us returned to school, but this time I was driving my own car with McDowell to help. Charlie and his wife decided to go to Texas for the next month and live off base. McDowell and I split the driving chore. I started flying again on the 31st. It was a tough school with very demanding flying. They let us relax for a few flights by flying in the front seat to keep up our proficiency in landing the aircraft. During January I made 19 flights with all but two in the TV-2. The other two were in the SNB-5 to practice low-level instrument flying under the hood. The flights in this aircraft were usually four hours long, but the actual time flying at the controls was shortened because more than one student was aboard. The rest of the time was spent trying to stay awake. The course was tough, and we were pushed hard every minute. One day half way through January, it started out clear and warm with the wind from the southeast. By noon, the temperature was in the low eighties just before a cold front came through with heavy rain, thunderstorms and strong wind. By evening the storm had blown itself out, but the cold air behind the front now blowing from the northwest caused the temperature to start dropping rapidly. When we came out of the officer's mess that evening after dinner, the temperature was down to freezing. A drop of almost 50 degrees! The effect of the cold front didn't last long, and we were back into the cockpit the following day. I finished this grueling course on the 28th after flying a series of four flights that took me to Arizona and back over two days. The entire time in the air was spent either under the hood (5.2 hours) or on actual instrument (1.4 hours). The jet aircraft we were flying had no autopilot, so it was hands-on flying all the time. I graduated from the school on January 29, 1954 with the following addition to my logbook:

TV-2: 27 flights, 38.7 hours, with 6.1 hours actual instrument flying,
SNB-5: 2 flights, 7.9 hours,
Eight GCA approaches,
Fifteen hours in the flight simulator.

Immediately after finishing school we checked out and had our orders stamped by the base Officer of the Day. The two of us returned to Moffett by car to start our instructor-pilot work. Charlie and his wife drove back separately. I wasted no time and began flying as an instrument instructor pilot (IP) for refresher training of naval aviators on February 3. It was a steady schedule of flying because we flew even if the weather was bad. Rain, fog, low clouds were not any reason for staying on the ground. The only time we didn't fly was when the field was closed by the airbase operations. During February at the end of three different flights, when it was time to land I took over the controls from the back-seat pilot and flew a Ground Control Approach (GCA) because of poor visibility or low clouds. The Moffett GCA crew was outstanding, and the TV-2 was a great instrument jet. The GCA crew was so good you could depend upon them to put you right on the centerline and 500 feet down from the beginning of the runway every time. Out of the all the days I flew, six days were double-flight days. It was a great way to increase flying time, and best of all; no one was shooting at me. Lots of flying time brings out the best and smoothest flying capability. During February I flew 19 flights for 31.8 hours and with three actual GCA approaches. It was not a bad schedule for the winter months. Moffett Field had two parallel runways about 10,000 feet long so there was limited waiting time for either landing or takeoff. The San Francisco Bay area was a great place to fly.

From our flying altitude it was beautiful because the hills were all green from the winter rain. With the back-seat pilot doing the flying my job was to keep track of any other aircraft to avoid the possibility of a mid-air. There were seldom any, because all commercial flights were either at 23,000 feet or below, and we normally flew higher. I took my wife's camera along and took many pictures of the area while the back-seat pilot was controlling the aircraft. The picture shows the Golden Gate Bridge to the right. Just in front of the tip tank is the area called "Twin Peaks."

During March I flew 33 flights for a total of 64.3 hours. There were 13 days when I once again flew twice each day. On five of the days in March the weather was overcast with either low clouds or fog, so each one was flown using the Moffett Radio Range for approach to the field. The ceiling or the visibility wasn't below minimums so I did not have to use the GCA unit for a final approach. We seldom flew with the same pilot, but on occasion I went all the way with one. There were five flights in the refresher syllabus for qualified pilots. Most of the pilots did not like to fly on instruments. For me, however, I had developed a taste for instrument flying and enjoyed the challenge. It paid off later when bad weather caught up with me during several cross-country flights.

During April I was in the air almost every weekday and flew 37 flights for 64.5 hours. There were 15 days when I flew twice each day. I couldn't get enough flying. Just as in March, five of these days the weather was overcast with either low clouds or fog. Again, each one was flown using the Moffett Radio Range for approach to the field, but in addition two approaches required the use of the GCA unit. Flying as many GCA approaches as I did, I found that my approach and descent on the glide path was steady and smooth all the way. Frequently there were only minor corrections from the GCA controller. The Squadron Commanding Officer changed the game, so starting that month we started flying with the same pilot for the entire five flights. It made it much better.

There was one pilot who got more than he bargained for. On April 27, 1954, I was scheduled for the fourth flight of the usual five flights for instrument renewal with the same Navy pilot. I did my pre-flight check of the aircraft, checking the fuel levels in the various tanks. This aircraft had seven tanks, so it always took a little time to unscrew each and visually check. All was okay, and we climbed aboard. I climbed into the front seat with the other pilot in the rear seat. Settled into the cockpit, I gave the starter jeep the thumbs up, and with auxiliary power started the jet engine. While the engine rpm was at idle, I signaled for the crew to unplug the starter, and we were ready to taxi out to the runway. After clearance from the control tower, I lowered the canopy to within a few inches so we could have some cool air in the cockpit while taxiing out to the duty runway. The aircraft engine was functioning normally, and with clearance from the tower I taxied out on to the duty runway and lined the aircraft up between the white lines while closing and locking the canopy. I passed the controls over to the pilot in the rear seat. He took over and held the brakes as he moved the throttle forward to full power. All indicator lights were "in the green," and with both all set, he released the brakes, and we started down the runway. He was a smooth pilot, and the practice instrument takeoff was neat and clean. After I raised the landing gear and then the wing flaps, he started his climb to 30,000 feet to start flying the course work. In a few minutes I noticed that the aircraft drifted into a slight right wing down position. He corrected it, but it started again. I asked him over the intercom if there was something wrong. He answered that he had been putting in trim to account for a heavy wing. I took the controls and could immediately feel the heaviness of the right wing. We had a problem!

I figured that the right tip tank was not transferring fuel. I cut off the transfer on the left tip tank so as not to further increase the effect of the fuel weight in the right tip tank. He came out from under the hood as I banked the aircraft into a turn and started back to Moffett. I let down to 5,000 feet to feel the effect on the aircraft by the uneven weight in the landing configuration. It was not very good below 150 knots because the plane gave indications of being uncontrollable. I kept the gear down to burn up as much fuel as possible and notified the Moffett control tower that I had a problem and declared an emergency. I received immediate clearance for my approach and landing. The crash crews manning the fire trucks were already out in full force spaced down the runway off in the grass as I made a straight-in approach and crossed the end of the runway with the extra air speed to give positive control. I held the plane off the runway to bleed off the airspeed as much as possible until I felt the right wing getting heavy. I touched the plane down on the runway as gently as possible. We were well above the maximum weight for landing. It rolled straight and level for a few more hundred feet, and then the right wing began to drop further as the plane lost more air speed. It kept dropping as I started to brake hard to stop the aircraft as soon as possible. The fire trucks were racing after us in case the tip tank struck the runway and started losing fuel or in the worse case caught fire. The plane stopped on the runway near the right-hand side with the right tip tank about six inches from the cement. That was too close for comfort! I had opened the canopy once the speed had dropped low enough so we could get out if there was a fire. Fully stopped I cut the engine off, and we waited for the ladder to arrive.

The flight-line jeep soon arrived with the ladder, and we both climbed out. We rode back to the hanger in the jeep, leaving the aircraft for the ground crew to bring back to the hanger using a tractor. After the aircraft was towed back to the hanger the mechanics found that the transfer pump on that tip tank had failed. It was just my luck to get an airplane with a problem.

The following day we flew twice to finish the course for the pilot. By then I had learned I would be transferred to the advance training command and assume duties of a flight instructor. Besides my jet flying I also flew three flights in the SNB-5, for 7.8 hours. I had to fly another checkout flight in the SNB-5 for night flying. Then I flew a cross-country to NAAS El Centro at night and returned for night flying qualification requirements with LCDR McDowell. It sure was different buzzing along at 8,000 feet. We flew down the central valley then through the mountain pass to El Centro. It was a beautiful night, but I did not enjoy looking out and seeing the mountains on either side. I was too used to looking down at them, rather than from the side. I had one fun flight on the April 15th. I was able to get a scheduled flight in VF-153's new F9F-6 swept-wing aircraft. Ensign Bud Marler had arranged for me to take a flight with him doing the duty as chase pilot. I flew the F9F-6 on one flight for 1.5 hours all over northern California. It sure had a lot more speed and power than the last F9F I flew. I took the opportunity to engage the "flying tail" and flew it through the speed of sound, Mach 1. All together I flew 31 flights that month for a total of 56.7 hours.

I would have liked to stay at Moffett because the flying was great, and the area was wonderful with so much to see and do. But that was not to be. I finally received orders to report to NAS Corpus Christi for assignment to a training unit in the advance training command. At first the staff at NAS Corpus Christi wanted to assign Charlie and me to NAAS Beeville flying the propeller driven T-28. Charlie led the fight, and he finally convinced them that with all that jet experience and instrument flying we should be assigned to a jet-training unit. We then received our new orders to NAAS Kingsville, assigning us to ATU-202 to be flight instructors in the F9F-2 unit.

I had no idea what this part of Texas was like, so it was a total shock to see this vast empty place. It was only May, but it was hot, dusty, and the wind blew out of the southeast every day. My wife and I were both a little down in the dumps when we first saw what the rental houses looked like. We soon found out that a new housing project had been built close to the base and the apartments were all new. It was filled with Navy families, and once we moved in, things began to look a little better. Neither of us could get used to the heat. I had been in the Corpus Christi area during my advance training, but there was a big difference between the two places. We settled in, and I started my job of becoming a flight instructor.

I checked out in the F9F-2 at the end of May, making four flights, for six hours. Two flights were for touch-and-go landings, since I hadn't flown this aircraft type for over eight months. In the course of becoming accustomed to the F9F-2 again, I discovered that there were a number of the aircraft at Kingsville that had been originally assigned to VF-831 several years before. My life began to settle down into the routine of flying five days, traveling with my wife on the weekends, and getting settled into some sense of normalcy.

In June, I flew the F9F-2 for 23 flights and 33.0 flight hours. On June 26 a hurricane in the Gulf of Mexico threatened the Texas coast around Corpus Christi, and the Navy ordered that all flyable aircraft be flown inland to escape the strong wind. The jets were to fly to a US Air Force Base outside of Austin, Texas. I was one of the last to leave Kingsville because the aircraft I was assigned had to have some maintenance completed before it could be flown. The advance weather condition caused by the hurricane was moving closer when I finally left. It was a short distance to Austin, and I was in the air about 40 minutes before landing at the air base. The airfield was covered with Navy planes; they were parked all over every available hard surface. The ground crew was overwhelmed trying to re-fuel such a large number of aircraft. Soon after arriving the flyaway was called off because the hurricane changed direction and headed into Mexico. I was lucky enough to get re-fueled in a short time, because I wanted to leave for Kingsville before the weather became worse. The ground crew had started re-fueling the aircraft that had landed last rather than the first ones that had landed. All fueled up, I went into the base operation for flight clearance and before anyone could change their minds I had a jeep take me out to my aircraft. I was soon airborne and headed for Kingsville.

The weather was clear at Austin, but the storm clouds were evident as I reached my halfway point. With plenty of fuel, I dropped down to stay below the clouds. I learned later that after I left they stopped allowing planes to return because the weather at Kingsville started deteriorating rapidly with low clouds and heavy rain showers. I was still operating under Visual Flight Rules (VFR), but the cloud cover was getting darker as I crossed over the highway from Alice, Texas, to Corpus Christi. At this point, I was close enough to NAS Kingsville to be able to convince the tower controller to let me land. I changed my fight plan to Instrument Flight Rules (IFR) and proceeded on instruments. The rain became very heavy, with the ceiling and visibility lowering by the minute. I was cleared by the control tower to contact Ground Control Approach (GCA) to start my approach pattern. I reduced my altitude to 2,000 feet while lowering my seat to make it easier to fly instruments. I was in the clouds and settled in flying the gauges while I made contact with the GCA unit. Their search radarscope picked me up, and they gave me a vector to put me on my downwind leg and ordered me to descend to 1,000 feet. Reaching 1,000 feet I lowered my landing gear and went through my landing check-off list. The controller gave me another vector to start my crosswind leg. After my turn on to the crosswind leg the rain became so heavy that GCA lost me on their radarscope. Fortunately I spotted the lights of the petrochemical plant that was several miles directly northwest of the runway 13-31 and started a turn to line up on the runway heading, 130 degrees just as the controller saw me again on his radarscope. Rolling out of the turn I was handed off to the GCA approach controller.

Just then I flew into another heavy rain area, and my position was lost on the radarscope. Fortunately the GCA approach controller was able to pick me up again as I came out of the heavy rain area and the approach controller guided me towards the spot in the sky to start the beginning of my glide path. On the controller's orders to start my descent from 1,000 feet I dropped my landing flaps and the aircraft began to slowly settle at the proper rate to stay on the GCA glide slope. The turbulence from the strong wind from the left was buffeting the aircraft and it was difficult to stay on the glide path heading. I had to fly slightly into the wind or "crab" so the aircraft would stay on the ground track of the runways centerline.

Just as I reached about 100 feet above the runway I broke out of the overcast and was able to set the plane down on the runway even with the crosswind. I had to keep up the crab until almost the end. When the wheels touched down, there was so much water on the runway that I looked more like a speedboat than an airplane, throwing up a large spray of water from my main landing gear. It was worse when the air speed dropped and the nose wheel touched down. But with the strong wind and the drag of the water on the wheels it didn't take long before I was slowed to a crawl. I thanked the GCA controller for his great guidance and taxied slowly back to the ramp area. The taxiways were hard to follow with all the water on the field. This area of Texas is so very flat that the water drains away very slowly. When I got close to the hanger, the ground crew pushed the door open far enough for me to gun the engine and roll into the hanger. Crossing the entrance, I shut the engine off and came to a stop inside. They quickly closed the hanger doors against the wind, and I was able to climb out without getting too wet. All my instrument training and actual instrument flying paid off very well. I was a little tense because of the heavy rain and turbulence, but I felt completely in control.

In early July, I began to give refresher instrument check rides to Naval Aviators needing their instrument rating updated. These checkout rides were in the TV-2 just as it was when I was at Moffett. I flew 12 flights for 21.9 hours in the TV-2. I also flew the F9F-2 for 19 flights for 28.4 hours. I found several more of the F9F-2 aircraft that were assigned to the training unit that were ones I had flown before when they were part of VF-831. On July 13, I had a deferred emergency when a hydraulic line failed in the engine section of the aircraft filling the cockpit with blue smoke. I first thought I had a fire, but there were no fire warning lights on, and I could soon smell the recognizable odor of the hot hydraulic fluid. The control tower gave me clearance for a straight-in approach. When on final with no hydraulic pressure I blew the landing gear down with the emergency air bottle. It was the second time I had to use the emergency air bottle. With no hydraulic pressure I would have to make a no-flap landing. With the higher air speed needed for a no-flap landing, I used almost the entire 10,000-foot runway to get the aircraft stopped. In addition to the higher landing speed for a no-flap landing, the braking ability on the main gear was not all that good because it also depended upon hydraulic pressure as well.

During the first part of August I flew 18 flights for a total of 27.6 hours. Of these, five flights were in the TV-2 for nine hours and 13 flights in the F9F-2 for a total of 16.6 hours. There was an opening for a ground-school instructor and being a rather junior officer I was assigned to take this job. So at the end of August I was transferred to ground school as an instructor in flight safety and F9F-2 engineering. It was a change in the pace for me. I would not be flying that much because of the class schedule. The students coming into advance training spent two weeks in classroom work before they took their first flight in the F9F-2. I thought the course work was weak and didn't really cover the essentials I felt that they should learn. I approached the officer in charge of ground school, a Marine major, and laid out my case. He was interested, so he said for me to develop a detailed lesson plan and final test. I started this effort along with my regular class work.

In September, I flew only three flights in the TV-2 as an Instructor Pilot for instruments for the other training squadron, ATU-200, flying students for their final instrument check ride. I put only 4.9 hours into my logbook. I also started taking two classes at the small college in Kingsville, Texas A. & I. As long as I was going to be in Kingsville I wanted to add some more college credits to move me further towards a bachelor degree. I knew I would, sometime in the future, be assigned to go back to school full time to complete my last two years under the Navy program and obtain my degree, but I wanted to keep my study habits up.

During October, I continued my main duties as a ground-school instructor as well as a substitute F9F-2 instructor and an instructor pilot for instruments. I enjoyed my studies at the college and made friends with the history professor. I got an interesting view on US History from the Texas point of view. My wife had her history books from her courses at Brown University. You would think these two sets of books were written about two different counties!

During November, I started my check out in the SNB-5 to become re qualified as a twin-engine pilot. Even though I had flown it many times before, I had to get another check ride. I would then be available for utility flights for the various training units at both fields. The north field was for the jets, while the south field was for the two-propeller advance-training units. I flew three flights for a total of 6.2 hours. The first was a check ride, and the second was an instrument check ride. The last one was to build up flight time. Whenever I went to operations to fly I called ahead to schedule the aircraft and also to let them know I would take passengers. Some of the enlisted crew needed flight time to qualify for flight pay. I became very popular with this small group because I would load up the aircraft and take them on a sight-seeing tour of south Texas. I often enjoyed making the flight interesting by pointing out items on the ground. I also had fun by letting one of my fuel tanks run dry while flying at a reasonable altitude. When this happened the engines stopped. The sailors in the back of the airplane were often sitting with their eyes closed. The lack of engine sound certainly startled them to become wide-awake. I quickly switched to another tank and the engines started right up. Continuing my college course it was time to prepare for my two final exams that were coming up in December.

In December, qualified as an SNB-5 first pilot, I flew the aircraft 4 times for 7.5 hours. I started practicing flying under the hood to increase my instrument capability in this aircraft. I flew with the ground school officer in charge so I could build up my flight time, and he could take a refresher series of flights. It was a lot of fun, and we learned from each other. When the training command closed down for the Christmas holiday I took a break from flying, teaching, and college class work. My wife and I drove north to visit our families in New Jersey and Rhode Island. We returned to Kingsville on January 1, 1955 after a long round trip of over 3,800 miles.

January was a full flying month, flying the SNB-5, TV-2 and the F6F-5. There were two flights in the SNB-5 for 3.3 hours, one flight in the TV-2 for 1.4 hours and three flights in the F6F-5 for 7.6 hours. The latter was made up with a familiarization flight and then a ferry flight to Pensacola, Florida. The other naval aviators in the flight had not flown the F6F, so I was appointed the flight leader. It was interrupted at Lake Charles when one member of the flight crashed landed his F6F in a farmer's field after running out of gas east of the air base. We had started out fully loaded with fuel including a belly tank. In my briefing, I stressed that we would takeoff on the left tank and once at cruising altitude we switched over to the belly tank. When we reached Lake Charles, we then had almost emptied the belly tanks and we were to switch to the right tank. The weather had gotten overcast when we reached the Lake Charles area and ferry flights were to be flown using Visual Flight Rules (VFR) so I had dropped down to a 1,000 feet to stay under the clouds. Unfortunately, one of the pilots did not switch over when I gave the order, and his engine stopped because of fuel starvation. He quickly lost altitude and made successful wheels-up crash landing in a farmer's field. I immediately set up a rescue pattern. Ordering the remaining pilots to circle the crash site while I flew north to the main east west highway. I contacted the Lake Charles tower on guard channel and they quickly launched a rescue helicopter. I was circling a small road intersection waiting for the helicopter. Once I spotted it, I led it to the crash site to pick up the pilot. The other joined up with me and I headed towards the Lake Charles air base. We could not make it to Pensacola with the fuel we had on board, so landing at the base was the only option. It also turned out that the weather was getting worse, and I wanted to get the flight on the ground. Everyone landed okay, and we were finally allowed to get into operations and find out about the condition of the downed pilot. He was only shook up. That made two of us. We were stuck at Lake Charles for an extra day because the weather was too poor for VFR flying. The following day we were able to leave and made it to Pensacola in a little over two hours. Back at Kingsville I was called before the accident board for my statement. I did not receive any official comment over this mess. Unofficially, I did get a pat on the back for my handling of the crash and rescue. The airplane was going back to Pensacola to be made into a drone. These drones were used in gunnery testing and other flights where the aircraft was to be destroyed. We just did it sooner!

February produced a total of 7.4 hours. I flew 4.8 hours in the SNB-5 and 2.6 hours in the TV-2. I flew to Austin, Texas on a utility flight in the SNB to fly a maintenance crewman to repair a grounded F9F-2 aircraft that was flown by a student. Much of the flight was on instruments, 1.8 hours. My instrument practice had again paid off with a smooth flight, radio range approach and a VFR landing. Around Kingsville I also had six practice GCA approaches, five in the SNB-5, the other in the TV-2. These were all under the hood rather than actual. At ground school, the new lesson plan on safety was introduced to an incoming class. I warned them that it was going to be more difficult and they must pay close attention and learn the safety rules. Also, the new lesson plan for F9F engineering was started and the examination also had a lot more detailed questions. Unfortunately, a number of the students didn't take my warning very seriously, so at the end of the two weeks they failed the tests. That meant they had to repeat the course. There were some very unhappy cadets, but I wanted future aviators to know their stuff. I was not the most popular instructor on the air base.

March was much the same, four flights, three in the SNB-5, and one in the TV-2 for a total of 8.6 hours. On two of the flights I acted as instrument instructor for another naval aviator taking a refresher course. My All Weather Flight School training allowed me to continue instructing in instruments. April was a repeat of ground school teaching, attending college classes, flying a little and trying to stay cool as the heat in south Texas was going higher and higher. Summer comes early in this area. I flew only three flights, one in the SNB-5 and two in the F9F-2 flights for a total of 5.8 hours. One of the F9F-2 flights was a night flight when I was escorting a flight of students during their introduction to night flying. Flying with students at night was not the most relaxing thing to do. It required a lot of attention to keep all the aircraft in sight and keep them safe. Night formation flying is not easy and with students doing it one can become very tense.

May turned out to be a much busier flying month with an extended cross-country flight to San Diego, California, and return. I hadn't flown instruments in the TV-2 in a while, so to prepare for this trip I flew a flight in the back seat to sharpen up my instrument flying. Also the last leg was to be at night to fulfill my night-flying hours, a yearly requirement. I carried another flight instructor out with me because he was going on leave, and I gave him a ride to San Diego. It was an easy flight across Texas, and we landed at El Paso. After re-fueling we proceeded to fly the next leg to our western destination, NAS North Island at San Diego. We arrived in the late morning because of the time difference of two hours. I got the aircraft re-fueled while I grabbed a quick lunch for the trip back. I wanted to get to El Paso at dusk so my takeoff after refueling would be at night as well.

The third leg went off with out a hitch, and I was happy to be on schedule. Checking in to operations after landing, I made arrangements for the aircraft to be refueled. I then got with the weather people for an up date on the weather to NAAS Kingsville via San Antonio. There was no frontal activity, but there was the possibility of local thunderstorms in the area coming in off of the gulf. That was standard for the south Texas area. After a pre-flight of the aircraft I fired up the engine and with clearance from the tower taxied out to the duty runway. On the way I received my clearance from Air Traffic Control (ATC). Cleared to take-off, I lined up on the runway, went to full throttle and started my takeoff roll. As soon as I was air borne I cleaned up the aircraft raising first the landing gear, then the flaps, built up the airspeed, and started my climb to the east. The sunset was almost complete but as I climbed to my cruise altitude of 35,000 feet I could still see the sunlight behind me. It soon disappeared, and I was alone with a heaven full of stars. The moon was not due to rise until half way through my flight. I had estimated it would take me about 1.7 hours to reach Kingsville. About 100 miles out from San Antonio I contacted ATC and asked if I was correct on the time for the moon to show. He said he would check and radio back that it had. I could not see anything and was mildly concerned. I requested the weather and when he radioed back it wasn't too good. A large thunderstorm had rolled in from the Gulf of Mexico and it was currently over Corpus Christi moving to west northwest. I began to notice lighting streaks ahead at my altitude. Anticipating the storm I requested a change in my altitude to 40,000 feet from the ATC controller. He granted it, and said I was the only one out at this altitude in all of south Texas. He then radioed back that the storm was closing in on San Antonio and that a commercial airliner had turned away because of the storm. *Great*, I thought. Requesting the weather at Kingsville from ATC he reported that it was raining heavily. The weather all around was getting bad. As I reached San Antonio, I started to climb some more to stay above the storm. I realized when I reached 49,000 feet that I was in the storm, and the airplane could go no higher. I turned towards a heading for Kingsville wanting to fly out of this monster storm. At this altitude, I had only five-knots between stall airspeed and compressibility for the TV-2. Not the best situation to be in. The ice crystals in the thunderhead created a large amount of static electricity, and it showed up as purple streaks all over the canopy. Pretty, but I was too busy to enjoy this scenic activity. The heavy static had knocked out my low-frequency automatic directional finder (ADF) radio so that instrument was useless. I could not use it to home in on the Kingsville radio. When I believed I was close enough, I broadcast a radio call to the Kingsville Control Tower. My first attempt was unsuccessful. A few minutes later I tried again. This time I got a response. They were glad to hear from me, and the feeling was mutual. They requested a long count so they could take a bearing on my UHF voice radio broadcast. After a moment, they gave me a heading to follow. The storm clouds began to thin out at my altitude so I started a slow descent to get to a lower altitude.

Even with the cabin heat full on it was cold in the cockpit. The outside air was a nice cold -55 degrees. I rode a few knots below the mach needle as I descended to 40,000 feet. The next long count showed that I was somewhere above the station so I started my instrument let down. Even at 4,000 feet a minute, it is a long way from 40,000 feet. At 30,000 feet I made 90-degree turn to the right and then a 270-degree turn to the left to come back on the opposite heading all the while letting down at 4,000 feet a minute. I reached 20,000 feet and repeated the same procedure, this time stopping my let down at 5,000 feet and after another long count, they determined I was back over the air base. I started my final let down to 2,500 feet in a shallow 180 degree turns. As I approached 2,500 feet the GCA units long range radar picked me up on their radarscope and notified the control tower operator. The control tower operator cleared me to contact the GCA unit, and I switched over to their radio frequency.

Their welcome voice came in loud and clear. They had me on their radarscope, and I started letting down headed for the downwind leg under their control. It was still raining hard, and the noise of it hitting the aircraft was so loud I could hear it in spite of my helmet. I was ordered to make a 90-degree left turn to my crosswind leg. During this turn I kept going in and out of heavy rain. They advised me that they were having difficulty trying to maintaining radar contact. I gave them a "Roger" message and continued. I did have enough fuel for two maybe three passes. On their orders, I made another 90-degree turn onto the final approach heading and lowered my landing gear and flaps and made my adjustment to my power setting. I hit the point in the sky to start my descent on the glide path and began my descent. In this aircraft I had found that all that was necessary was to drop the speed brakes, and the plane started settling at the proper rate. It was still raining hard. They were going to talk me in to within 100 feet of altitude, but as I got lower I still couldn't see much. Just as I leveled out at 100 feet I spotted the runway lights, and with great delight settled the aircraft on the runway. Once again I made like a speedboat. I realized my flight suit was rather wet, and it wasn't from the rain. I needed to wait at the end of the runway for a jeep to lead me in. All the taxiway lights were out of order because they had been drowned in all the rainwater. Again the ground crew opened the hanger doors, and I did a repeat of my earlier wet flight. This time, however when the nose section door was opened, the inside was filled with ice. The aircraft had been so cold that when the rainwater had come in around the gun ports it froze into solid ice. I figured I could collect my bag the next day. I had been in the air for 7.3 hours during the four flights. Once on the ground, out of the aircraft, I realized that I was one tired guy. The month ended with seven flights and 11.5 flight hours.

June started out okay with news that I might be reassigned back to the training squadron as a flight instructor flying the F9F-2 as well as an instrument instructor pilot. I flew three flights in the first few days in the F9F-2 and a flight in the TV-2 for two hours. This flight was at night to continue keeping up my qualifications in this aircraft. In mid-month I piloted the SNB-5 for a two-hour flight and then was asked to ferry some personnel to the main base at Corpus Christi and return. Then on Monday the 27th I was assigned to fly with a student who had failed his instrument course, but returned for one more try. The disposition review board at Kingsville had given him a rejection to continue in the flight program, as did the staff of the Advance Training Command. Admiral Glover, head of the Advance Training Command, however, over ruled the rejections. On June 27, 1955 I reviewed his flight jacket and found that he had been rated as a below-average student. He was an eager student, but the reports were damning. I spent some time with him going over the three check rides we were going to fly.

On the first flight I did the takeoff and after we were airborne had him go under the hood and continue the climb to altitude. One of my means to determine how smoothly a student flew was to have him just fly straight and level and then to make shallow turns to heading and such simple flying. This showed me what he could do. This student was careless and let the aircraft drift too far before correcting the drift. I tried to get him to relax and let the airplane fly itself. He wasn't using the trim tabs very well either. Basically he was not a good pilot. How he made it this far was amazing. Maybe he was marginal flying around in the clear sky, but he was very poor flying on instruments. I had him continue with air work and then directed him to start the let-down towards Kingsville. After we reached 2,500 feet, I took over, and he came out from under the hood. I made the usual approach to the field, flying towards the duty runway, and did an overhead carrier break pulling a tight turn towards the downwind leg. With wheels and flaps down I made the 180-degree descending turn to a short straightaway and touchdown smoothly about 500 feet down the runway. I talked to him after the flight covering things he needed to think about for the next flight on Tuesday. I stressed that he had not developed a good scan on the flight instruments as well as he was too tense.

Early Tuesday morning I was scheduled with him for another flight. I went over with him about his scanning of the flight instruments and also flying the aircraft with a light, relaxed touch. Flying on instruments did not need a lot of control stick movement, just pressure. Also, he was to make an instrument takeoff as part of the check out. He seemed to be in good spirits, so we went out to the flight line and did a pre-flight of the aircraft. He climbed in first and settled into the rear seat and followed and settled into the front seat. When all set, I fired up the engine and gave the signal to the ground crew to pull the chocks. We rolled out to the duty runway without a pause because the ground traffic was light at this hour. It was just before seven in the morning. We moved to takeoff position on the runway and locked the brakes. He then took control, and when the tower cleared us he added throttle to full and then released the brakes. He maintained his heading and we rolled smoothly down the runway. As the air speed reached 90 knots he lifted the nose wheel off the deck and we danced along on the main gear until we reached flying speed.

Just as we lifted off the runway, he suddenly pulled the control stick back, and we went into a steep climb. I yelled at him to get off the controls and immediately pushed the stick forward to the left land corner. We had already started into a stall as the right wing dropped about 45 degrees. I yanked the landing-gear handle up and noticed the engine power was dropping off. "Good God!" he had pulled the throttle back as well. I slammed the throttle forward and started my hand for the emergency tip tank jettison button on the lower part of the instrument panel to lighten the aircraft. Those two tanks, when full, weighed about one and a quarter tons, and with them off I could make the plane a lot lighter. I never made it. We hit the ground at the end of the runway with a terrible impact. The aircraft continued skidding on its belly into the brush for about 500 feet. When the airplane stopped I tried to move and found that I had no strength and I was in unbelievably intense pain.

We needed to get out if there was a fire, but someone was looking out for me, because there was no fire. The smell of dust and JP fuel was very strong, but there was no way I had enough strength to pull the emergency release to open the canopy. I learned later that I was suffering from shock. Noticing that there were a lot of red lights glowing on the instrument panel I thought, *Hey, I have electrical power,* and hit the canopy open switch, and up it went. That is when I heard the engine running. I tried to kill it, but the throttle just flopped around. The linkage was broken. I reached for the emergency fuel shutoff, and I had just enough strength to be able to break the safety wire protecting the switch and kill the engine. The first crash truck arrived moments later, and soon they were all around us. I was almost blinded by the pain that came over me in great waves. I was not going to pass out, not with the problem I had.

The medical crew reached the accident site in short order, and the doctor climbed up the ladder to get to me and in one swift moment raised my flight suit arm and jabbed me with a load of morphine. After questioning me, he organized the crew to get me out of the cockpit. He knew I had probably broken my spinal column. How to get me out without doing further damage was going to be tough. First the crew had to wait while an ordnance man could be brought out and safety the ejection seats. The impact had armed them. Once done, they were able to remove the canopy and then get the student out. He appeared not to be in too bad shape. To get me out without doing further damage was going to be a problem. It turned out that a member of the crash crew was a wrestler, and he was really strong. While others held his feet, he stood on the nose of the aircraft and squatting down reached into the cockpit over the windscreen to lift me up. I could not help him because I had lost all use of my legs. As he lifted me up, others braced my body so it remained locked in one position. They got me almost horizontal and then slid a stretcher in under me so I could be placed face down on my stomach. Securing me on the stretcher they were able to gently lower me down to the ground. They then put another stretcher on top of me, put strap around me and were able to flip me over without my body moving. All this took over an hour. The morphine didn't help that much, but managed to keep the screams down that were generated by the intense pain inside me. The ambulance slowly drove me away from the crash site to the base hospital. After stabilizing my condition with fluids and stitching up a cut I had received on my chin from hitting my flight suit zipper, I was taken by ambulance the 60 miles to the Corpus Christi Naval Hospital. It was a very painful ride even with the amount of painkiller I had received.

Chapter 18
The Going Gets Tough

I arrived by ambulance in the late morning at the Naval Hospital located on the grounds of the Corpus Christi Naval Air Station. The ride from Kingsville was a blur of continuous pain that was magnified by every bump in the road. It was all I could do to repress the screams that rose from my throat. It was pure, burning hell. The crew carefully took me to the Sick Officer Quarters (SOQ) wing of the hospital. After a review of my current medical condition by the medical staff, I was then taken to the laboratory for X-rays to determine the extent of my internal injuries. The x-rays showed that I had smashed my first lumbar vertebra in my lower back. The bone fragments had penetrated my spinal column causing an unknown amount of nerve damage. I was in shock, and my condition was critical. I was placed in a private room with a corpsman overseeing my condition 24 hours a day. The shock was treated with a continuous stream of saline fluid dripping into my arm. The day ended with a large dose of morphine, and I finally fell into a drugged sleep. I drifted between sleep and pain for days depending upon when I got a needle full of morphine. One of the painful parts of me was my feet. They were hyper sensitive, and I could not even stand a light touch without having a horrible pain shoot through me. During one of the days, the Commanding Officer of the hospital made the rounds of the wards. He stopped in to see me, and after a briefing by my doctor on my condition he turned to me and assured me that I would get the best of care. As he left he reached out and patted me on the foot. The nurse made a valiant try to stop him, but when he made contact I let out a scream. He was very upset and apologized as he left. I felt bad about that scream, but the pain had been so intense it just came out. Slowly my condition improved, and my team of doctors' thought I had responded well enough that I could withstand surgery to fix my back.

On Monday the next week, in the early morning, I was taken to surgery at the hospital and operated on to fix my back. The pair of surgeons, one Navy and the other a civilian, spent almost six hours carefully removing the bone splinters from around the spinal column and fusing my spine around the shattered vertebrae. The loss of the vertebrae resulted in the loss of almost an inch in my height. I did not wake up from this operation for three days, as I was kept well supplied with morphine for pain, as they wanted to keep me as quiet as possible. I was not put into a body cast, but was just lying flat on my back. I slowly began to come to the surface and recognized the staff and my wife who was by my side every day. I was completely paralyzed from the waist down from the moment of the crash, and the operation did nothing to change my status.

As I became aware of my surroundings, I found myself on a miserable bed called a "Stryker frame." It was narrow and was designed so that the body could be turned over every four hours to reduce the chance of getting bedsores. It consisted of a long oval metal frame with a canvas stretched in the middle. On top of this was a thin layer of foam rubber, then a sheet. To flip me over, first a sheet was laid on top of me followed by the layer of foam rubber. Then another frame similar to the bottom frame was placed on top of the foam rubber. The top frame was bolted just like the bottom frame to the head and foot of the vertical section that sat on the floor. The last thing that was done was to place three large cargo straps around this entire "sandwich" with me being the filling. These straps were tightened so that my body could not move. I could barely breathe they were so tight. A crank was inserted in the plate at the foot of the bed and when all was ready the entire bed was flipped over. I soon got so used to this crazy activity that it did not bother me at all. At first it was just plain terror to be rotated around. Between the painkiller and lots of bottles of blood, saline water and glucose dripping into me, I stayed alive for the first week after the operation. I ate nothing for many days. I did manage to get a small amount of liquid food down a little later in the beginning of the following week, but I learned that trying to eat or drink fluids lying on my back or stomach was not easy. Often after eating, my messed up nervous system rejected the food in my stomach, and I had to press the call button for a corpsman to clean me up. I was helpless as a newborn baby. I was so weak that I could not hold a full glass of anything. The first month was the worst period I have ever had in my life. The pain was constant with frequent cramps in my legs and feet. It was then that I learned that the pain in my lower body was going to be my constant companion for the rest of my life. It was not a very comforting thought.

The days went slowly by. For countless hours my lovely wife sat by my side. It must have been horrible for her to witness the misery and difficulties I went through. She was a tower of strength in my many moments of despair. The surgeon told her that the best he hoped for was for me to be able to use a wheelchair. She kept silent and did not tell me this news until much later. The days passed slowly. The night hours were filled with the torments of pain, mental agony, or drug-induced sleep. Through this ordeal the Navy nurses and corpsmen that took care of me were wonderful. They were compassionate and very professional. I could not have asked for a better team than those who helped me pull through this ordeal. The changes I hoped for did not come for weeks and weeks. I was in a state of suspense. I was in deep despair that I would have to live the life of a cripple. I had lost everything I had worked so hard to reach. There were many times that I cursed and damned that stupid student. He suffered only a cracked vertebrae and was discharged a month after the accident. I did not see him ever again. That was the lowest point in my life. I only knew it was the weekend because of the reduced staff on the ward. The day of the month was not important. The only thing that was important was when I could get the next shot of Demerol. I was a first-class junkie.

July and August passed slowly with little difference among the days. As time passed I began to adjust to the hospital routine. The thermometer arrived at seven in the morning followed by breakfast. Soon after came my morning sponge bath and my ration of pills. Gads, I must have taken hundreds of pills while I was in the hospital. The weekdays were better than the weekends because there was activity in the ward. There were only a few officers in the other rooms who stayed a short time and were gone. I was getting to be an old timer, so the staff was my only contact within the ward. My wife was always there during the afternoon for moral support and conversation. Once she left, and the sun had set, the dreaded night started. I got my shot of Demerol at 10:00 P.M. to ease the pain and let me sleep. I usually awoke after four hours and they fed me Seconal to put me back to sleep. When they woke me up in the morning it tasted like an army had marched through my mouth. By then I could take fluids, and so I got my jolt of caffeine from good old Navy coffee.

In mid-September I was lying on the frame, covered only by a sheet with a small pillow under my head, looking at my toes sticking up at the end of the bed. The physical therapist who visited me in my room to start the rehabilitation process said to me, "Think hard about moving a muscle."

What the hell did she mean? How do I move them? We take for granted that we can move them. I stared at my feet, and with mental determination willed those toes to move. Nothing happened at all. It was a bunch of junk as far as I knew. I kept at it, however, because I wanted it so bad. As I lay there staring at those toes, my right big toe twitched. *Did it really move?* I tried again to think about making it move. Suddenly it did! I let out a yell, and that brought a corpsman running. I said to him, "Watch the toe; watch my right toe, and tell me if it is my imagination." It moved, and he smiled with me. When the doctors found out they were just as excited. That meant that my nerves to my lower body where not completely gone. When Beverly came in that day after lunch, and I told her what had happened, she broke into a big smile; tears streamed down both our cheeks. It was exciting for us. I never thought I could get so excited over the movement of one toe. The future looked a lot less bleak. How much of my damaged nerve would return was yet unknown to me at that time, but there was hope.

About this time the doctor told me that he wanted to stop the painkiller medicine I received everyday. I thought that wouldn't be any big deal because the pain had decreased to the point that I could function okay during the day. The more I ate, the stronger I got, and was able to keep my mind off of the pain. He gave me two weeks to make the break. I could have it for two weeks, and then go "cold turkey" at the end, or I could try to go a day without it. I thought, I'd try the day off routine because what could happen? I usually got this shot at 10:00 P.M. The first night I was tired and sleepy by ten o'clock, so it seemed that I could just doze off and go to sleep. Boy, was I wrong! By ten after the hour, my body was calling for a shot. I tried to ignore the sensations, but my palms began to sweat and my body began to have cramps. I was a full-fledged junkie. I took the shot the first night and vowed to work harder the next day to get real tired. I was so beat that next night that I finally went to sleep from shear exhaustion about 3:00 A.M. I was determined to break this hold the painkiller had on me. It took everything I had to make it through the two weeks, but I did it. I was free of the medicine. But just as a smoker thinks about a cigarette, there were times when I thought that one shot of Demerol would be just fine.

By the end of September, my back had finally healed well enough for me to sit up. But before I could sit up I was fitted with a back brace to keep me from doing any twisting to damage the fusing of the vertebrae. When this back brace arrived I was transferred to a regular hospital bed so I could sit up with my legs over the side. The first time I sat up, the blood drained from my head and my feet turned purple. I almost passed out. It took a while before my body began the adjustment to being upright. I had been horizontal for many weeks. At first, because I was so weak, I could sit up for only about 20 minutes at a time. The first time I was helped into a wheelchair, the corpsman wheeled me down to the nurse's station to be weighed. Holding me upright they obtained my first weighing. I topped the scales at 108 pounds. My normal weight before the accident was 140 pounds. Every morning and afternoon I got up and sat in a chair placed close to the bed. At first I needed a lot of help, but I soon could make it on my own. I kept at it and I forced myself to do it five to ten minutes longer each week. To keep my mind active I started to read again. Between physical therapy and reading I began to feel my way towards getting better. It was going to be a long road to independence, but at this time I did not know how long.

I had started a full series of sessions with the physical therapy team to first build my shoulder muscles so I could use crutches. That wasn't difficult because they were unaffected by the crash. I sat in the wheelchair and pulled weights. It sure felt good to move my arms. The condition of my leg muscles was another matter. Because they had not moved for so long, the muscles had badly atrophied. The first task was to stretch these muscles so the process to strengthen them could start. The corpsman had to manually move my legs, and as he bent the legs at the knees, the pain was terrible. It felt like a red-hot needle was being pushed into the joint. There was no easy way to do it. To help, they first lowered me on a stretcher into a very large tank of hot water and turn on the two big whirlpool machines. This tank, called a Huber tank, was big enough to put my entire body under water up to my neck. After about 20 minutes I soaked up a lot of heat. Near the end, they tossed in a handful of soap and I got my daily bubble bath. After drying me off, I was moved into another room so the corpsman could stretch my leg muscles. I had them put a wet face cloth in my mouth so I could not scream out loud or bite my tongue. I wanted them to do it, but I didn't want them to ease up because it hurt so bad. After a session with them I was completely exhausted. I ached for hours, and there was no relief from the pain. No matter, each day it got easier and easier. I learned just how much pain I could take. What is that old saying, "When the going gets tough, the tough get going"?

Finally, being stretched out, I could start to work on my legs to build up what muscles responded. Not all the muscles reacted, because the nerves to these muscles were too damaged as the result of the crash. Sitting on a bench, I was to raise my lower legs to bring them into a horizontal position. The first time I tried it I could not raise the leg with a shoe on it. The shoe was just too heavy. I kept at it, and a few days later could do it. From there, they kept adding weights. First it was a metal shoe, and then it was with a metal bar through the metal shoe. Soon after came the extra weights to continue the process. My left leg got stronger but my right leg just couldn't get past the twenty-five-pound mark. I tried to work on the muscles on the back of the leg, but they were the ones that were affected the most. I never was able to get much out of them.

Not all was misery. On one occasion while lying on the bed in the therapy area, after a workout, the cute Navy physical therapist was trying to get me to move my muscles in my butt. I was lying on my stomach and really wasn't getting it. I had no feeling or sensation in my buttocks so I really didn't know what she meant. She marched out in front of me and with her butt about a foot in front of my face she showed me what she meant. She sure did wiggle her butt muscles. She suddenly realized what she was doing and turned red in the face and ran out of the room. The two corpsmen with me could not stop laughing. It took her a number of days before she could face me again. She was one great lady.

The days passed slowly with small improvements each week. I pulled weights twice a day to strengthen my shoulder muscles so I could support myself, first between the parallel bars and then on crutches. I worked on my leg muscles, but found that only a few responded to my workout. My right leg lagged behind my left leg and never gained much strength, but got the most important muscles in my legs to work, so I did not have to look forward to wearing leg braces. My overall strength was coming back, and my appetite improved. Earlier, when I was on the striker frame, the doctors' were trying to help me keep my food down. I jokingly said to him that a shot of booze might help. My doctor, Lieutenant Philip James, had been a flight surgeon with a carrier air group and knew a lot about naval aviators. That evening just before dinnertime the corpsman came walking in carrying a small tray that was covered over with a cloth napkin. With a big grin and great fanfare he uncovered the tray, and there sat a shot glass of medicinal booze. I sipped this, and it went down without trouble. Gads, did it taste wonderful. It took about one minute before the alcohol was absorbed, and it hit me. I was soon high as a kite. It sure helped my outlook plus it helped me with my food intake. For many days, I had a cocktail for lunch and dinner. The corpsmen got a big kick out of this unorthodox medical therapy. But it worked—that was all that mattered. Being on a big food-intake schedule I added two more feedings during the day. I had a milk shake with an egg beaten up in it at ten and three o'clock. I was beginning to gain weight on this schedule.

The summer in south Texas came to an end, and a week before thanksgiving I felt well enough to get out of the hospital. The doctors were not so inclined, but Beverly figured out a plan. She invited the corpsmen who had taken such good care of me to a homemade Thanksgiving meal. With three of them with me, the doctors gave in, and I escaped from my hospital room for the first time in five months. It was wonderful to see the outside world, but by the time the corpsmen helped me back to the hospital that evening I was completely beat. It was a terrific boost to my mental state. Within the four weeks between Thanksgiving and Christmas I was allowed to live in our apartment for the weekends, and by the end of January I become an outpatient. Slowly I was learning how to move around on crutches. For anyone who has had to use crutches they can remember the first time they faced a flight of stairs. It took me some time to feel comfortable going down. Once I taught myself the best way, stairs no longer became a fearful obstacle.

I was spending my time improving my mind as well as my body. I began to devour books at a high rate. I had the time and I embarked on a project to read almost all the books written by Sir Winston Churchill. I accomplished my goal before I left the hospital. I also started rereading my math books from my first two years at Brown University to become knowledgeable again of the course work that I had almost completely forgotten. It had been seven years since I sat in a college classroom. One heck of a lot time had passed, so it was going to be rough to get back into the study habit.

The next major effort was to learn to drive a car again. I finally figured out that the best way to drive was with both feet, right on the gas pedal, left ready to use the brake. It was a good thing that we had an automatic shift car. At first I was no speed demon, but I got used to this technique and have used it ever since. Spring came early in south Texas, and I began to plan for my discharge from the hospital. I was going to be placed on the temporary disabled retirement list for three years and then be reevaluated. I also set the wheels in motion to go back to college. I re-applied to Brown University. But I was concerned about how I could face the ice and snow of a New England winter using crutches, so I decided to apply to Stanford University as well. We both loved the San Francisco Bay area when I was stationed at NAS Moffett Field before my second tour, and after we were married and thought it was well worth the try. I was accepted to Brown, but within a week I received my acceptance to Stanford. I declined Brown's acceptance letter and gladly accepted Stanford's letter. This made the future a lot brighter.

So, after a very long ten-months period of hospitalization and learning to use what muscles responded I was ready to face the world. With the aid of crutches I managed to regain enough use of my legs to go out into the world and try to live as close to a normal life as possible. I retired from the Navy on May 1, 1956 with full disability. That crash almost a year earlier was my last view from the cockpit and the end of my flying career.

My new life after graduation from Stanford took me into the dawn of the new world of computers. I wrote my first computer program while at Stanford in October 1957. I may not fly an airplane anymore, but I learned to make the computer fly into many new adventures. No matter what, the old saying is still with me. "You can take the pilot out of the airplane, but you can never take the airplane out of the pilot."

Appendix 1

Plane Director Instruction and Meaning

Movement	Meaning
Both arms upraised	Command to follow
Both arms upraised and moving backwards	Add throttle and move forward
Right fist closed, arm pointing downwards, left arm up and moving backwards	Apply brake to turn aircraft left
Left fist closed, arm pointing downwards, right arm up and moving backwards	Apply brake to turn aircraft right
Horizontal palms together then opened	Lower wing flaps
Horizontal palms open then closed	Raise wing flaps
Arms out stretched then folded across chest	Fold wings

Arms across chest then outstretched	Unfold wings
Both arms upraised and both fist closed	Stop
Arms vertical with palms together & then opened	Unlock tail wheel
Arms vertical with palms opened & then closed	Lock tail wheel
Both arms horizontal & Pointing to another director	Passing control to next director
Patting head and pointing One arm away	Passing control to pilot
Arms lowered with thumbs Pointing outwards	Chocks removed
Arms lowered with thumbs Pointing inwards	Chocks in place

Appendix 2

Landing Signal Officer (LSO) Instructions and meaning

Action	Instruction
Cut, right paddle crossed neck	Cleared to land
Fast, left paddle straight out, right paddle lowered 45 degrees	Reduce airspeed
High, paddles overhead in a "V"	Lower altitude
Low, paddles lowered in a "V	Increase altitude
Roger, paddles held horizontal	Approach OK
Slow, paddles moved together and then pulled back	Increase airspeed
Wave off, paddles overhead waving rapidly across each other	Not cleared to land

Glossary

AAA
Antiaircraft Artillery Rapid-fire cannon or machine guns, often aimed by radar

AD Skyraider
Heavily armed propeller driven aircraft used for ground attack. Carried bombs, napalm, and rockets. Also armed with 20-mm cannons used for strafing.

Air Officer
Ship's officer responsible for aviation matters in an aircraft carrier. Also call the "Air Boss."

Air-to-air
Referring to attacking enemy aircraft with forward firing machine guns or cannons

Air-to-ground
Bombing, rocketing or strafing enemy targets either under the control of a forward air controller or target of opportunity deep behind enemy lines. Troops, truck, bridges, etc.

Altimeter
An aircraft instrument connected to an aneroid barometer showing height in feet above sea level

Angle of attack
Angle of the wing relative to the forward flight path of the airplane. On any aircraft, too great an angle of attack will cause the wing to stop flying, as airflow across the upper surface is cut off

Angels
Fighter Director code to denote thousands of feet, i.e. 20,000 feet, angels 20.

Arresting gear
An arrangement of wires on a carrier flighty deck that stops an airplane after the tail hook has engaged it. *Essex*-class carriers have nine wires.

ASW
Antisubmarine warfare. Task assigned to VC-11

ATAR
High-Velocity Anti-Tank Aircraft Rocket fired from an attacking aircraft at a ground target. Explosive warhead similar to a 5-in. amour-piercing shell from a cannon

Barricade
Collapsible arrangement of vertical webbing rigged on an aircraft carrier to arrest an airplane that does not engage the arresting wire and the two barriers.

Barrier
Collapsible fence on a carrier flight deck that stops those airplanes whose tail hook has missed the arresting wires. For propeller aircraft it has several strands of wires across the flight deck to engage the propellers.

Barrier, Davis
Collapsible fence on a carrier flight deck that stops those airplanes whose tail hook has missed the arresting wires. For jet aircraft it has vertical webbing that is activated by the nose wheel pulling up an arresting wire from the deck that engages the main landing gear of the airplane.

Bingo
Minimum fuel for a comfortable and safe return to base.

Bogey
An unidentified and potentially hostile aircraft

Bore sight
Sight to align guns and sighting devices

Bounce-drill
Practice touch-and-go landings

CAG
Commander of the Carrier Air Group

CAP
Combat Air Patrol. Normally a division operating under the control of the ship's CIC Fighter Director Officer. The CAP is the earlier protection against hostile aircraft

CAS
Close Air Support; aircraft under the control of a forward air controller either on the ground or airborne who directs friendly attacking aircraft on a specific target in support of friendly ground forces.

Cat Shot
A carrier takeoff assisted by a hydraulic powered catapult. A "cold cat shot," one in which insufficient launch pressure has been set into the device, can cause the aircraft to crash on takeoff.

Catwalk
Walkway just below flight deck level, providing shelter and fore and aft access

CIC
Combat Information Center on a carrier. Manned by crew specializing in communication and radar. Continuously searches the area around the task force using air surveillance radar. The FDO uses this information to control the CAP.

Chock
A U- shaped device placed around an aircraft's main landing gear to prevent the aircraft from moving forward or aft. Can be made out of wood or metal.

Clock Position
Position of an object outside an aircraft as if its nose were at 12 o'clock. The tail is at 6 o'clock

CO
Commanding Officer. Refers to the commanding officer of the squadron or the ship

COD
Carrier On-Board Delivery aircraft used to transfer personnel and high priority cargo to and from the carrier deck.

CQ
Carrier qualification. A set number of carrier takeoffs and landings required in training and period intervals of all carrier flight crews. Also, "Carqual."

Cherokee Strikes
A code name assigned to deep support missions by the task force. Name was derived because ADM J J Clark's ancestry.

Cumulonimbus
Ultimate manifestation of growth of a cumulus cloud formation; dense with considerable vertical up and down drafts, lightning, thunder, and often hail.

Division
Tactical subdivision of a squadron in an air group. Made up of two two-plane sections. Also, administrative unit which men are divided on board ship.

Desoto
An automobile manufactured by Chrysler Corporation until the mid-50s.

Dud
Used in two different contexts: the first is an aircraft "dud" when it has an engine, electrical, or hydraulic problem. The second use involves air-to-ground ordnance that fails to explode.

Essex-class carrier
A class of World War II carrier displacing 27,500 tons; after the war, a number were modernized to accommodate high-performance jet aircraft.

Feet dry
Radio code indicating an aircraft or group of aircraft has crossed the coast inbound

Feet wet
Radio code indicating an aircraft or group of aircraft has crossed the coast outbound.

Flak
Antiaircraft gun fire usually automatic cannons firing explosive shells.

Flaps
A rear extension of the aircraft wing that can be lower by degrees to achieve greater lift at critically lower speeds

Flare
The nose-up landing posture normal for most landing aircraft. Used by carrier aircraft landing on a "straight" deck carrier.

FAC
Forward Air Controller. Can be either on the ground or airborne and controls friendly aircraft in support of friendly ground forces.

FCLP
Field Carrier Landing Practice. Used to train carrier pilots learning the approach technique to landing on a carrier at sea.

FDO
Fighter Director Officer. A member of the carrier CIC crew specializing in the controlling of ASW and CAP defensive forces.

G, G-loading, Gee

High-performance aircraft subjects airframes and occupants to centrifugal forces far beyond simple gravity. One-G equals normal gravity; a pilot and plane pulling 4-Gs in a turn or pullout will feel the forces equal to four times the weight of gravity.

G-suit

Nylon trousers that wrap around the legs and abdomen. Filled automatically with compressed air in high-G maneuvers, the G-suit helps prevent the pooling of blood in the lower extremities, thus retarding the tendency to lose consciousness.

GCA

Ground Control Approach, pilots making an IFR approach to a large airfield under the control of a specialized unit using radar. Consists of a search radar and an approach radar. The later radar is used by a controller to direct an aircraft to a point over the duty runway at airfield minimums of visibility and height above the ground

Gyro horizon

A gyro-stabilized instrument providing a horizontal reference for aircraft in instrument flight, when the natural horizon is not available.

HVAR

High Velocity Aircraft Rocket fired from an attacking aircraft at a ground target. Explosive warhead similar to a 5-in. shell from a cannon

Hold

A command to stay in one place. Usually issued by a control tower operator

IFF

Identification—friend or Foe, an electronic device that transmits a signal when a radar beam set it off. The signal then will show up on a radar screen.

IFR

Instrument Flight Rules, permitting safe flight operations in conditions of limited visibility

Jinx or Jinxing
Maneuvering continuously in both horizontal and vertical planes to present as unpredictable a target as possible.

Load up
The depositing of carbon particle of an engine spark plugs while idling at low rpm with full mixture.

LSO
Landing Signal Officer. Air group members with considerable experience in carrier landing, responsible for assisting others onto the deck and for grading their efforts.

Merge, Merged Plot
The point which an intercepting aircraft guided by radar, and the bogey are within visual contact.

Mach Number
Based on the ratio of the speed of an aircraft (true airspeed) to the speed at which sound travel under the same conditions. At Mach 1 the aircraft is traveling at the local speed of sound.

Magneto
An electrical device that controls the energy to the spark plugs. Normally there are two per engine, one for the forward and the other for the rear set of spark plugs. Each magneto can be tested separately. Similar to the older the automobile distributor

MiG-15
Soviet-manufactured aircraft built by Mikoyan-Gurevich flown by the communist forces.

Milk run
Aircraft mission with minimum danger by the enemy

Military Power
Maximum jet engine power, 100%

Mixture Control
A lever located on the throttle quadrant that controls the fuel air mixture being used by the engine. Full forward is a rich mixture, part way back is a lean mixture, and full back is all fuel is cut off

Morning Heckler
Specialized night fighter and bomber who takes off before dawn to attack enemy road and railroad traffic, returning at dawn to the carrier.

NAAS
Naval Auxiliary Air Station, usually a airfield with some support facilities associated with a Naval Air Station

NAF
Naval Auxiliary Field, usually a airfield with runways but no support facilities associated with a Naval Air Station.

NAS
Naval Air Station, usually a large airfield with support facilities

Night Heckler
Specialized night fighter and bomber who takes off at dusk to attack enemy road and railroad traffic, returning three hours after at night to the carrier

Out
Radio code: end of transmission, reply is neither requested nor desired, never used with "Over."

Over
Radio code: end of transmission, but reply is requested

Pigtail
An electrical connector between the aircraft and the rocket motor. Carries an electrical signal that ignites the rocket motor when the pilot pushes the firing button on the control stick.

Pitch, Pitching
The movement of the aircraft about a horizontal axis, wingtip to wingtip

Ramp
Curved section of the aft end of the flight deck

Roger
LSO signal that landing approach is satisfactory (see appendix 1)

Roll, Rolling
The movement of the aircraft about a horizontal axis nose to tail

SCAR
Sub-Caliber Aircraft Rocket, a small air-to-ground missile used in training containing a white powder to mark the impact point.

Section
A unit of two aircraft

Shuttle
Part of the catapult to which the bridle is attached. The other part is attached to the aircraft.

Slipstream
The turbulent blast of air created by a propeller-driven aircraft

Spin
An uncontrollable rotation of the aircraft after a stall about a vertical axis. The spin may be right side up or inverted.

Split-S, Split-es
An acrobatic maneuver in which an aircraft reverse direction 180 degrees by turning in the vertical rather than the horizontal plane. Often a violent half roll to an inverted position

Squadron
A unit of usually 16 aircraft and 24 pilots

Stall
To lose the amount of forward speed necessary to maintain lift

Tally-ho
Visual sighting by a member of an intercepting combat group of a targeted aircraft

TARCAP
Fighters stationed around an air strike assigned to protect the strike aircraft from enemy aircraft.

Tie Down
A rope, cable or wire to secure the aircraft while parked. On an airfield the tie down is attached to a ring secured in the cement or asphalt of the parking area. On board ship the tie down are attached to metal grating anchored in the fight deck.

Touch-and-go landing
A landing in which the pilot applies full takeoff power after touching down with the intent of taking off rather than coming to a full stop, See Bounce drill.

Turn-and-bank
A gyroscopic instrument for indicating the direction and rate of turn and degree for coordinated flight. Instrument has two parts: a needle for the first two conditions and a ball for the third condition. Thus called "needle-ball."

VA
Navy attack squadron usually flying the Douglas AD Skyraider

VC
Navy composite squadron designation. Air group normally contains four such special mission aircraft. VC-3, a night attack detachment flying the F4U-5NL, VC-11 a ASW detachment flying the AD-4W; VC-35 a night attack detachment flying the AD-4NL; and VC-61 a photographic detachment flying the F9F-2/5.

VF
Navy fighter squadron flying either the F4U-5 or the F9F-2/5

Wilco
Voice-radio directive: If you understand and will comply with the order given, the reply is "Wilco."

Wingman
Second pilot in the two-aircraft pair. Responsible for ensuring that his leader's tail remains clear. The smallest Navy air combat unit.

Wing over
An acrobatic maneuver to reverse direction in the horizontal plane.

XO
Executive Officer. Refers to the executive officer of the squadron or the ship

Yaw, Yawing
The movement of the aircraft about a vertical axis passing through the center of gravity. It also can be called "Skidding"

Printed in the United States
101110LV00007B/44/A